KETOGENIC DIET

Destiny Lawson

500 High-Fat Diet Recipes, The Rapid Weight-Loss Solution, Scientifically Proven, Low-Carb, Fat-Burning Machine

Table of Contents

Introduction

I want to thank you and congratulate you for downloading the book, "KETOGENIC DIET: 500 **High-Fat Diet Recipes, The Rapid Weight-Loss Solution, Scientifically Proven, Low-Carb, and Fat-Burning Machine**".

This book contains proven steps and strategies on how to lose weight with the ketogenic diet.

Ketogenic diet is a special diet that allows you to eat a high amount of fat alongside sufficient protein, while reducing carbs in your daily diet.

The main goal of the diet is to enhance overall health by using fats as the main source of energy which will in turn reduce the risk of developing various health conditions which are attributed to diets with too much carbohydrate content.

The ketogenic diet forces the body to enter a state known as ketosis, which allows to body to use fat as its main energy source.

The Ketogenic diet can also improve an individual's nutritional and health status through consumption of nutrient-dense foods like fruits and vegetables that are rich in dietary fiber and antioxidants, both of which are essential in reducing levels of free radicals and toxic elements that accumulate in the body.

Other health benefits of Ketogenic diet include higher levels of energy, effective fat and weight loss, regulated blood sugar and cholesterol levels, and promote healthy aging and increased longevity by increasing the amount of beneficial nutrients and antioxidants in the diet.

Thanks again for downloading this book, I hope you enjoy it!

Chapter 1 KETO BREAKFAST

Delicious Keto-Omelette

Ingredients:
- 3 organic eggs
- 1 tsp. butter
- 1 tsp. olive oil
- 2 links breakfast sausage, sliced
- 1 tbsp. onion, chopped
- 1 tbsp. green bell pepper, diced
- 1 tbsp. parmesan cheese
- Salt and pepper to taste

Directions:
1. Using a non-stick pan, heat the oil and butter. Sauté the onions and then bell peppers. Once the onions are translucent, add the sausage.
2. In a small bowl, beat the three eggs until well mixed. Season with salt and pepper.
3. Pour the beaten eggs over the sautéed vegetables and sausage. Reduce heat to medium-low. Cook for 30 seconds.
4. Sprinkle the parmesan cheese on top of the omelette.
5. Cook the eggs for another 30 seconds and then fold the omelette in half.
6. Flip the omelette carefully and cook for another 30 seconds.
7. Serve and enjoy.

Garlic Mushrooms Eggs

Ingredients:
- 1 tbsp. butter

- 1 tsp. olive oil
- ½ c. sliced shitake or oyster mushrooms
- 1 tsp. garlic, chopped
- 2 organic eggs
- Salt and pepper to taste

Directions:
1. In a non-stick pan, heat the butter and oil. Sauté the chopped garlic until light brown.
2. Add in the mushrooms and cook for about 3 minutes. Season with salt and pepper.
3. Set the mushrooms aside.
4. Using the same pan, fry two eggs – sunny side up style. Cook under low heat for about a minute. You can choose to have it over easy or well done.
5. Serve the eggs on a plate and place the sautéed mushrooms on the side.

Refreshing Cheese Tacos

Ingredients:
3 strips bacon
1 oz. cheddar cheese (shredded)
1/2 avocado
2 tbsp. butter
1 cup mozzarella cheese (shredded)
6 large eggs
Salt and pepper to taste

Directions:
1. Start by fully cooking the bacon. Either in an oven for 15 to 20 minutes at 375□F or stovetop.
2. Heat a clean pan on medium heat, and add 1/3 cup of mozzarella.
3. Heat the cheese until it just begins to bubble and turn brown on the side touching the pan. Pay close attention here! It will only take a few seconds for the cheese to jump from brown to burned.
4. Slip a spatula under the cheese and gently unstick it from the pan.
5. Now use a pair of tongs and drape the cheese over a wooden spoon that should be resting over a bowl or pot. Allow the cheese to cool and form a taco shell shape.
6. Repeat steps 2 to 5 with the rest of your mozzarella.
7. Now add your butter and eggs to the pan and cook completely, adding salt and pepper to suit your taste.

8. Divide the eggs equally between your cheese shells.
9. Slice the avocado and divide the slices evenly between the tacos.
10. Chop or crumble your bacon, and again divide equally between the tacos.
11. Last step! Sprinkle your cheddar cheese over the tops. Enjoy

Yummy Ham Breakfast

Ingredients:

12 eggs
4 cups of diced broccoli
2 cups of diced ham
½ cup each of mozzarella and grated cheddar cheese

Directions

Preheat the oven to 375° F.
Lightly blanch broccoli for about 3 minutes in boiling water.
Wisk the eggs and add cheese, ham, and broccoli
Pour into a suitable oven-proof dish and leave to cook for around half an hour.

Rasher Bacon Breakfast

Ingredients:

6 eggs
4 rashers of bacon

½ cup of cream
Seasoning to taste

Directions:

Lightly fry bacon until crisp. Set aside and dice when cool.
Wisk together eggs, cream, and seasoning and scramble in the bacon fat.
Add bacon and serve.

Avocado Cheesy Breakfast Tacos

Ingredients:

1 cup Mozzarella Cheese, shredded
6 large Eggs
2 tbsp. Butter
3 strips Bacon
1/2 small Avocado
1 oz. Cheddar Cheese, shredded
Salt and Pepper to Taste

Directions:
1. Start off by cooking the bacon. Line a baking sheet with foil and bake 3 strips in an oven for about 15-20 minutes at 375F.
2. While the bacon is cooking, heat 1/3 cup of mozzarella at a time on clean pan on medium heat. This cheese will form our taco shells.
3. Wait until the cheese is browned on the edges (about 2-3 minutes). Slide a spatula under it to unstick it. This should happen easily if you're using whole milk mozzarella as the oil from the cheese will prevent it from sticking.
4. Use a pair of tongs to lift the shell up and drape it over a wooden spoon resting on a pot. Do the same with the rest of your cheese, working in batches of 1/3 cups.

5. Next, cook your eggs in the butter, stirring occasionally until they're done. Season with salt and pepper.

6. Spoon a third of your scrambled eggs into each hardened taco shell.

7. Then add sliced avocado on top.

8. Follow this by adding the bacon (either chopped or whole strips).

9. Lastly, sprinkle cheddar cheese over the tops of the breakfast tacos. Add hot sauce and cilantro if you'd like and enjoy!

Parmesan Basil Omelet

Ingredients:

4 large eggs
1½ tablespoons freshly-chopped basil leaves
¾ cup grated parmesan cheese
2 thin slices of cooked ham, minced
1 small avocado, pitted and sliced
2 tablespoons coconut oil
Pinch of sea salt

Directions:

Whisk together the eggs and parmesan cheese. Add in the basil, ham and sea salt. Mix well. Heat the coconut oil in a pan over medium-high flame. Once the oil is hot, pour in the egg mixture and cook for 30 seconds. To prevent the egg from burning, use a spatula to push the sides of the egg towards the center.

Flip the omelet and cook the other side for 1 minute. Once the omelet is cooked, remove it from the heat and transfer it to a serving plate.

Top the omelet with avocado slices and serve.

Spaghetti Squash Carbonara

Ingredients:
- 1 small spaghetti squash
- 6 ounces bacon (roughly chopped)
- 1 large tomato (sliced)
- 2 chives (chopped)
- 1 garlic clove (minced)
- 6 ounces low-fat cottage cheese
- 1 cup Gouda cheese (grated)
- 2 tablespoons olive oil
- Salt and pepper, to taste

Directions:
1. Preheat the oven to 350°F.
2. Cut the spaghetti squash in half, brush with some olive oil and bake for 20–30 minutes, skin side up. Remove from the oven and remove the core with a fork, creating the spaghetti.
3. Heat one tablespoon of olive oil in a skillet. Cook the bacon for about 1 minute until crispy.
4. Quickly wipe out the pan with paper towels.
5. Heat another tablespoon of oil and sauté the garlic, tomato and chives for 2–3 minutes. Add the spaghetti and sauté for another 5 minutes, stirring occasionally to keep from burning.
6. Begin to add the cottage cheese, about 2 tablespoons at a time. If the sauce becomes too thick, add about ¼ cup water. The sauce should be creamy, but not too runny or thick. Allow to cook for another 3 minutes.
7. Serve immediately.

Gluten-Free Pancakes

Ingredients:
- 6 eggs
- 1 cup low-fat cream cheese
- 1 ½ teaspoons baking powder

- 1 scoop protein powder
- ¼ cup almond meal
- ½ teaspoon salt

Directions:

1. Combine the dry ingredients in a food processor. Add the eggs one by one, and then the cream cheese. Process until you get a batter.
2. Slightly grease a skillet with cooking spray and place over medium-high heat.
3. Ladle the batter into the skillet. Gently rotate the skillet to create round pancakes.
4. Cook for about 2 minutes on each side.
5. Serve pancakes with your favorite topping.

High-Protein Breakfast

Ingredients:
- 3 tablespoons chia seeds
- 3 tablespoons flax seeds
- 2 ounces coconut flour
- 1 cup soy milk
- ⅔ cup water
- ½ tablespoon ground cinnamon
- Pinch of nutmeg
- 2 scoops of vanilla protein powder

Directions:

1. Combine all the ingredients and set aside for the night. It is best to keep the bowl in the fridge.
2. In the morning, bring the soaked ingredients to a simmer and cook until the mixture thickens. You can also enjoy it without cooking, to fully benefit from all the vitamins and minerals in the ingredients.
3. Serve with your favorite topping.

Tasty Flaxseed Crepes with Yogurt

Ingredients:
- 8 large egg whites
- ½ cup plain yogurt
- 4 tablespoons ground flaxseeds
- ½ cup soy milk

Directions:
1. Combine the flaxseeds with the milk and mix well until smooth and free of lumps.
2. Beat the egg white and add to the flaxseeds mixture little by little.
3. Slightly grease a nonstick skillet with cooking spray. Ladle the batter and cook for about 60-90 seconds on one side and 10-15 seconds on the other.
4. Top with yogurt and serve.

Bacon Breakfast Mash

Ingredients:

6 rashers of bacon
2 cups of cubed cauliflower
1 cubed onion
2 cloves of freshly ground garlic
Season to taste
1/2 teaspoon of powdered garlic

Directions:

Fry bacon till nice and crisp. Set aside to cool and crumble.
Using the bacon grease; fry the onion, fresh garlic, and cauliflower over a medium heat.

When the cauliflower begins to turn brown, add the rest of the seasoning and bacon. Mix well and serve immediately.

Delicious Pepper Flake Sausage and Eggs

Ingredients:

½ pound pork (finely ground)
½ teaspoon of sage (dried)
Salt and pepper as required
A pinch of flaked red pepper (replace with garlic powder if you want something with a little less zing)
¼ sweet onion (diced finely)
¼ cup of zucchini (diced)
12 free range eggs
1 big avocado (cubed)

Directions:
Set your oven to 350°F.
Set your stove at medium heat and warm up a large frying pan. Season the pork and fry until it loses all traces of pink. Remove the pork and set to one side, taking care to leave the grease in the frying pan.
Fry the zucchini and onion until they are tender. (It will take around five minutes). Mix the onion/ zucchini and pork together. Mix in the eggs until well-combined.
Grease a muffin pan with 12 compartments using coconut oil. Divide the mixture between all the compartments.
Bake for about half an hour or until the egg is completely cooked. Serve with some avocado on top.

Cinnamon French Toast Muffin

Ingredients:
1 tsp. cinnamon
2 tbsp. erythritol
1 tsp. vanilla extract
1 tbsp. butter (unsalted)
2 tbsp. coconut oil
1/2 tsp. salt
1/4 tsp. nutmeg
1/4 cup heavy cream
1/4 cup peanut butter
1/4 cup toasted almonds (crushed)
6 large eggs
2/3 cup almond flour
10 drops liquid stevia

Direction:
1. Preheat your oven to 350□F.
2. If your almonds aren't already toasted, grind them up in a food processor and add them to a pan heated to medium-high. Keep a close eye on them and stir occasionally.
3. Add your peanut butter, coconut oil, and butter to a bowl and microwave until completely melted (about 40 seconds). Mix completely.
4. Mix your erythritol, salt, cinnamon, almond flour, and nutmeg in a separate bowl.
5. Combine your melted butter mixture, the dry ingredients, and the heavy cream. Stir and mix completely.
6. Divide the mixture evenly in a cupcake tray and top with your toasted almonds.
7. Bake for approximately 20 to 25 minutes.
8. Give them about 5 minutes after removing from the oven to cool, and then remove from the cupcake tray. Allow them to cool for at least 15 minutes and top with whipped cream.

Parmesan, Ham and Basil Omelet

Ingredients:
4 large eggs
1½ tablespoons freshly-chopped basil leaves
¾ cup grated parmesan cheese

2 thin slices of cooked ham, minced
1 small avocado, pitted and sliced
2 tablespoons coconut oil
Pinch of sea salt

Directions:

Whisk together the eggs and parmesan cheese. Add in the basil, ham and sea salt. Mix well. Heat the coconut oil in a pan over medium-high flame. Once the oil is hot, pour in the egg mixture and cook for 30 seconds. To prevent the egg from burning, use a spatula to push the sides of the egg towards the center.
Flip the omelet and cook the other side for 1 minute. Once the omelet is cooked, remove it from the heat and transfer it to a serving plate.
Top the omelet with avocado slices and serve.

Butter Tuna Mayo Breakfast

Ingredients:
- 2 organic eggs
- 4 asparagus spears
- 2 oz. fresh tuna sashimi
- 1 tsp. garlic wasabi mayo
- 1 tbsp. butter
- 1 tsp. olive oil
- Salt and pepper to taste

Directions:
1. In a small bowl, beat the two eggs with a whisk. Season with salt and pepper.
2. Using a non-stick pan, heat the butter and oil. Pour in the beaten eggs and stir around to make scrambled eggs. Cook for a minute and then set aside.
3. Using the same pan, cook the asparagus spears. Cook for about 3 to 5 minutes. Set aside.
4. Thinly slice the fresh tuna sashimi using a paring knife.
5. On a large plate, place the scrambled eggs, asparagus spears, tuna sashimi, and garlic wasabi mayo.
6. Serve and enjoy.

Almond Vanilla Coconut Donuts

Ingredients:

4 tbsp. almond flour
1 tbsp. coconut flour
1 tsp. vanilla extract
1 tsp. baking powder
4 tbsp. erythritol
3 oz. cream cheese
3 large eggs
10 drops liquid stevia

Directions
1. Add all of your ingredients to a bowl or pitcher and combine with an immersion blender. A food processor will also work for this step if you don't have an immersion blender.
2. Make sure that all your ingredients are well blended and smooth.
3. Heat your donut maker and spray with your grease of choice. Coconut oil always gives your cooking a savory finish!
4. Pour your mixture into the donut maker. Don't fill all the way to the top, leave some room (say 10%) to give your donuts space to rise.
5. Let the mixture cook for 3 minutes, and then flip and cook a further 2 minutes.
6. Remove the cooked donuts and repeat steps 3 to 5 for the rest of your batter.

Spinach Savory Green Waffles

Ingredients:

1 bunch spinach, washed, drained and chopped
4 eggs
3 bacon strips, cooked and chopped
1 tablespoon full-fat coconut milk
Pinch of salt and black pepper

Directions:

Place the coconut milk and eggs in a bowl then whisk them together. Gradually fold in the chopped spinach and mix well. Season the egg mixture with salt and pepper.

Grease the waffle iron with cooking spray and turn on the heat. Pour the egg mixture into the heated pan and sprinkle chopped bacon on top. Close the waffle iron and let the dish cook for 3 minutes. Once the waffle is cooked, use a fork to remove it from the pan and transfer it to a serving plate.

Coconut Biscuit Sausage Gravy

FOR THE BISCUITS

½ cup coconut flour

½ cup almond flour

2 teaspoons baking powder

1 teaspoon garlic powder

½ teaspoon onion powder

½ teaspoon salt

½ cup shredded Cheddar cheese

¼ cup butter, melted

4 eggs

¾ cup sour cream

FOR THE SAUSAGE GRAVY

1 pound ground breakfast sausage

1 teaspoon minced garlic

1 tablespoon almond flour

1½ cups unsweetened almond milk

½ cup heavy (whipping) cream

1½ teaspoons freshly ground black pepper

½ teaspoon salt

To make the biscuits

1.

Preheat the oven to 350°F degrees.

2.

Line a baking sheet with parchment paper.

3.

In a large bowl, combine the coconut flour, almond flour, baking powder, garlic powder, onion powder, and salt. Slowly incorporate the Cheddar cheese.

4.

In the center of the dry ingredients, create a well for adding the wet ingredients.

5.

Into this well, add the melted butter, eggs, and sour cream. Fold together until a dough forms.

6.

Use a spoon to drop biscuits onto the prepared baking sheet, placing them 1 inch apart.

7.

Bake the biscuits for 20 minutes, or until firm and lightly browned.

To make the sausage gravy

1.

Heat a large saucepan over medium-high heat. Add the ground sausage, breaking it up with spoon and browning it on all sides.

2.

Once the sausage browns, add the minced garlic. Cook for 1 minute.

3.

Once the garlic is fragrant, sprinkle in the almond flour. Reduce the heat to medium-low. Allow the almond flour to incorporate with the grease to develop a light roux, stirring constantly, about 5 minutes.

4.

Slowly add the almond milk to the roux, stirring constantly.

5.

Add the heavy cream. Increase the temperature to medium-high, stirring and reducing the mixture for 3 minutes.

6.

Reduce the heat to medium-low. Add the pepper and salt. Stir for 1 minute to incorporate.

7.

Check the biscuits and remove the baking sheet from the oven when ready. Cool the biscuits for 5 minutes.

8.

Reduce the heat again under the sausage gravy to low. Simmer while the biscuits cool.

9.

Once the biscuits are cool, plate 1 biscuit per person and top with ⅓ cup of gravy.

Poached Egg Spring Soup

Ingredients
- 32 oz. of chicken broth
- 2 regular-sized eggs
- 1 head romaine lettuce, chopped
- 1 pinch of salt, to taste

Directions:

1. Boil the chicken broth.
2. Turn the heat down, then poach the eggs in the broth for around 5 minutes or until slightly runny.
3. Get the eggs and transfer into separate bowls.
4. Place the chopped romaine lettuce in the soup, and cook for 3 to 5 minutes or until wilted slightly.
5. Using a ladle, transfer the broth into the 2 bowls.
6. Serve while hot and enjoy immediately.

Yummy Brie Balls & Salted Caramel

Ingredients
- 4 oz. of Brie cheese, chopped roughly
- 2 oz. of salted macadamia nuts
- ½ tsp. of caramel flavor

Directions:

1. Place all ingredients in a small-sized food processor and pulse until a coarse dough is formed or around half a minute.
2. Using a spoon, form 6 balls from the mixture.

3.   Serve and enjoy immediately. If desired, refrigerate for no more than 3 days before consuming.

Tasty Steak and Eggs

Ingredients:
- 4 oz. of sirloin steak
- 3 large-sized eggs
- 1 Tbsp. of butter
- 1 Tbsp. of olive oil
- ½ avocado
- Salt & pepper to taste

Instructions
1.   Heat the olive oil in a pan and cook the steak until the desired doneness is achieved.
2.   While waiting for the sirloin to cook, get another pan and heat the butter until it is completely melted. Fry the eggs until the yolks reach the preferred level of doneness and the egg whites have set. Dash a pinch of salt & pepper.
3.   Remove the sirloin steak from the pan and slice it into bite-sized pieces. Season with some salt & pepper.
4.   Cut the avocado into smaller slices. Sprinkle with some salt.
5.   Assemble everything on a plate.
6.   Serve and enjoy immediately.

Bacon Carbonara Balls

Ingredients
- 3 oz. of bacon, cooked
- 3 oz. mascarpone
- 2 large-sized eggs (hard-boiled, use the yolks only)
- ¼ tsp. black pepper, freshly ground

Directions:

1.   Chop the cooked bacon into crumbs.
2.   Place the egg yolks, pepper, and mascarpone in a small-sized bowl. Use a fork to mix everything well.
3.   Form 6 balls from the mixture.
4.   Put the bacon crumbs on a medium-sized plate. Roll the balls through, making sure each ball is evenly coated.
5.   Serve and enjoy immediately. If preferred, refrigerate first before serving, and use within 3 days.

Gluten Free Casserole Cristo

Ingredients
*   3 batches of cream cheese pancakes
*   (2) 6-oz packages of bacon
*   1 ½ cups of shredded Swiss or Gruyere cheese
*   ½ cup of warmed sugar-free pancake syrup

Directions:

1.   Grease a medium-sized baking dish.
2.   Put a layer of cream cheese pancakes (4 pcs) at the bottom and around halfway up the sides.
3.   Place a layer of bacon, and then sprinkle with half a cup of cheese.
4.   Bake for 15 minutes at 3750 F or until heated all over.
5.   Take the dish out of the oven and then evenly pour warm syrup on top.
6.   Cut the dish into six squares
7.   Serve and enjoy while warm.

Delicious Bacon and Avocado Balls

Ingredients:

- 4 slices of bacon
- 1 medium-sized avocado, pitted & peeled
- 1 Tbsp. of bacon fat
- 1 Tbsp. of green onions, chopped finely
- 2 Tbsp. of cilantro, chopped finely
- 1 small-sized jalapeño pepper, seeded & chopped finely
- 2 Tbsp. of coconut oil
- 1/3 tsp. of sea salt

Directions:

1.   Put a non-stick skillet over heat set at medium. Cook the bacon slices until they turn golden. This should take around 4 minutes for each side.
2.   Drain the excess oil from the bacon using a paper towel. Set the bacon fat aside in a glass container. Allow the bacon to cool.
3.   Chop two of the bacon slices into crumbs.
4.   Cut the remaining 2 slices of bacon into 3 pieces each. Set them aside for later. They will serve as the bases of the balls.
5.   Using a fork, mash the avocado in a small sized bowl. Pour the cooled bacon fat and coconut oil. Add the onion, jalapeño, cilantro, salt, and bacon crumbles. Mix all the ingredients well.
6.   Refrigerate for half an hour, at least.
7.   Remove the mixture from the refrigerator.
8.   Spoon out the mixture and make 6 balls.
9.   Arrange the bacon pieces previously set aside on a plate. Put one avocado ball on top of each piece of bacon.
10.   Serve immediately and enjoy. If preferred, refrigerate for no more than 3 days before consuming.

Cream Cheese Bacon Jalapeño Balls

Ingredients

- 3 oz. of cooked bacon (reserve the fat)
- 3 oz. of cream cheese
- 1 Tbsp. of cilantro, chopped finely
- 2 Tbsp. of reserved bacon fat
- 1 tsp. of jalapeño pepper, seeded & chopped finely

Directions:

1.   Get a cutting board and chop the cooked bacon into bits.
2.   Get a small-sized bowl and mix the jalapeño, cream cheese, cilantro, and bacon fat well. From the mixture, form 6 balls.
3.   On a medium-sized plate, spread out the bacon crumbs. Individually roll the balls, making sure that each one is coated evenly.
4.   Serve and enjoy immediately. If preferred, refrigerate first before serving, and use within 3 days.

Delight Salami & Olive Rollups

Ingredients :

- 3 oz. of cream cheese
- 12 pcs. of large, pitted kalamata olives
- 1 (1 oz.) slices of Italian salami

Directions:

1.   Place the cream cheese and olives in a small-sized food processor, and process until a coarse dough consistency is achieved.
2.   Using a spoon, form 3 balls from the cheese mixture.
3.   Put a ball each on the salami slices. Wrap each ball with a salami, secured by a toothpick.
4.   Serve and enjoy immediately. If preferred, refrigerate first before serving, and use within 3 days.

Cheddar Egg, Sausage

Ingredients
- 3 oz. of breakfast sausage
- 1 large-sized egg
- 1 slice of cheddar cheese
- 1 Tbsp. of olive oil
- Chives or green onion for garnish

Directions:

1. Heat olive oil in a pan, and cook the egg (over easy) and breakfast sausage.
2. Remove from heat and transfer to a plate
3. Add a cheddar slice.
4. Arrange or layer the rest of the ingredients as desired.
5. If preferred, sprinkle some hot sauce.
6. Top everything with sliced green onions or chives.
7. Serve and enjoy immediately.

Sausage Butter Muffin Sandwich

Ingredients:

4 large eggs
200 grams breakfast sausage
½ cup chicken stock
4 tablespoons melted unsalted butter
Pinch of sea salt and black pepper
Hot sauce

Directions:

To make the muffin loaves, pour 2 tablespoons of butter on a frying pan over medium flame. Once the butter begins to heat up, place 4 round biscuit cutters on the pan. Place an egg into each biscuit cutter then prick the yolks with a fork. Sprinkle each egg with salt and pepper. Slowly pour the chicken stock into the pan, making sure that the liquid stays outside the biscuit cutters. Cover the pan, adjust the flame to low and cook the eggs for 3-4 minutes. Once the eggs are cooked, slowly remove them from the pan and let it cool.

To make the sausage patty, pour the remaining butter onto the pan and heat it up over medium flame. Create 2 thick and round patties with the breakfast sausage then place them on the pan. Cook each side for 3 minutes.

To assemble the sandwich, place 2 eggs on a plate. Place a sausage patty over each egg, squeeze some hot sauce over it then cover each patty with the remaining eggs.

Creamy Morning Omelet

Goat cheese (3 Tbsp.)
Salt
Eggs (2)
Olive oil (3 Tbsp.)
Kefir (1 c.)
Chopped spinach (1/2 lb.)

1.In order to get started on this recipe, combine the kefir and the spinach together in the food processor and let them mix together until the mixture is pretty smooth.
2.Once that is done, you can bring out a skillet and heat up the olive oil. Pour your prepared spinach mixture into this skillet and cook on a medium heat for a bit.
3.Increase the temp for a bit and let these cook a little longer before taking off the heat.
4.While the spinach mixture is going, you can beat the eggs before you pour them into the frying pan. Fry the egg on both of the sides for a minute on both sides and then move it over to a plate.
5.Add in the spinach and fold it in half. Sprinkle with the ricotta cheese and then serve.

Pesto Muffins

Red pepper (1/4 tsp.)
Pesto (3 Tbsp.)
Salt (1 tsp.)
Goat's cheese (1/2 c.)
 Eggs (4)
Halved Kalamata olives (1/4 c.)
Chopped tomato (1)
Chopped spinach (3 ½ oz.)

1.For this recipe, you will need to take out a muffin tin and prepare it with some paper liners. Turn on the oven and let it have time to heat up to 350 degrees.
2.Combine together the pepper, salt, pesto, goat's cheese, Kalamata, and the tomatoes. Taking the eggs one at a time, whisk them on a high setting so that they become incorporated well.
3.Use a nice scoop or your spoon and place this mixture into the tins you set out. You can then get them into the oven and let them bake so that you can place a toothpick into the eggs so that they come out clean.

Garlic Kale and Eggs Benedict

Ingredients:
- 2 large eggs
- 1 tablespoon cream cheese
- 1 garlic clove (peeled and crushed)
- ½ stick butter
- 2 teaspoons coconut oil
- 3 ounces baby spinach
- Salt and pepper to taste

Directions:
1.   Melt 1 teaspoon coconut oil in a large skillet. Sauté the garlic for 2–3 minutes until golden brown.
2.   Add the spinach.
3.   Cook for 5 minutes, covered. Remove from heat but leave the cover on.

4.	Melt 1 more teaspoon of coconut oil in another skillet.

5.	Crack 1 egg and separate the white from the yolk. Crack the other whole egg in the bowl with the egg white. Add these eggs to the skillet and cook for 2 minutes.

Hollandaise Sauce

1.	Meanwhile, melt the cream cheese to form a creamy sauce.

2.	Blend the remaining egg yolk in a food processor for 20 seconds and add some salt and pepper. Then begin to add the butter and cream cheese mixture about a quarter at a time while continuously blending until smooth.

3.	Serve the eggs on a bed of spinach leaves, topped with sauce.

Honey Crunchy Sunflower Seed Cereal

Ingredients:

1 ½ cups raw sunflower seeds

1 ½ tablespoons ground cinnamon

2 cups coconut shreds

1 teaspoon coconut oil

½ teaspoon sea salt

2 medium eggs

½ cup organic honey

2 cups full-fat coconut milk, chilled

Directions:

Prepare a parchment-lined baking sheet and preheat the oven to 350°F.

Grind the sunflower seeds and coconut shreds in a food processor. Once both ingredients are fully chopped, add in the eggs, honey, salt, cinnamon and coconut oil. Process the mixture for 1-2 minutes.

Using a spatula, place the mixture into the baking sheet and press downwards and sideways for an even thickness. Place the cereal in the oven and bake for 15 minutes.

Once the cereal is ready, remove it from the oven and let it cool for 20 minutes. Use a wooden spoon to lightly tap and break the cereal into small bits.

Place the cereal into individual bowls and pour the chilled coconut milk on top of it. Serve immediately.

Deviled Eggs Salad

Ingredients:
- 2 organic eggs
- 1 tsp. mayonnaise
- ¼ tsp. Dijon mustard
- ¼ tsp. fresh parsley, minced
- Pinch of smoked paprika
- Salt and pepper to taste
- 1 c. fresh spinach leaves

Directions:

1.   Using a medium-sized casserole, place the two organic eggs with four cups of cold water. Place over high heat and wait for the water to boil. As soon as it boils, turn off the flame and leave the eggs for 10 minutes.
2.   In a small bowl, mix the mayonnaise, mustard, parsley, paprika, salt and pepper. Set aside.
3.   Remove the eggs from the hot water and peel off the shell. Slice the eggs in half and separate the egg yolks from the egg whites.
4.   Mix in the egg yolks in the bowl of mayonnaise mix. Mash the yolks and mix well.
5.   Place back the egg yolk mix to the egg white cups.
6.   Serve the deviled eggs on a bed of fresh spinach leaves. Enjoy.

Almond Friendly Pancakes

Ingredients:
- 2/3 c. organic almond flour
- 2 organic eggs
- 2 oz. full cream cheese (room temperature)
- 1 tsp. organic baking powder
- 2 tsp. organic stevia

- 1 tsp. vanilla extract
- 1 tsp. olive oil

Directions:

1.   In a mixing bowl, combine the almond flour, organic eggs, baking powder, stevia, vanilla extract, and cream cheese. Use an electric hand mixer for better results.
2.   The batter should be a bit runny and a little lumpy.
3.   On a non-stick flat skillet, brush over the olive oil. Place 1/3 cup of the batter. Cook each side for about 3 minutes or until brown.
4.   Serve with a side of organic maple syrup.

Coconut Pancakes and Bacon Strips

Ingredients:
10 bacon slices, cooked
1 cup almond flour
½ cup coconut flour
5 large eggs
½ teaspoon baking soda
¼ cup coconut milk
¼ cup water
12 drops liquid stevia
¼ cup Erythritol
¼ cup egg white protein
½ cup melted unsalted butter

Directions:
Whisk together the eggs, coconut milk, water and liquid stevia. Set this aside.

In another bowl, mix together the almond flour, coconut flour, baking soda, Erythritol and egg white protein. Slowly pour the egg mixture into the dry ingredients. Mix the pancake batter thoroughly.

Heat the butter in a pan over medium flame. Using a wooden spoon, pour a strip of batter into the pan, making sure its shape mimics the shape of the bacon strip. Place a strip of bacon in the middle of the pancake and wait for the sides to bubble. Flip the pancake and continue cooking for a minute or two. Follow the same process for the remaining batter until you have 10 bacon pancakes. Serve warm.

Spicy and Savory Breakfast Patties

Ingredients:

900 grams ground chicken meat
1 large egg, beaten
1 teaspoon garlic powder
2 teaspoon sea salt
1 teaspoon onion powder
½ teaspoon fresh thyme
¼ teaspoon chili flakes
1 teaspoon ground black pepper
1 teaspoon chopped parsley
¼ teaspoon nutmeg
¼ teaspoon paprika
2 teaspoons chopped dried sage
3 tablespoons olive oil

Directions:

Place the ground chicken and egg in a bowl and mix well. Gradually blend in the garlic powder, salt, onion powder, thyme, sage, nutmeg, paprika and chili flakes into the chicken mixture. Form the spiced mixture into 16 round patties then set aside.
Heat the olive oil in a pan over medium flame. Place the patties on the hot oil and cook for 3-5 minutes. Flip each patty over and cook the remaining side for 3 minutes. Place the breakfast patties on a plate and serve while hot.

Chive And Bacon Omelet

Ingredients:

1 oz. cheddar cheese
1 tsp. bacon fat
2 slices bacon (cooked)
2 stalks cheddar
2 large eggs
Salt and pepper to taste

Directions:

1. Make sure your chives are chopped, cheese shredded, eggs are cracked and mixed, and bacon cooked before you begin. Omelet making tends to be a fast process so keep on your toes and don't waste time completing these steps later!
2. Heat your bacon fat in a pan on medium-low heat.
3. Add your eggs, chives, and salt and pepper to the pan.
4. Cook until you can see the edges start to set, and then cook for another 30 seconds.
5. Immediately add your bacon to the center of the omelet, and turn off the heat.
6. Sprinkle your cheese on top of the bacon.
7. Fold two edges of the egg on top of the bacon/cheese pile. The melted cheese should hold the egg in place.
8. Repeat step 7 with the rest of the egg. This will create a slightly burrito shaped omelet.
9. Flip the omelet over, and allow it to cook a little longer in the pan (it'll still be warm).
10. Feel free to sprinkle some extra chive, cheese, or bacon on top.

Herbed Bacon and Egg Cups

Ingredients:

½ tablespoon chopped fresh chives
½ tablespoon chopped fresh parsley
12 bacon strips

8 eggs
½ cup cottage cheese
½ cup shredded cheddar cheese
2 jalapeno peppers, deseeded and minced
½ teaspoon garlic powder
Pinch of salt and ground black pepper
Olive oil

Directions:

Lightly grease 12 muffin cups with olive oil and set aside. Preheat the oven to 350°F.
Place the bacon in a pan over medium flame and cook until light golden brown but not crispy.
Cool the bacon for 2 minutes, then place a strip inside each muffin cup, circling the sides of the
vessel. Set aside.
Whisk together the eggs, chives, parsley, cheeses, jalapeno peppers, garlic powder, salt and
pepper in a mixing bowl. Pour the egg mixture into each bacon-lined cup, making sure that some
space is left on the top so as to prevent the egg from overflowing.

Almond High-Fiber Keto Oatmeal

Ingredients:
4 cups coconut milk
¾ cup flaxseeds
1 cup ground almonds
½ cup finely-chopped cauliflower
½ cup cottage cheese
¼ cup heavy cream
3 tablespoons unsalted butter, melted
1 teaspoon cinnamon powder
¼ teaspoon allspice
½ teaspoon vanilla
½ teaspoon nutmeg
10 drops liquid stevia
3 tablespoons Erythritol

Directions:

Pour the coconut milk inside a saucepan and mix in the cauliflower. Heat the mixture over medium-high flame.

Once the mixture starts to boil, season it with cinnamon, allspice, vanilla and nutmeg. Mix well. Gradually add in the stevia, Erythritol and flaxseeds and mix until the oatmeal starts to thicken. Pour the melted butter, cottage cheese and heavy cream into the oatmeal mixture and continue cooking for 5 minutes. Turn off the heat then spoon the oatmeal into individual bowls. Sprinkle chopped almonds on top of each bowl of oatmeal. Serve while hot.

Ham and Egg Cupcake

Ingredients:

- ½ doz. Organic eggs
- 6 slices big circular Canadian bacon
- 1 c. grated cheddar cheese
- 1 c. fresh baby arugula leaves
- Salt and pepper to taste
- 1 tsp. olive oil

Directions:

1. Preheat the oven in 320°F.
2. Take out a 6-cup regular muffin pan. Brush each cup with olive oil. Place a slice of Canadian bacon in each cup. Make sure to press down the bacon to take the shape of the muffin cup.
3. Sprinkle over a pinch or two of grated cheese and add a couple of arugula leaves.
4. Season with salt and pepper.
5. Crack an egg in each cup and season again with salt and pepper.
6. Bake these for 20 minutes.
7. Serve with a side of sour cream and enjoy.

Honey Mustard Bacon-Cheddar Eggs Breakfast

Ingredients

12 hard-cooked eggs
1/2 cup mayonnaise
4 bacon strips, cooked and crumbled
2 tablespoons finely shredded Cheddar cheese
1 tablespoon honey mustard
1/4 teaspoon pepper

Directions
Slice eggs in half lengthwise; remove yolks and set whites aside.
In a small bowl, mash yolks.
Stir in the mayonnaise, bacon, cheese, mustard and pepper. Stuff into egg whites.
Refrigerate until serving.

Spinach Greek Frittata

Ingredients:

*   3 tablespoons Olive oil
*   10 eggs
*   5-ounce baby spinach
*   1-pint grape tomatoes, sliced
*   4 scallions, sliced
*   8-ounce feta, crushed
*   1-2 teaspoons salt
*   ½ teaspoon fresh and ground pepper
*   Optional: ¼ cup pitless Greek black olives

Directions:
1.   Preheat the oven to 350° F and add oil in a casserole. Keep it in the oven for 5 minutes.

2.	Whisk eggs, pepper, and salt together.
3.	Add the following in order; tomatoes, scallions, spinach and feta.
4.	Take out the casserole from the oven.
5.	Transfer mixture to casserole and bake it for 25 to 30 minutes to get puffed and golden in color.

Garlic Scrambled Eggs with Sauce

Ingredients
2 eggs
1 leek, chopped
1 tablespoon vegetable oil
1 clove garlic, minced
3 tablespoons tomato sauce

Directions

In a small bowl, stir together eggs and chopped leek.
Heat the oil in a small skillet over medium heat. Add the egg mixture and cook until set.
Return skillet to heat and add garlic.
Saute garlic briefly then add tomato sauce. Pour warm sauce over eggs and serve.

Tasty Zucchini and Eggs

Ingredients
2 teaspoons olive oil
1 zucchini, sliced
1 egg, beaten
Salt and pepper to taste

Directions
Heat a small skillet over medium heat.
Pour in oil and saute zucchini until tender.
Spread out zucchini in an even layer, and pour beaten egg evenly over top. Cook until egg is firm.
Season with salt and pepper to taste.

Spicy Scrambled Eggs

Ingredients:

8 eggs
½ cup of cream
Seasoning to taste
A teaspoon of coconut oil/butter
½ cup of onion (diced)
½ cup of ham (diced)
½ cup of peppers (diced)
1 cup of mature cheddar (grated)
1 pinch of chili flakes (optional)

Directions:

Beat the eggs, cream, and seasoning together.
Warm up a frying pan over medium heat. Add in the eggs, stirring so that the eggs scramble.
Add the rest of the ingredients, except the cheese.
Add the cheese when almost done and serve immediately.

Garlic Bacon Hash

Ingredients:

6 rashers of bacon
1 onion (diced)
2 cups of cauliflower (diced)
2 crushed cloves of garlic
Seasoning to taste

Fry bacon until crisp and set aside to cool. Chop into bite sized bits.
Using the same pan, mix in the rest of the ingredients and fry over medium heat for a few minutes until it browns.
Add bacon just before serving.

Hearty Breakfast
(Serves 6)
12 eggs
4 cups of broccoli (diced)
2 cups of ham (diced)
½ cup each of mozzarella and cheddar cheese (grated)

Directions

Preheat the oven to 375° F.
Lightly blanch broccoli for about 3 minutes in boiling water.
Wisk the eggs and add cheese, ham, and broccoli
Pour into a suitable oven-proof dish and leave to cook for around half an hour.

Delight Easy Breakfast

Ingredients:

6 eggs
4 rashers of bacon
½ cup of cream
Seasoning to taste
Lightly fry bacon until crisp. Set aside and dice when cool.
Wisk together eggs, cream, and seasoning and scramble in the bacon fat.
Add bacon and serve.

Double Cream Poppy Seed Muffins

Ingredients:

- ¾ cup almond flour
- ¼ cup flaxseed meal
- 1/3 cup natural sweetener like Erythritol
- 1tsp baking powder
- ¼ cup unsalted butter
- ¼ cup double cream
- 2 tbsp poppy seeds
- 3 eggs
- 3 tbsp lemon juice
- 1 tsp vanilla extract
- Natural sweetener to taste

Directions:

- Preheat the oven to 350.
- Put together the flour, erythritol, flaxseed, and seeds
- Liquefy the spread. Blend it into the flour with the cream and eggs. Make a smooth hitter.
- Include the rest of the ingredients.
- Put 10 cupcake molds onto a heating plate. Pour the blend equally over them. Silicone molds are awesome for holding the normal cost down.

Have a go at serving by slicing down the middle and setting margarine or cream cheddar in the middle of the parts. They can make an incredible breakfast or snack.

Onion & Bacon Pie

Ingredients

5 slices bacon, chopped
1 large onion, sliced thin, 5 1/2 ounces
8 ounces Monterey jack cheese, shredded
6 eggs
1 cup heavy cream
1/2 teaspoon salt
1 teaspoon chili powder

Directions

Sauté the bacon and onion until the bacon is cooked and the onion is tender and slightly caramelized. Place the cheese in a greased pie plate; top with the bacon and onions.

Beat the eggs, cream and seasonings; pour over everything. Bake at 350° for 35-40 minutes until a knife inserted in the center comes out clean.

Let stand 10 minutes before cutting.

Broccoli Brunch Casserole

Ingredients

1 pound pork sausage
6 ounces ham, diced
10 ounces frozen broccoli, cooked and drained
8 ounces Monterey jack cheese, shredded
8 ounces cheddar cheese, shredded
3/4 cup parmesan cheese, 3 ounces
8 ounces cream cheese, softened
1/2 cup heavy cream
12 eggs
1/2 teaspoon onion powder
1/2 teaspoon Spicy Seasoning Salt
Pepper, to taste

Directions

Brown the sausage; drain the fat. Place the sausage in a greased 9x13" baking pan. Add the ham, cheeses and chopped broccoli; toss lightly to combine.

Beat the cream cheese briefly until creamy; gradually beat in the cream.

Whisk in the eggs and seasonings; pour over everything in pan. Bake at 350° 45-50 minutes or until a knife inserted in center comes out clean. Let stand 10 minutes before serving.

Makes 12 Servings

Per Serving: 508 Calories; 41g Fat; 31g Protein; 4g Carbohydrate; 1g Dietary Fiber; 3g Net Carbs

Dilicious Chicken Enchilada Pie

Ingredients:

1/3 cup onion, chopped, 1 3/4 ounces
1 tablespoon butter
1 1/2 cups diced cooked chicken
1/2 cup green enchilada sauce
1 tablespoon cilantro, chopped, optional
2 eggs
1/2 cup mayonnaise
1/4 cup heavy cream
6 ounces cheddar cheese, shredded
Salt and pepper, to taste

Directions

Sauté the onion in the butter until tender; combine with the chicken, enchilada sauce and cilantro in a greased pie plate.

Beat the eggs with the mayonnaise, cream and a little salt and pepper. Mix about 1/3 of the cheddar cheese into the chicken mixture.

Top with the remaining cheese and pour the custard evenly over the top.

Bake at 350° 35 minutes. Let stand 10 minutes before serving.

Scrambled Eggs with Roasted Red Peppers & Avocado

Ingredients
1/2 tablespoon butter
2 eggs
1/2 roasted red bell pepper, about 1 1/2 ounces
1/2 small avocado, coarsely chopped, about 2 1/4 ounces
Salt, to taste

Directions

In a small, nonstick skillet, heat the butter over medium heat. Break the eggs into the pan and break the yolks with a spoon; sprinkle with a little salt.

Stir to scramble and continue stirring until the eggs are starting to set up. Quickly add the peppers and avocado.

Cook and stir until the eggs are set to your liking. Adjust the seasoning, if needed.

Makes 1 Serving

Per Serving: 317 Calories; 26g Fat; 14g Protein; 9g Carbohydrate; 5g Dietary Fiber; 4g Net Carbs

Chive Mushroom & Spinach Omelet

Ingredients
2 tablespoons butter, divided

6-8 fresh mushrooms, sliced, 5 ounces
Salt and pepper, to taste
Pinch garlic powder
4 eggs, beaten
1 ounce Swiss cheese, shredded
1 handful fresh baby spinach, about 1/2 ounce
Chives, chopped, optional

Directions

In a very large skillet, sauté the mushrooms in 1 tablespoon butter until tender; season with salt, pepper and garlic powder.

Remove the mushrooms from the pan and keep warm. Heat the remaining tablespoon butter in the same skillet over medium heat.

Beat the eggs with a little salt and pepper and pour into the hot butter; swirl the pan to coat the entire bottom of the pan with egg. As soon as the egg is nearly set, place the cheese over half of the omelet.

Top the cheese with the spinach leaves and hot mushrooms. Let cook a minute or so to start wilting the spinach. Carefully fold the empty side of the omelet over the filling and slide onto a serving plate and sprinkle with chives, if desired.

Alternately, you could make two omelets using half of the mushroom filling, spinach and cheese in each.

Butter Green Chile Scrambled Eggs

Ingredients
1 tablespoon butter
3 eggs
Salt, to taste
1 ounce cheddar cheese, shredded
1 tablespoon green chile salsa
1 tablespoon sour cream

Directions

Heat the butter in a small nonstick skillet over medium-high heat. As soon as the butter has melted, crack the eggs into the skillet. Sprinkle with salt then add the cheese.

Cook the eggs, stirring constantly just until they are set or are done to your liking. Remove the eggs to a dinner plate. Serve topped with the salsa and sour cream.

Walnut Crusted Salmon

Ingredients :
½ cup walnuts
2 tablespoons sugar free maple syrup
1/2 tablespoons Dijon mustard
¼ teaspoon dill
2/3 ounce salmon fillets
1 tablespoon olive oil
4 or 5 spinach leaves
Salt
Pepper

Directions:

☐ Preheat the oven to 350°F.
☐ In a food processor, pulse together the walnuts, maple syrup and spices, then add the mustard.
☐ Heat the oil on a medium heat using a large skillet.
☐ With the skin side down, fry the salmon fillets for around three minutes.
☐ Add the mixture onto the top of the fish.
☐ Once the underside is cooked, bake in the oven for 8 minutes.
☐ Serve over the spinach.

Low Carb Breakfast Skillet

Ingredients
6 large eggs
1/2 package of bacon
2 tbsp of salted Butter
2 tsp of pepper
1/2 medium onion
1 cup cheddar cheese

Directions

Cook bacon, while the bacon is cooking, dice up the 1/2 onion. Place the pepper, butter, and onions into a skillet over medium heat and cook until the onions are lightly brown, stirring occasionally.

Scramble the eggs in a mixing bowl while waiting for your onions to brown. Once the onions are lightly brown, pour in the eggs and cook until eggs are done.'

Add the cheese to the eggs, and mix until the cheese is melted.

Crumble up the crisp bacon, and add it to the mix. Serve in a bowl

Pizza Breakfast Frittata

Ingredients:
- 12 eggs
- 9oz spinach ripped into smaller pieces
- 1oz pepperoni
- 1 tsp garlic, minced
- 5oz mozzarella cheese
- ½ cup ricotta cheese

- 4 tbsp oil
- ¼ tsp nutmeg
- Seasoning to taste

Directions:

- ☐ Preheat the oven to 375
- ☐ Blend the eggs, flavors, and oil together
- ☐ Include the cheddar and spinach
- ☐ Add to a skillet, sprinkle with some additional mozzarella cheddar on top
- ☐ Add the pepperoni to make it resemble a pizza
- ☐ Put in the broiler and prepare for 30 minutes

Yummy Flaxseed Morning Muffin

Ingredients:
- 2 tbsp. organic flaxseed
- 1 tbsp. self-rising flour
- 1 tsp. baking powder
- 1 tbsp. butter (room temperature)
- 1 tbsp. fried pepperoni, chopped
- 1 organic egg

Directions:
1. Preheat the oven to 300°F.
2. In mixing bowl, combine the flaxseed, flour, baking powder, and butter. Mix well using a wooden or rubber spatula.
3. Add in the fried pepperoni. Mix well to make sure the pepperonis are covered with the sticky batter.
4. Add in the beaten egg. Mix well.
5. Using an individual muffin cup, place the mix in the cup. Make sure to grease the cup first with a little oil or butter.
6. Bake for 25 minutes.
7. Serve and enjoy.

Salsa Sausage Quiche

Ingredients
1 pound pork sausage
8 ounces cheddar cheese, shredded
3 eggs
1 cup salsa

Directions

Crumble and brown the sausage; drain the grease. Place the sausage in a greased 10-inch pie plate.

Top with half of the cheese. Beat the eggs and salsa; pour over the cheese and spread it evenly (see my update below for an alternate method).

Bake at 350° 30 minutes or until the quiche is firm in the center. Sprinkle with the remaining cheese; bake 5 more minutes until the cheese is melted. Let stand 10 minutes before serving.

Otherwise the quiche will be too soft to remove from the pan.

Yummy Sausage Quiche with Mushrooms

Ingredients
1 pound pork sausage
1/2 pound fresh mushrooms, sliced
1 small onion, chopped, 2 1/2 ounces
8 ounces cheddar cheese, shredded
6 eggs
1/2 teaspoon salt
Dash pepper

1 cup heavy cream

Directions
Brown the sausage along with the mushrooms and onions; drain the fat. Put the sausage mixture in the bottom of a large pie plate.

Top with the cheese. Beat the eggs, salt and pepper, then beat in the cream. Slowly pour the egg mixture evenly over the sausage and cheese.

Bake at 350° for 35-45 minutes until a knife inserted in center comes out clean. Let stand about 10 minutes before cutting.

Cheesy Avocado Baked Eggs

1 avocado, halved lengthwise, pitted
2 eggs
4 tablespoons shredded Colby cheese, divided
⅛ teaspoon salt, divided
⅛ teaspoon freshly ground black pepper, divided
1.
Preheat the oven to 475°F.
2.
Scoop out enough avocado from each half so an egg fits. Place each avocado half in a ramekin, setting it into the ramekin, cut side facing up.
3.
Using two small bowls, carefully crack an egg into each. Do not break the yolk.
4.
Spoon one yolk into each avocado half and fill to the brim with egg white.
5.
Sprinkle 2 tablespoons of Colby cheese over each avocado half. Season evenly with the salt and pepper.
6.
Place the ramekins in the preheated oven carefully so the avocado halves don't tip over.
7.
Bake 15 to 20 minutes, or to your desired doneness.

Butter Bacon Asparagus Wrap

Ingredients:
4 bacon slices
12 asparagus spears, divided
1 teaspoon minced garlic
½ teaspoon onion powder
½ teaspoon salt, divided
¼ teaspoon freshly ground black pepper, divided
1 tablespoon butter
4 eggs

Directions:

1.
Preheat the oven to 400°F.
2.
Wrap one bacon slice around each bundle of three asparagus spears. Place each bundle on a parchment-lined baking sheet.
3.
Sprinkle the garlic, onion powder, ¼ teaspoon of salt, and a pinch of pepper over the bundles.
4.
Place the tray in the preheated oven. Bake for 12 minutes, or until the bacon crisps.
5.
In a large skillet over medium-high heat, melt the butter. Crack the eggs in pairs into the skillet. Try to keep the yolks intact.
6.
Cook the eggs to your desired doneness, about 5 minutes for a runny egg. Season with the remaining ¼ teaspoon of salt and the remaining pepper.
7.
Remove the asparagus from the oven.
8.
Remove the eggs from the skillet, placing two eggs atop two bundles of asparagus per serving.

Garlic Scotch Eggs

Ingredients:

½ cup breakfast sausage
½ teaspoon garlic powder
¼ teaspoon salt
⅛ teaspoon freshly ground black pepper
2 hardboiled eggs, peeled

Directions:
1.
Preheat the oven to 400°F.
2.
In a medium bowl, mix together the sausage, garlic powder, salt, and pepper. Shape the sausage into two balls.
3.
On a piece of parchment paper, flatten each ball into a ¼-inch-thick patty.
4.
Place one hardboiled egg in the center of each patty and gently shape the sausage around the egg.
5.
Place the sausage-covered eggs on an ungreased baking sheet and into the preheated oven.
6.
Bake for 25 minutes. Allow 5 minutes to cool, and then serve.

Low Carb Smoked Sausage & Swiss Cheese Quiche

Ingredients
1/2 pound smoked sausage

6 ounces Swiss cheese, shredded
6 eggs
3/4 cup heavy cream
1/2 teaspoon salt
1 teaspoon chives, minced

Directions

Peel the skin off the smoked sausage and cut in half lengthwise. Cut each half into halfmoons.

In a medium bowl, whisk the eggs. Add the cream, salt and chives; whisk well.

Arrange the cheese and sausage evenly in the bottom of a greased 9-10 inch glass pie plate.

Pour the egg mixture over the cheese. Bake at 350°, 35-40 minutes, until a knife inserted in the center comes out clean.

Tamari Marinated Steak Salad

Ingredients
- 2.5 oz. of salad greens
- 6 to 8 pcs. of cherry or grape tomatoes, halved
- ½ pc. of red bell pepper, sliced
- 4 pcs. of radish, sliced
- 1 Tbsp. of olive oil
- ½ Tbsp. of fresh lemon juice
- Salt, to taste
- ½ lb. of steak
- ¼ cup of tamari soy sauce (gluten-free)
- Avocado or olive oil for cooking the steak

Directions:
1. Marinade steak in gluten-free tamari soy sauce.
2. Get a mixing bowl.
3. Start preparing the salad by mixing the tomatoes, bell pepper, salad greens, and radishes with the lemon juice and olive oil. Sprinkle some salt, to taste.
4. Divide and transfer the salad into 2 plates.
5. Put avocado oil (or olive oil) in the frying pan. Set heat on high setting.
6. Cook (or grill) the marinated steak to the preferred doneness level.
7. Transfer the steak into a platter. Set aside for a minute.
8. Slice the steak into strips, and distribute evenly on top of the 2 plates of salad.

Chicken Bites Wrapped in Garlic Bacon

Ingredients
- 1 large-sized chicken breast, cut into around 25 bite-sized pieces
- 8 to 9 thin bacon slices, cut into 3 pcs. each
- 6 pcs. of crushed garlic or 3 Tbsp. of garlic powder

Instructions
1. Pre-heat oven to 4000 F.
2. Get a baking tray and line with aluminium foil.
3. Put crushed garlic or garlic powder in a mixing bowl
4. Dip each bite-sized chicken piece in garlic.
5. Wrap each piece of chicken with a short piece of bacon.
6. Arrange the bacon-wrapped chicken on the tray. Make sure to have enough space between each chicken piece on the baking tray so they will not touch one another.
7. Place the tray in the oven and bake for 25 to 30 minutes. If possible, turn the chicken pieces after 15 minutes.

Garlic Chicken Cherry Tomatoes

Ingredients

1 /2 pound chicken breasts, skinless and boneless

1 pound cherry tomatoes

2 garlic cloves, crushed

1 cup water

½ cup pitted green olives

¼ cup red wine (tart flavor)

1 teaspoon olive oil

1 teaspoon kosher salt

1 teaspoon dried oregano

1 spring fresh basil

¼ teaspoon hot pepper flakes

Directions:

- Heat your pressure cooker with the oil.
- Once hot, add the chicken breasts and brown on both sides.
- Place the cherry tomatoes into a plastic bag and tie – crush the tomatoes until they are open, but not squashed.
- Remove the chicken from the pressure cooker and pour in the tomatoes and juice.
- Add the hot pepper flakes, salt, wine, water, oregano, garlic, and mix together.
- Add the chicken back into the cooker and stir it around to coat.
- Close the lid and cook on high pressure for 12 minutes.
- Stir and rest for 5 minutes.
- Serve with green olives and basil

Yummy Sardines Mustard Salad

Ingredients :

- 4 to 5 oz. (1 can) of sardines in olive oil
- ¼ pc. of cucumber, peeled and cut into small dice
- 1 Tbsp. of lemon juice
- ½ Tbsp. of mustard
- Salt & pepper, to taste

Directions:

1. Drain the sardines of excess olive oil.
2. Mash the sardines.
3. Mix the sardines, lemon juice, diced cucumber, mustard and salt & pepper. Make sure the ingredients are well-combined.
4. Transfer the ingredients to a serving dish and serve.

Spicy Sesame Sour Meatballs

Ingredients:

16 ounces ground beef
16 ounces ground pork
4 green onions, chopped
3 chili peppers, chopped
¼ cup almond flour
6 tablespoons sesame seeds
2 tablespoons soy sauce
1 ½ tablespoons sesame oil
1 ½ tablespoons extra-virgin olive oil
1 teaspoon ginger powder
1 teaspoon salt
1 teaspoon garlic powder

Directions:

1. Put the ground beef, ground pork, green onion, and chili peppers into a large bowl.
2. Mix until well incorporated.
3. Add soy sauce, ginger powder, salt, and garlic powder to the bowl.
4. Mix until well incorporated.
5. Sift in the almond flour.
6. Mix until well incorporated and flour has been thoroughly absorbed.
7. Divide the mixture into 20 meatballs, rolling them as you go.
8. Put a large pan with the sesame oil and extra-virgin olive oil over medium-high heat.
9. When the oil begins to sizzle, place about 10 meatballs in the pan.
10. Cover with a lid and let the meatballs sizzle for 4 minutes.
11. Uncover and roll the meatballs over to the un-cooked side.
12. Re-cover pan and let sizzle again until cooked all the way through.
13. Repeat steps 9-12 with the remaining ten meatballs.
14. Roll meatballs in sesame seeds.
15. Plate and serve with your favorite keto-friendly dipping sauce!

Soy Sauce Shrimp Curry

Ingredients:

1 tsp. fish sauce
1 tbsp. peanut butter
1 tsp. ginger (minced)
1 tsp. roasted garlic (crushed)
1 tbsp. soy sauce
1/4 tsp. xanthan gum
1/2 tsp. turmeric
3 tbsp. cilantro (chopped)
2 tbsp. coconut oil
1 spring onion (chopped)
1 cup vegetable stock
1/2 cup sour cream
1 cup coconut milk
5 oz. broccoli florets
2 tbsp. green curry paste
6 oz. shrimp (cooked)
1/2 lime (juiced)

Directions:

1. Heat a pan over medium, and add the coconut oil. When hot, toss in the garlic, spring onion, and ginger.
2. Stir for a few minutes; and once cooked, add 1 tbsp. of the green curry paste. Along with your soy sauce, turmeric, peanut butter and fish sauce.
3. Continue to stir and cook for several minutes.
4. Now add the vegetable broth and coconut milk.
5. Add the xanthan gum, and mix completely.
6. When you notice the mixture begin to thicken, toss in the broccoli.
7. Continue to stir, and add the cilantro.
8. Lastly; add the shrimp and mix everything up. Allow it to cook for a few more minutes to allow the shrimp taste to develop.
Serve with your sour cream on top and enjoy!

Delicious Keto Burritos

Wrap Ingredients:
1 cup broth of your choice, heated
½ cup coconut flour
4 tablespoons butter
2 tablespoons ground psyllium husk
½ teaspoon salt
½ teaspoon garlic powder

Stuffing Ingredients:
64 ounces skirt steak
6 jalapenos, chopped
1 can tomatoes (whole)
2 onions, chopped
2 sweet peppers, chopped
2 chili peppers, chopped
6 tablespoons ketchup (sugar-free)
2 tablespoons apple cider vinegar
4 teaspoons cumin
2 teaspoons chipotle powder
2 teaspoons garlic powder
Dash of salt and pepper

Wrap Directions:

1.   Place coconut flour, ground psyllium husk, salt, and garlic powder in a bowl. Stir until all ingredients are well incorporated.
2.   Mash the butter into the mixture until well incorporated.
3.   Put the mixture into a high-power blender or food processor and add the hot broth. Pulse until butter is fully melted and substance is thick.
4.   Take the dough out of the blender and mold into a large rectangle.
5.   Slice into 12 pieces.
6.   Roll each piece of dough out over a piece of parchment paper. They don't have to be perfectly round – what's important is spreading them evenly.
7.   Take a lid or plate and place it over the rolled-out dough to make a perfectly round circle. Trim away uneven edges.
8.   Put a pan greased with coconut oil over medium heat.

9.   Place a wrap onto the pan once it is hot.
10. Allow the bottom side to brown before flipping and letting the top side to brown.
11. Repeat steps 8-10 for the remaining 11 wraps.

Stuffing directions:
1.   Put all stuffing ingredients into a crock pot.
2.   Leave the ingredients to cook for 3 ½ hours on low heat.
3.   Stir ingredients. Let cook for another 3 ½ hours on low.
4.   Shred steak into bite sized pieces.
5.   Fill each wrap with a portion of the crock pot mixture.
6.   Fold two sides of the wrap into each other until they almost touch. Grab the bottom of the wrap and roll upwards; having the first two folds on either side while rolling.
7. Serve and enjoy!

Hot and Spicy Pork Taco Wraps

Ingredients:

10 iceberg or Boston lettuce leaves, washed and drained
400 grams lean ground pork
1 cup tomato salsa
½ teaspoon garlic powder
¼ teaspoon cumin
½ teaspoon onion powder
¼ teaspoon ground black pepper
1 tablespoon olive oil
Slices of avocado, bell peppers and red onions

Directions:

Place the ground pork, garlic powder, cumin, onion powder and black pepper in a bowl. Using your hands, knead the spices into the meat.

Heat the olive oil in a skillet over medium flame. Place the spiced ground pork on the skillet and cook it until the meat becomes brown.

Once the meat is cooked, turn off the flame and drain the excess oil from the cooked pork. Pour the salsa over the pork and mix well.

To assemble the taco wraps, place a lettuce leaf on a plate, spoon the pork mixture on top of it then place some chopped avocadoes, peppers and onions. Fold or roll the lettuce leaf to secure the pork inside it. Serve immediately.

Tasty Bacon Meatball Skewers

Ingredients:

5 bacon slices
450 grams ground pork
½ teaspoon salt
½ teaspoon ground black pepper
½ teaspoon onion powder
½ teaspoon garlic powder
½ teaspoon turmeric powder
½ cup olive oil
Chunks of tomato, cucumber and pineapple

Directions:
Place the bacon and ground pork in a food processor and blend well. Season the meatball mixture with salt, pepper, onion powder, garlic powder and turmeric powder.

Form the mixture into 20 meatballs and place it on a parchment-lined baking sheet. Bake the meatballs in a 170°F oven for 12 minutes. Let the meatballs cool on a wire rack for 10 minutes.

To serve, place a chunk of tomato, cucumber, pineapple and meatball through a small skewer. Place the skewers on a serving plate and drizzle with olive oil.

Dijon Mustard Zesty Chili Crab Cakes

Ingredients:

3 cups fresh crab meat
2 large eggs
2 tablespoon coconut flour
4 tablespoons minced green chilies
1 tablespoon minced garlic
1 teaspoon Dijon mustard
½ teaspoon mayonnaise
Pinch of sea salt and black pepper
3 tablespoons olive oil

Directions:

In a large bowl, mix together the crab meat, eggs, chilies, garlic, mustard and mayonnaise. Season the mixture with salt and pepper then gradually add the coconut flour to thicken its consistency. Mix well.
Form the mixture into 10 round patties and set aside.
Heat the olive oil in a large pan over medium-high flame. Place the crab cakes on the pan and cook each side for 3 minutes or until golden brown.

Avocado Tuna Mayonnaise Meatballs

Ingredients:

280 grams canned tuna fish, drained
1 medium avocado, peeled, pitted and diced
1 cup chopped celery
¼ cup cottage cheese
¼ cup mayonnaise

¼ teaspoon onion powder
¼ teaspoon paprika
1/3 cup almond flour
1 cup olive oil
Pinch of salt and ground black pepper

Directions:

Transfer the tuna to a mixing bowl and season it with salt, onion powder, paprika and pepper. Mix well.
Add in the avocado, celery, cheese and mayonnaise. Slightly mash the ingredients together.
Form 12 meatballs from the tuna avocado mixture then roll it in the almond flour. Set aside.
Heat the olive oil in a pan over medium-high flame. Once the oil is hot, fry the meatballs until the sides are golden brown. Let it cool for 5 minutes then serve.

Cumin Hot and Spicy Pork Taco Wraps

Ingredients:

10 iceberg or Boston lettuce leaves, washed and drained
400 grams lean ground pork
1 cup tomato salsa
½ teaspoon garlic powder
¼ teaspoon cumin
½ teaspoon onion powder
¼ teaspoon ground black pepper
1 tablespoon olive oil
Slices of avocado, bell peppers and red onions

Directions:

Place the ground pork, garlic powder, cumin, onion powder and black pepper in a bowl. Using your hands, knead the spices into the meat.
Heat the olive oil in a skillet over medium flame. Place the spiced ground pork on the skillet and cook it until the meat becomes brown.
Once the meat is cooked, turn off the flame and drain the excess oil from the cooked pork. Pour the salsa over the pork and mix well.

To assemble the taco wraps, place a lettuce leaf on a plate, spoon the pork mixture on top of it then place some chopped avocadoes, peppers and onions. Fold or roll the lettuce leaf to secure the pork inside it. Serve immediately.

This recipe yields 2 servings.

Pineapple Bacon Meatball Skewers

Ingredients:

5 bacon slices
450 grams ground pork
½ teaspoon salt
½ teaspoon ground black pepper
½ teaspoon onion powder
½ teaspoon garlic powder
½ teaspoon turmeric powder
½ cup olive oil
Chunks of tomato, cucumber and pineapple

Directions:

Place the bacon and ground pork in a food processor and blend well. Season the meatball mixture with salt, pepper, onion powder, garlic powder and turmeric powder.

Form the mixture into 20 meatballs and place it on a parchment-lined baking sheet. Bake the meatballs in a 170°F oven for 12 minutes. Let the meatballs cool on a wire rack for 10 minutes.

To serve, place a chunk of tomato, cucumber, pineapple and meatball through a small skewer. Place the skewers on a serving plate and drizzle with olive oil.

Zesty Chili Crab Cakes

Ingredients:

3 cups fresh crab meat
2 large eggs
2 tablespoon coconut flour

4 tablespoons minced green chilies
1 tablespoon minced garlic
1 teaspoon Dijon mustard
½ teaspoon mayonnaise
Pinch of sea salt and black pepper
3 tablespoons olive oil

Directions:

In a large bowl, mix together the crab meat, eggs, chilies, garlic, mustard and mayonnaise.
Season the mixture with salt and pepper then gradually add the coconut flour to thicken its
consistency. Mix well.
Form the mixture into 10 round patties and set aside.
Heat the olive oil in a large pan over medium-high flame. Place the crab cakes on the pan and
cook each side for 3 minutes or until golden brown.

Ginger Spicy Pork Tenderloin

Ingredients
2 tablespoons chili powder
1 teaspoon salt
1/4 teaspoon ground ginger
1/4 teaspoon dried thyme
1/4 teaspoon ground black pepper
2 (1 pound) pork tenderloins

Directions
In a small bowl, mix together chili powder, salt, ginger, thyme, and black pepper. Rub spice mix
into pork tenderloins. Place meat in a baking dish, cover, and refrigerator for 2 to 3 hours.
Preheat grill for medium heat.
Brush oil onto grill grate, and arrange meat on grill. Cook for 30 minutes, or to desired doneness,
turning to cook evenly.

Delicious Steamed Corned Beef

Ingredients
1 (12 ounce) can corned beef
1/4 green bell pepper, chopped
1/4 onion, chopped
1 teaspoon vegetable oil
2 teaspoons tomato paste
1/4 cup water
1/4 teaspoon crushed red pepper flakes
1/4 teaspoon dried thyme
Salt and pepper to taste

Directions
Heat the oil in a skillet over medium heat. Add onion, green pepper, red pepper flakes and dried thyme; cook and stir until the onion is beginning to brown, about 7 minutes.
Reduce the heat to low and stir in the tomato paste and season with salt and pepper.
Simmer for 3 minutes then stir in the water.
Mix in the corned beef and then let it simmer until most of the liquid has evaporated

Pan-Fried Salmon with Zesty Balsamic Sauce

Ingredients:
2 150-gram salmon fillets
2 tablespoons white wine
1 tablespoon organic ketchup
1 tablespoon fish sauce
2 teaspoons olive oil
2 tablespoons coconut aminos
1 tablespoon balsamic vinegar
2 teaspoons chopped garlic
1 teaspoon chopped ginger
2 teaspoons organic honey

Directions:
Mix together coconut aminos, honey, fish sauce, balsamic vinegar, garlic and ginger in a bowl.
Place the salmon fillets in the balsamic mixture and marinate for 15 minutes.

After 15 minutes, drain the liquid from the salmon fillets and set aside.

Heat the olive oil in a pan over medium-high flame. Once the oil is hot, place the salmon fillets on the pan, skin side down. Fry for 3 minutes, then slowly flip the fillets and cook for another 3 minutes. Pour the balsamic marinade into the pan and let it boil with the fish.

Take out the fried fish from the pan and set aside. Pour the ketchup and white wine into the boiling marinade and cook for 5 minutes or until the sauce has reduced. Turn off the heat and cool for 5 minutes.

Place the salmon fillets on a plate and drizzle the sauce over it. Serve immediately.

BBQ Pork Ribs with Spinach Bean Salad

Ingredients :

1 ½ pounds baby back pork ribs
1 cup barbecue sauce
1 pinch salt
1 pinch ground black pepper
1 tablespoon olive oil
1 diced onion
1 ½ cups water
1 cup dried cannellini beans
1 bay leaf
1 finely chopped garlic clove
6 ounces fresh spinach

Directions:
- [ ] Cut the ribs apart and coat them with the barbecue sauce on all sides.
- [ ] Sprinkle the ribs with salt and pepper and place into the steamer basket – set aside.
- [ ] Heat the pressure cooker on medium heat and add the oil.
- [ ] Stir in the onion and sauté until soft.
- [ ] Add the water, beans, bay leaf, and stir.

- [ ] Lower the steamer basket containing the ribs into the pressure cooker and close. Cook for 20 minutes on high pressure.
- [ ] Place the lid of the pressure cooker on your countertop upside-down and lift the steamer basket out of the pressure cooker. Place the basket on the lid
- [ ] Remove the bay leaf and throw away.
- [ ] Mix in 1 teaspoon salt, garlic and the spinach.
- [ ] Spoon the bean mixture into a large casserole dish which is big enough to hold the ribs all in one layer.
- [ ] Arrange the ribs on top of the bean mixture and brush with what is left of the barbeque sauce.
- [ ] Broil the casserole until the sauce is caramelised.

Yummy Pork & Hominy Stew

Ingredients
2 cups dry hominy kernels, soaked overnight
4 cups water
2 pounds boneless pork, sliced into two chunks
2 bay leaves
2 dried ancho chilies
1 teaspoon dried Mexican oregano
1 teaspoon 0.
cumin powder
3 cloves garlic
3 teaspoons salt
1 fresh red bell pepper

Directions:

- [ ] Add the soaked hominy and the water to the pressure cooker.
- [ ] Cook on a high pressure at 15 minutes.
- [ ] Once cooked, open the lid and add the meat, bay leaves, dry ancho chilies, oregano, cumin, garlic, and salt.

- ☐ Close the lid and cook again on high pressure for 10 minutes.
- ☐ Open the lid and allow to rest for 10 minutes.
- ☐ Discard the bay leaf and remove the ancho chilies.
- ☐ Puree the chilies, two spoons of hominy from the cooker, fresh pepper, and garlic into a paste and put back into the pressure cooker.
- ☐ Simmer for 5-10 minutes.
- ☐ Serve

Chicken Noodle Soup

Ingredients:

- 3 cups of chicken broth
- 1 pc. of chicken breast (around ½ lb.), cut into small pcs.
- 1 pc. of green onion, sliced or chopped
- 1 stalk of celery, sliced or chopped
- 1 pc. of zucchini, peeled
- ¼ cup of cilantro, chopped finely
- Salt, to taste

Directions:
1. Dice the chicken breast.
2. Heat a saucepan with avocado oil.
3. Sauté the chicken pieces until cooked.
4. Add the chicken broth to the diced chicken, and simmer.
5. Add the chopped celery into the saucepan.
6. Add the chopped green onions into the saucepan.
7. Prepare the zucchini noodles. You can use a potato peeler to make long strands or use other methods such as using a food processor (w/ shredding attachment) or spiralizer.
8. Add the zucchini noodles and the chopped cilantro into the pot.
9. Allow to simmer for a few more minutes. Dash with a pinch of salt to taste.
10. Transfer to a bowl and serve while hot. Enjoy!

Tuna Avocado Salad

Ingredients
- 4 oz. tuna (canned)
- 1 medium-sized egg, hard-boiled, peeled, & chopped
- ½ pc. of avocado
- ½ stalk of celery, diced
- 2 Tbsp. of mayonnaise
- ½ tsp. of fresh lemon juice
- 1 tsp. of mustard
- Salt & pepper to taste

Directions:

1. In a small-sized bowl, mix the tuna, celery, and avocado.
2. Stir in the mayonnaise, lemon juice, mustard, and spices and then add the chopped egg.
3. Mix everything well.
4. Serve and enjoy immediately, or if preferred, allow to cool in the refrigerator for up to an hour first.

Macadamia Curried Tuna Balls

Ingredients
- 3 oz. of tuna in oil, drained
- 1 oz. of crumbled macadamia nuts
- 2 oz. of cream cheese
- ¼ tsp. of curry powder, divided

Directions:

1.   Process the tuna, half of the curry powder, and cream cheese in a small-sized food processor. It should take about half a minute before the desired smooth and creamy consistency is achieved.

2.   Form 6 balls from the mixture.

3.   Place the remaining curry powder and crumbled macadamia nuts on a medium-sized plate.

4.   Roll the balls individually to make sure each one is evenly coated.

5.   Serve and enjoy immediately. If preferred, refrigerate first before serving, and use within 3 days.

Chicken Skin Crisps Egg Salad

Ingredients
*   Skin from 3 to 4 pcs. of chicken thighs
*   1 large-sized hardboiled egg, yolk only, chopped
*   1 large-sized hardboiled egg, peeled & chopped
*   1 Tbsp. of fresh parsley, chopped finely
*   1 Tbsp. of mayonnaise
*   ¼ pc. of garlic clove, minced
*   ½ tsp. of sea salt

Directions:

1.   Set oven to 3500 F and preheat.

2.   Lay out the skins on a cookie sheet. Make sure they are as flat as possible.

3.   Allow to bake for 12 to 15 minutes or until the skins become crispy and light brownish. Make sure they don't burn.

4.   Take the skins from the cookie sheet and transfer to a paper towel. Allow to cool for a few minutes.

5.   Combine the egg yolk, egg, mayonnaise, garlic, sea salt, and parsley in a small-sized bowl and mix well.

6.   Halve each piece of crispy chicken skin.

7.   Put a Tbsp. of the egg salad mixture on top of each chicken crisp.

8.   Serve and enjoy right away.

Sunday Roast Chicken

Ingredients :

1/2 cup dry white wine
2 lemons, cut in half
6 large cloves garlic
1 (4 pound) whole chicken
1 1/2 teaspoons cold butter
2 tablespoons Dijon mustard
Salt and pepper to taste

Directions :

Preheat an oven to 425 degrees F (220 degrees C). Pour the wine into a 10-inch cast-iron skillet; set aside.

Place the lemon halves and garlic cloves into the cavity of the chicken. Slide half of the butter underneath the skin of each breast. Rub the chicken all over with Dijon mustard, then season to taste with salt and pepper. Place into the cast-iron skillet.

Bake the chicken in the preheated oven for 15 minutes, then reduce heat to 350 degrees F (175 degrees C), and continue baking until no longer pink at the bone and the juices run clear, about 1 hour more. An instant-read thermometer inserted into the thickest part of the thigh, near the bone should read 180 degrees F (82 degrees C). Remove the chicken from the oven, cover with a doubled sheet of aluminum foil, and allow to rest in a warm area for 15 minutes before slicing.

Lemon Stuffed Chicken

Ingredients:

1 (3 pound) whole chicken
2 cups stuffing mix
2 lemons
1/4 teaspoon salt
1/4 teaspoon paprika
1/4 teaspoon dried rosemary
1/4 teaspoon dried sage
2 tablespoons olive oil

Directions
Preheat oven to 350 degrees F (175 degrees C).
Stuff the bird with the prepared stuffing and rub the skin with the olive oil. Cut 1 lemon in half; cover the opening of the bird with a lemon half and stuffing (save the other half for garnish). Pour the juice of the second lemon over the bird. Season the bird with the salt, paprika, rosemary and sage.
Cover and bake in preheated oven for 1 to 2 hours. Remove the cover half way through baking to brown. Baste often.

Rosemary Pork Roast

Ingredients :

3 pounds pork tenderloin
1 tablespoon olive oil
2 cloves garlic, minced
3 tablespoons dried rosemary

Directions
Preheat oven to 375 degrees F (190 degrees C).
Rub the roast OR tenderloin liberally with olive oil, then spread the garlic over it. Place it in a 10x15 inch roasting pan and sprinkle with the rosemary.
Bake at 375 degrees F (190 degrees C) for 2 hours, or until the internal temperature of the pork reaches 160 degrees F (70 degrees C).

Spicy Pork Sausage

Ingredients
1 pound fresh, ground pork sausage
1 tablespoon crushed red pepper
1 1/2 tablespoons ground cumin
3 cloves garlic, finely chopped
Salt to taste

Directions
In a bowl, mix together with your hands Pork sausage, red pepper, cumin, garlic and salt. Form patties. Fry in a skillet over medium heat until well done.

Mustard Cabbage Roll Corned Beef

Ingredients:

1 tbsp. erythritol
1 tbsp. bacon fat
1 fresh lemon
1 tbsp. brown mustard
1 tsp. whole peppercorns
2 tsp. Worcestershire sauce
1 tsp. mustard seeds
1/4 tsp. cloves
1/4 allspice
1/2 tsp. red pepper flakes
2 tsp. salt
1/4 cup coffee
1 medium onion
1/4 cup white wine
15 large cabbage leaves
1.5 lbs. corned beef
1 bay leaf (crushed)

Directions:

1. In a slow cooker, combine all your spices, liquids, and the corned beef.
2. Turn the slow cooker to low, and leave for 6 hours.
3. When ready, bring a pot of water to boiling, and add all cabbage leaves as well as the sliced onion.
4. After 3 minutes remove the cabbage leaves, and dump them in some ice water for a further 4 minutes. Remember the onions should still be in the boiling water!
5. Slice the meat and dry off the cabbage leaves. Remove the onion from the water.
6. All the fillings into each cabbage leaf, and give a squirt of lemon juice overtop for good measure.
Enjoy!

Sausage Chili Soup

Ingredients:

2 tsp. chili powder
2 tsp. garlic (minced)
2 tsp. cumin
1 tsp. Italian seasoning
1 green bell pepper
6 cups raw spinach
1/2 medium onion
1 can tomatoes with jalapenos
1.4 lbs. hot Italian sausage
2 cups beef stock
1/2 tsp. salt
1 red bell pepper

Directions:

1. Tear the sausage into chunks and cook on the stove until fully cooked.
2. Slice your peppers; and add them, tomatoes, all spices, and beef stock to a crock pot.

3. Top the crock pot with the sausage and mix.

4. Fry your onions and garlic until the garlic begins to brown.

5. Add the onions and garlic to the crock pot, and top with the spinach.

6. Turn the crock pot to high, and cook for 3 hours.

7. After 3 hours, open it up and give everything a stir, then cook a further 2 hours. Serve

Bamboo Curry Chicken

Ingredients:

4 tablespoons coconut oil

¼ cup diced onion

1 cup bamboo shoots

1 pound boneless chicken thighs, diced

1 teaspoon minced fresh ginger

1 tablespoon curry powder

1 tablespoon paprika

1¼ cups coconut milk

¼ cup heavy (whipping) cream

¼ teaspoon salt

⅛ teaspoon freshly ground black pepper

Directions:

1.

In a large skillet over medium-high heat, heat the coconut oil for about 1 minute. Add the onion, bamboo shoots, and chicken meat. Cook for 5 minutes.

2.

Stir in the ginger, curry powder, and paprika. Continue cooking for 2 to 3 minutes more.

3.

Add the coconut milk and heavy cream. Reduce the heat to medium-low. Simmer for about 15 minutes. Season with salt and pepper.

4.

Serve over with rice

APC Scallions Chicken

Ingredients:
1 onion, finely chopped
½ cup finely chopped scallions
3 tablespoons soy sauce
1 tablespoon apple cider vinegar
1 tablespoon olive oil
2 teaspoons chopped fresh thyme
2 teaspoons Splenda, or other sugar substitute
1 teaspoon liquid smoke
1 teaspoon salt
1 teaspoon allspice
1 teaspoon cayenne pepper
1 teaspoon freshly ground black pepper
½ teaspoon nutmeg
½ teaspoon cinnamon
1 whole chicken, quartered
1.
In a medium bowl, mix together the onion, scallion, soy sauce, cider vinegar, olive oil, thyme, Splenda, liquid smoke, salt, allspice, cayenne pepper, black pepper, nutmeg, and cinnamon.
2.
In a large dish, place the chicken pieces skin-side down. Pour the marinade over it. Marinate covered, in the refrigerator, for at least 4 hours.
3.
When ready to cook, preheat the oven to 425°F.
4.
Place the baking dish with the chicken into the preheated oven. Cook for 30 minutes.
5.
Remove the baking dish from the oven. Turn the chicken skin-side up. Return the pan to the oven. Cook for 20 to 30 minutes more, or until the internal temperature checked with a meat thermometer reaches 165°F.
6.
Cool the chicken for 5 minutes before cutting and serving.

Sesame Broiled Chicken

Ingredients:

4 bone-in, skin-on chicken thighs
¼ teaspoon salt
¼ teaspoon freshly ground black pepper
2 tablespoons soy sauce
2 tablespoons sugar-free maple syrup
1 tablespoon sesame oil
1 teaspoon minced garlic
1 teaspoon red wine vinegar
½ teaspoon crushed red pepper flakes

1.
Season the chicken with the salt and pepper. Set aside.

2.
In a bowl large enough to hold the chicken, combine the soy sauce, maple syrup, sesame oil, garlic, vinegar, and red pepper flakes. Reserve about one-quarter of the sauce.

3.
Add the chicken thighs to the bowl, skin-side up. Submerge in the soy sauce. Refrigerate to marinate for at least 15 minutes.

4.
Preheat the oven to broil.

5.
Remove the chicken from the refrigerator. Place the thighs skin-side down in the baking dish.

6.
Place the dish in the preheated oven, about six inches from the broiler. Broil for 5 to 6 minutes with the oven door slightly ajar. Turn the chicken skin-side up. Broil for about 2 minutes more.

7.
Turn the chicken again so it is now skin-side down. Move the baking dish to the bottom rack of the oven. Close the oven door and broil for another 6 to 8 minutes.

8.
Turn the chicken again to skin-side up. Baste with the reserved sauce. Close the oven door and broil for 2 minutes more.

9.

Remove the chicken from the oven. With a meat thermometer, check the internal temperature. It should reach at least 165°F.

10.
Cool the chicken for 5 minutes before serving.

Broccoli Coconut Curry

Ingredients:

2 tsp. red boat fish sauce
1 tsp. garlic (minced)
2 tsp. soy sauce
1 tsp. ginger (minced)
1/2 cup coconut cream (or coconut milk)
4 tbsp. coconut oil
1 cup broccoli florets
1 tbsp. red curry paste
1/4 onion
1 large handful spinach

Directions:
1. Add 2 tbsp. coconut oil to a pan on medium-high.
2. Chop your onion, and add it as well as the garlic to the pan.
3. When the garlic begins to brown, turn heat down to medium, and add broccoli.
4. Stir everything together, and when the broccoli is partially cooked, move everything to one side of the pan.
5. Add the curry paste to the open side of the pan, and let cook for 60 seconds.
6. Now toss the spinach on top of the broccoli until it begins to wilt, then add the coconut cream and rest of the oil.
7. Stir everything together, and add the fish sauce, ginger, and soy sauce. Let simmer for 10 minutes.
Enjoy!

Turkeys Meatballs

Ingredients:

1/2 salt
1/2 pepper
3 sprigs thyme
2 large handfuls of spinach
3 small red chilies
10 slices bacon
2 lbs. ground turkey
1/2 green pepper
2 large eggs
1 oz. pork rinds
1 small onion

Directions:

1. Line a baking sheet with foil, and place bacon on top. Preheat oven to 400 F.
2. Bake the bacon for 30 minutes, or until desired crispiness is reached.
3. While the bacon is cooking, add all ingredients (except ground turkey and spinach) to a food processor and mince well.
4. Add the minced mixture to the ground turkey and mix well.
5. Once the bacon is done, drain the fat into an individual container.
6. Now form 20 meatballs from your mixture and place on the same baking sheet that you used before.
7. Cook meatballs for 20 minutes or until the juice begins to run clear.
8. Skewer 2 to 3 pieces of bacon to each meatball.
9. Now in a food processor, blend the spinach, leftover bacon fat, and any spices you wish until you have a paste.
Serve the meatballs on top of the paste and enjoy!

Bacon Wrapped Pork Chops

Ingredients
6 (1 inch thick) boneless pork chops
6 tablespoons process cheese sauce
12 slices bacon

Directions
Preheat the oven to 350 degrees F (175 degrees C). Fry the bacon in a skillet over medium heat until cooked through but still flexible. Wrap two slices of bacon around each pork chop and top with a tablespoon of cheese sauce. Place the pork chops in a baking dish.
Bake for 1 hour in the preheated oven.

Bacon & Goat Cheese Salad

Ingredients:
- ½ pound goat cheese
- ½ pound bacon slices
- 14-ounce avocados, peeled and pitted
- Half a lemon, juiced
- 8 tablespoons mayonnaise
- 8 tablespoons olive oil
- 2 tablespoon heavy cream
- ½ teaspoon salt
- ½ teaspoon ground black pepper
- ¼ cup chopped parsley
- 4-ounce walnuts
- 1-ounce arugula lettuce

Directions:

1. Set oven to 400 degrees F temperature and let preheat.
2. Line a large baking dish with baking paper and set aside until required.
3. Slice goat cheese into ½ inch rounds and place in the prepared baking dish.
4. Place baking dish on the upper rack of the oven and bake for 5-8 minutes until top is nicely golden brown.
5. In the meantime, place a medium-sized frying pan over medium heat, add bacon slices and fry for 2-3 minutes per side or until crispy.
6. Prepare salad dressing by whisking together lemon juice, mayonnaise, olive oil and cream until blended.
7. Season with salt and black pepper, add parsley and stir until combined, set aside until require.
8. Divide lettuce leaves among four salad plates and top with chopped avocado.
9. Top with fried bacon and goat cheese and sprinkle with nuts.
10. Drizzle with prepared salad dressing and serve immediately.

Yummy Nacho Chicken Casserole

Ingredients:

1 ¾ pounds boneless, skinless chicken thighs
1 ½ teaspoon chili seasoning
2 tablespoons olive oil
4 ounces cream cheese
4 ounces cheddar cheese
1 cup green chilies and tomatoes
3 tablespoons parmesan cheese
¼ cup sour cream
16 ounces pack of frozen cauliflower
1 jalapeno pepper
Salt
Pepper

Directions:

☐ Preheat the oven to 375°F.
☐ Cut the chicken into chunks and season.

- ☐ Brown the chicken over a medium heat.
- ☐ Add the cream cheese, sour cream and cheddar cheese and mix.
- ☐ Add the tomatoes and green chilies.
- ☐ Transfer to a baking dish.
- ☐ Cut the jalapeno into pieces.
- ☐ Spread the cauliflower over the top of the baking dish mixture and sprinkle the pepper over the top.
- ☐ Bake in the oven for 15-20 minutes

Bacon, Avocado and Chicken Sandwich

Ingredients
3 eggs
3 ounces cream cheese
1/8 teaspoon cream of tartar
¼ teaspoon salt
½ teaspoon garlic powder
1 tablespoon mayonnaise
1 teaspoon sriracha
2 slices bacon
3 ounces chicken
2 slices pepper jack cheese
2 cherry tomatoes
¼ avocado

Directions:

- ☐ Preheat the oven to 300°F.
- ☐ Separate the three eggs into two different bowls – whites and yolks separate.
- ☐ Add the cream of tartar to the whites and whisk.
- ☐ Add the cream cheese to the yolks and beat.
- ☐ Fold the half the whites into the yolks, repeat for the rest.
- ☐ Place parchment onto a baking tray.
- ☐ Pour the mixture onto the paper into large circles and make a square.
- ☐ Sprinkle with garlic powder.Bake for 25 minutes.
- ☐ Cook the chicken and bacon in a skillet.
- ☐ Mix the mayonnaise and sriracha.
- ☐ Spread the mixture onto one side of the bread, and place the chicken on top.

- Add two slices of cheese and bacon, and halved tomatoes.
- Spread avocado mash on top and season.
- Put the 'lid' of the bread on top and serve.

Nutritional information
- Fat per serving – 28.3 grams
- Net carbs per serving – 2 grams
- Protein per serving – 22 grams
- Calories per serving – 361 calories

Sesame Chicken

Ingredients
1 egg
1 tablespoon arrowroot powder or corn starch
1 pound chicken thighs
2 tablespoons toasted sesame seed oil (1 tablespoon for chicken, 1 tablespoon for sauce)
Salt
Pepper
2 tablespoon soy sauce
2 tablespoon Sukrin Gold
1 tablespoon vinegar
1 centimeter cubed ginger
1 clove garlic
2 tablespoons sesame seeds
¼ teaspoon xanthan gum

Directions:

- Combine the arrowroot powder, corn starch and the egg.
- Coat the chicken in the mixture.
- Heat up the sesame seed oil and add the chicken, turning occasionally until cooked.
- Mix together the soy sauce, Sukrin Gold, ginger, garlic, xanthan gum, sesame seeds, and vinegar together.

- [ ] After the chicken is cooked, add the sauce to the same pan and stir for five minutes.
- [ ] Serve with extra sesame seeds.

Nutritional information

- [ ] Fat per serving – 36 grams
- [ ] Net carbs per serving – 4 grams
- [ ] Protein per serving – 45 grams
- [ ] Calories per serving – 520 calories

Garlic Chicken Kiev

Ingredients:

2 chicken breasts
4 tablespoons butter
2 cloves garlic
1 stalk green onion
Tarragon
Parsley
Salt
Pepper
1 ounce pork rinds
1 egg
¼ cup coconut flour

Directions:

- [ ] Preheat the oven to 350°F.
- [ ] Season the chicken with parsley, tarragon, salt, and pepper, to taste.
- [ ] Spread the butter on top of the chicken breast, the onion and chopped garlic.
- [ ] Roll up the chicken and hold together with toothpicks.
- [ ] Crush the pork rinds in a blender.
- [ ] Place the coconut flour in one bowl, the beaten egg in another, and the pork rinds in a third bowl.

First, dip the chicken into the flour, then into the egg, and then into the pork rinds – the chicken should be completely coated in all three.

Refrigerate for 30 minutes.

Fry the chicken on all sides.

Put the chicken into a baking dish and bake for 20 minutes. Serve

Yummy Keto Pizza

Ingredients:

- 2 tablespoons grated Parmesan cheese
- 1 tablespoon husk powder
- ½ teaspoon Italian seasoning
- ½ teaspoon salt
- 2 eggs
- 2 teaspoons olive oil
- 3 tablespoons tomato sauce
- 1.5 ounce shredded mozzarella cheese
- 1 tablespoon chopped basil

Directions:
1. In a large bowl place cheese, husk powder, Italian seasoning, salt and stir until just mix.
2. Add eggs and blend for 30 seconds using an immersion blender.
3. Switch on the broiler, set at high heat setting in the oven and let preheat.
4. Place a medium-sized nonstick frying pan over medium heat, add oil and let heat until smoking hot.
5. When the pan is hot, add prepared batter and spread evenly into a round crust.
6. Let cook until edges started to brown, then flip the crust for cook for a minute and transfer crust a baking tray.
7. Spread tomato sauce on the top of the crust, sprinkle with cheese and then place pizza into the oven.
8. Broil pizza until starts to bubbling and then remove from the oven.
9. Sprinkle with basil and slice to serve.

Lemon Chicken & Asparagus Stir-Fry

Ingredients:
- ☐ 1 ½ pounds chicken breast
- ☐ ¾ teaspoon salt
- ☐ 4 fluid ounce chicken broth
- ☐ 2 tablespoons soy sauce
- ☐ 2 teaspoons cornstarch
- ☐ 2 tablespoons water
- ☐ 2 tablespoons melted coconut oil, divided
- ☐ 1 bunch of asparagus
- ☐ 4 teaspoons minced garlic
- ☐ 1 tablespoon minced ginger
- ☐ 3 tablespoons lemon juice
- ☐ ¼ teaspoon ground black pepper

Directions:
1. Wash chicken, pat dry, cut into bite-sized pieces, season with salt and set aside until require.
2. In a small bowl pour chicken broth, add soy sauce and stir until combined.
3. In another small bowl combine cornstarch and water until mix well.
4. Place a large non-stick skillet pan over medium-high heat, add 1 tablespoon oil and let heat until hot.
5. Cut asparagus into 2-inch pieces, then add to pan and cook for 3-4 minutes or until tender-crisp.
6. Add ginger and garlic and cook for 1 minute or until fragrant.
7. Remove asparagus to a bowl and reserve the pan.
8. Increase heat to high, add remaining oil and half of the chicken.
9. Cook chicken pieces for 3-4 minutes until brown on all sides and cook through, stir twice.
10. Transfer cooked chicken pieces to asparagus bowl and cook remaining chicken pieces in the same manner.
11. Into the pan pour prepared soy sauce mixture, cook for 1-2 minutes and bring to boil.
12. Stir in lemon juice and made cornstarch mixture and bring to simmer, stir frequently.
13. Then add cooked chicken and asparagus and mix well.
14. Serve hot.

Chicken Skin Crisps Satay

Ingredients:
- Skin from 3 to 4 pcs. of chicken thighs
- 2 Tbsp. of chunky peanut butter
- 1 Tbsp. of coconut cream
- 1 tsp. of coconut oil
- 1 tsp. of jalapeño pepper, fresh, seeded & minced
- 1 tsp. of coconut aminos
- ¼ clove of garlic, minced

Directions:
1. Pre-heat oven to 3500 F.
2. Lay out the skins on a cookie sheet. Make sure they are as flat as possible.
3. Bake the skins for 12 to 15 minutes or until they become crispy and light brown. Make sure they don't burn.
4. Take the skins from the cookie sheet and transfer to a paper towel. Allow to cool for a few minutes.
5. Put the peanut butter, jalapeños, coconut oil, coconut aminos, and garlic in a small-sized food processor. Process until everything is well-blended or for around 30 seconds.
6. Cut the crispy chicken skins into 2 pieces. Make sure each one is approximately of the same size.
7. Put a Tbsp. of peanut sauce on top of each piece of chicken crisp.
8. Serve and enjoy immediately. However, if you find the sauce a bit runny, you can refrigerate it first for up to two hours before you use it.

Spicy Steak Salad with Cauliflower

Ingredients:

- [ ] 1 ½ pound beef flank steak
- [ ] 32-ounce baby spinach, stems removed
- [ ] 15-ounce cauliflower head, stem removed
- [ ] 1 teaspoon ground cumin
- [ ] 1 teaspoon salt, divided
- [ ] 1 teaspoon ground black pepper, divided
- [ ] 1 teaspoon ground turmeric
- [ ] 2 tablespoons melted coconut oil, divided
- [ ] ½ cup tomato sauce

Directions:

1. Set oven to 400 degrees F.
2. Wash steak, pat dry, cut evenly into four portions, then season with ½ teaspoon of each salt and black pepper, and cumin and set aside until require.
3. Rinse spinach, drain in a salad spinner and set aside until require.
4. Cut cauliflower into florets, then add to a medium sized bowl.
5. Add ½ teaspoon of each salt and black pepper, then add turmeric, olive oil and toss to coat well.
6. Spread seasoned cauliflower in a single layer on a baking tray, place the baking tray in the oven and roast for 12 minutes or until nicely golden brown and soft.
7. In the meantime, place a grilling pan over medium-high heat and let heat. Grease with coconut oil and once pan gets hot place seasoned steaks into the pan.
8. Switch heat to medium-low and cook for 5 minutes per side until cook through.
9. Remove steak from pan and let rest for 5 minutes before slicing into thin strips against the grain.
10. Assemble salad by combining spinach, tomato sauce and ¼ teaspoon of each salt and black pepper.
11. Add roasted cauliflower and toss to coat well.
12. Divide salad evenly among four serving plates, add steak slices and serve immediately.

Buffalo Chicken Salad Sandwich

Ingredients:

- [ ] 3 ½ tablespoons butter, unsalted
- [ ] 2 egg
- [ ] 2 tablespoons almond flour, divided

- 2 tablespoons husk powder, divided
- ½ teaspoon baking powder, divided
- ½ teaspoon cream of tartar, divided
- 2 tablespoons chicken broth
- 8 ounce cooked shredded chicken
- 1.3-ounce red pepper sauce
- 1/8 teaspoon garlic powder
- ¼ teaspoon salt
- 1 tablespoons minced celery
- 1 ½ tablespoons mayonnaise
- 2 tablespoons ranch dressing

Directions:

1. Take two wide microwave oven proof mug and crack an egg into each mug.
2. In a small microwave ovenproof bowl, place 2 tablespoons butter and microwave for 15 seconds or until melt entirely.
3. Pour this melted butter into equal portion over egg into each mug and then mix well.
4. Add 1 tablespoon almond flour, 1 tablespoon husk and ¼ teaspoon baking powder, ¼ teaspoon cream of tartar and 1 tablespoon chicken broth into each mug and stir until mix well and a soft dough comes together.
5. Wipe the edges of the mug and make the top of dough uniform.
6. Place mug in the oven and microwave for 60-75 seconds or until dough puff and inserted wooden skewer into mug comes out clean.
7. Tap mugs to take out the bun, cut in half and set aside until require.
8. Place a medium sized non-stick skillet pan over medium heat, add remaining butter along with pepper sauce, garlic powder, and salt.
9. Stir and cook until butter melt completely.
10. Then add chicken and minced celery to the pan, stir until mix well, let warm and then remove the pan from the heat.
11. Add mayonnaise to the chicken, stir until well combined.
12. For assembling burgers, top the bottom slice of each burger bun with the prepared chicken mixture and drizzle with a tablespoon of ranch dressing.
13. Cover with top slice of burger and serve immediately.

Onion Mug Meatloaf

Ingredients:
- 4-ounce ground beef
- 1 ounce shredded cheddar cheese
- 3 tablespoons tomato salsa, unsweetened
- ¼ teaspoon onion powder
- ½ teaspoon salt

Directions:
1. In a medium-sized bowl, place all the ingredients and using hands stir until mix thoroughly.
2. Transfer mixture in a wide microwave oven proof mug and smooth the top.
3. Place mug in the oven and microwave for 6-8 minutes at high heat setting or according to your oven cooking time.
4. Cook until meat isn't too dry.
5. Remove meatloaf from the oven and let cool slightly to room temperature before serving.

Ginger Tamari Broccoli Beef

Ingredients:
- 2 tablespoons coconut oil
- 8-ounce broccoli florets
- ½ pound cooked beef, thinly sliced
- 1 teaspoon minced ginger
- 2 teaspoons minced garlic
- 2 tablespoons tamari sauce

Directions:
1. Place a medium-sized skillet pan over medium heat, add oil and heat until hot.
2. Add broccoli and cook for 3-5 minutes until tender-crisp, stir occasionally.
3. Add beef and sauté for 2 minutes.

4.   Then add ginger, garlic and tamari sauce and transfer to serving bowl, serve straight away.

Roasted Shrimp with Zucchini Pasta

Ingredients:
- 2 medium zucchini
- 8-ounce shrimp, peeled and deveined
- 2 tablespoons olive oil
- 2 tablespoons butter, unsalted
- 2 teaspoons minced garlic
- ¼ teaspoon salt
- ¼ teaspoon ground black pepper
- 1 lemon, juiced and zested

Directions:
1.   Set oven to 400 degrees F temperature and let preheat.
2.   Slice zucchini into thin strip or use spiral and set aside until require.
3.   In a bowl place shrimps, add oil, butter, garlic, salt, black pepper, lemon juice and zest and stir until combined.
4.   Transfer mixture into a baking dish and roast for 8-10 minutes or until shrimps are cook through and pink.
5.   Add roasted shrimps to zucchini pasta, toss until mix well and serve.

Coconut Beef Tacos

Ingredients:
- 1.1 pound ground beef
- 2 tablespoons coconut oil

- 3.9 ounce chopped onion
- 2 teaspoons minced garlic
- ½ teaspoon salt
- ¼ teaspoon ground black pepper
- 1 teaspoon red chili powder
- ½ teaspoon ground cumin
- 1 tablespoon tomato puree
- 8 fluid ounce water
- 7.1-ounce avocado, peeled and pitted
- 5.3-ounce cherry tomatoes
- 3.5-ounce lettuce
- 1 medium cucumber, sliced
- 1 medium green bell pepper, sliced
- 4-ounce grated cheddar cheese
- 4 keto taco shells

Directions:

1. Crumble ground beef, rinse under running water, drain and squeeze out water and set aside until require.
2. Place a large non-stick skillet pan over medium-high heat, add coconut oil and let heat.
3. Add onion and garlic and cook for 2-3 minutes or until nicely golden brown, stir frequently.
4. Add ground beef to pan and cook for 3-5 minutes or until brown on all sides, stir frequently.
5. Add salt, black pepper, chili powder, ground cumin, tomato puree, water, stir until well combined and cook for 5-8 minutes or until meat is no longer pink.
6. In the meantime chop avocado and tomatoes, and warm taco shells.
7. Assembles tacos by filling shells with prepared beef filling, then top with chopped avocado and tomatoes, lettuce leaf, cucumber, bell pepper and lastly, cheese.
8. Serve immediately.

Yummy Chicken Stir-fry

Ingredients:
- 3.5-ounce red onion, chopped

- 0.5-ounce Thai chili pepper, deseeded and chopped
- 2.1-ounce red pepper, deseeded and sliced
- 4.2-ounce green pepper, deseeded and sliced
- 1.1 pound chicken thighs, boneless and skinless
- 1 tablespoon grated ginger
- 3-ounce coconut oil
- 8-ounce broccoli florets
- 2 tablespoons fish sauce
- 1 teaspoon salt
- 2 tablespoons lime juice

Directions:

1. Wash chicken pieces, pat dry and cut into thin strips. Set aside until require.
2. Place a large non-stick pan over medium-high heat, add 2 tablespoons of coconut oil and let heat.
3. When the oil is hot, add chicken pieces and cook for 3-5 minutes or until browned on all sides and meat is no longer pink.
4. Transfer chicken to a bowl and add remaining coconut oil into the pan.
5. Add onion, chili pepper and ginger to pan and sauté for 2-3 minutes until fragrant, stir frequently.
6. Add remaining peppers to pan and cook for 2-3 minutes until tender crisp.
7. Add broccoli, fish sauce, and salt and cook for 3 minutes until all the vegetables are tender-crisp.
8. Drizzle with lime juice, remove the pan from the heat and serve immediately.

Garlic Chicken Skin Crisps Alfredo

Ingredients
- Skin from 3 to 4 pcs. of chicken thighs
- 2 Tbsp. of cream cheese
- 2 Tbsp. of ricotta

- 1 Tbsp. of Parmesan cheese, grated
- ¼ pc. of garlic clove, minced
- ¼ tsp. of white pepper, ground

Directions:

1. Pre-heat oven to 3500 F.
2. Lay out the skins on a cookie sheet. Make sure they are as flat as possible.
3. Bake the skins for 12 to 15 minutes or until they become crispy and light brown. Make sure they don't burn.
4. Take the skins from the cookie sheet and transfer to a paper towel. Allow to cool for a few minutes.
5. Get a small-sized bowl and mix the pepper, garlic and cheeses. Mix everything until well-blended.
6. Cut the crispy chicken skins into 2 pieces. Make sure each one is approximately of the same size.
7. Put a Tbsp. of the Alfredo cheese mix on top of the chicken crisps.
8. Serve and enjoy immediately.

Cheesy Chicken Bacon

Ingredients:

3 tablespoons olive oil
4 boneless chicken breasts
½ teaspoon salt
¼ teaspoon freshly ground black pepper
1 tablespoon garlic powder
8 bacon slices
4 tablespoons butter
4 tablespoons Ranch Dressing (see here), or purchased bottled dressing
½ cup shredded Cheddar cheese, divided
½ cup shredded mozzarella cheese
½ cup grated Parmesan cheese
½ teaspoon dried parsley

1.

Preheat the oven to 350°F and prepare a baking dish with cooking spray.

2.

In a large skillet over medium-high heat, heat the olive oil for about 1 minute. Season the chicken breasts with the salt, pepper, and garlic powder. Add them to the skillet. Sear each breast for 5 minutes per side.

3.

Slice the bacon into small pieces, about 12 cuts per slice.

4.

Place the chicken into the prepared dish. Spread 1 tablespoon of butter and 1 tablespoon of ranch dressing over each breast.

5.

Top the chicken with the bacon, covering each breast completely.

6.

Place the dish in the preheated oven. Bake for 30 minutes. Remove from the oven.

7.

Sprinkle equal amounts of the Cheddar, mozzarella, and Parmesan cheeses over the bacon-topped breasts. Season with the dried parsley. Return the dish to the oven.

8.

Bake for another 10 to 12 minutes, or until the cheese melts.

9.

Remove the dish from the oven. Allow to rest for about 2 minutes before serving.

Chicken Stuffed Bell Peppers

Ingredients:

½ cup butter, divided
1 pound boneless chicken thighs
½ cup chopped onion
1½ cups Cauliflower "Rice" (see here)
¼ cup chopped scallions
½ cup chicken broth
2 teaspoons chili powder
1 teaspoon paprika
1 teaspoon salt
½ teaspoon cumin
½ teaspoon garlic powder
¼ teaspoon dried oregano

¼ teaspoon cayenne pepper (optional)
6 bell peppers, tops removed and seeded
1 cup shredded Mexican cheese blend
1.
Preheat the oven to 350°F.
2.
In a large skillet over medium-high heat, heat 6 tablespoons of butter. Add the chicken. Sear for 3 to 4 minutes on each side. Cover. Reduce the heat to medium-low. Cook for another 10 to 12 minutes. Check the chicken for doneness. Set aside to cool.
3.
Once cooled, shred the chicken into small pieces. Set aside.
4.
In a large skillet over medium-high heat, melt the remaining 2 tablespoons of butter. Add the onion. Cook for 3 to 4 minutes, until translucent.
5.
Add the Cauliflower "Rice" (see here), shredded chicken, scallions, chicken broth, chili powder, paprika, salt, cumin, garlic powder, dried oregano, and cayenne pepper (if using).

6.
Slice a thin piece from the bottom of each bell pepper so it will not tip over. Place the peppers open-side up on a baking sheet.
7.
Fill each bell pepper with an equal amount of the chicken mixture.
8.
Top evenly with the Mexican cheese blend.
9.
Place the sheet in the oven. Bake for about 30 minutes, or until the cheese browns.

Pork with Mushrooms

Ingredients
4 pork chops
1 (10.75 ounce) can condensed cream of mushroom soup
1 onion, chopped
2/3 cup water

Directions

Preheat oven to 350 degrees F (175 degrees C).
Place pork chops in a 9x13 inch baking dish. In a medium bowl combine the soup, onion and water. Mix well and pour mixture over pork chops. Cover dish with aluminum foil and bake in the preheated oven for 45 minutes. Remove cover and bake for another 15 minutes.

Smoked Salmon Rollups

Ingredients
- 3 oz. of crème Fraîche (or French sour cream)
- 1/8 tsp. of fresh lemon zest
- 3 slices of smoked salmon or lox
- 1/8 teaspoon fresh lemon zest
- 3 slices (1 oz.) of smoked salmon (lox)

Directions:

1. Mix the French sour cream and lemon zest in a small-sized bowl.
2. Evenly top each slice of salmon with of the mixture.
3. Individually roll each slice, and secure the rolls with toothpicks.
4. Serve and enjoy immediately.

Beef and Veggie Salad Bowl

Ingredients:

☐ 2 Tbsp dry red quinoa

- 2 cups mesclun greens
- 3 oz cooked lean beef, cubed
- 1/2 cup chopped broccoli florets
- 1/4 red bell pepper, chopped
- 2 tsp olive oil
- 1 tsp red wine vinegar

Directions:
Cook quinoa as instructed. Toss with greens, broccoli, beef, & pepper in a clean bowl. Whisk oil & vinegar for proper dressing.

Sunday Spring Vegetables Bowl

Ingredients:
- 2 oz dry whole-grain farfalle pasta
- 2 tsp olive oil
- 1/2 cup artichoke hearts
- 1/4 cup sliced red onion
- 1/4 cup peas
- 1 Tbsp chopped fresh mint

Directions:
Cook pasta as instructed and toss with oil, mint and vegetables. Season with salt & pepper to taste.

Mayonnaise Coconut Shrimp

Ingredients:

Oil for frying

1 cup unsweetened shredded coconut

½ cup unsweetened flaked coconut

¼ cup unsweetened coconut milk

½ cup mayonnaise

2 egg yolks

¼ teaspoon salt

⅛ teaspoon freshly ground black pepper

½ teaspoon garlic powder

1 pound shrimp, peeled and deveined, tails left on

FOR THE AIOLI

½ cup mayonnaise

2 tablespoons chili sauce, such as Huy Fong Foods brand

2 teaspoons freshly squeezed lime juice

1 teaspoon red pepper flakes

To make the coconut shrimp

1.

In a large pot, heat 2 inches of oil to 350°F for deep-frying.

2.

In a medium bowl, thoroughly mix together the shredded coconut, flaked coconut, coconut milk, mayonnaise, egg yolks, salt, pepper, and garlic powder.

3.

Using 1 to 2 tablespoons of batter, carefully form it around each shrimp, leaving the tails exposed.

4.

Immediately drop the battered shrimp into the preheated oil. Repeat with 2 to 3 more shrimp. Cook for 4 to 6 minutes, until golden brown.

5.

Remove the shrimp from the oil. Set aside to cool on a paper-towel-lined plate. Repeat the process with the remaining shrimp.

To make the aioli

1.

In a small bowl, thoroughly combine the mayonnaise, chili sauce, lime juice, and red pepper flakes.

2.

Serve immediately with the coconut shrimp.

Grilled Shrimp With Salad

Ingredients:

1 pound shrimp, peeled and deveined
2 tablespoons olive oil
½ teaspoon garlic powder
½ teaspoon salt, divided
⅛ teaspoon freshly ground black pepper
1 avocado, peeled, pitted, and diced
¼ cup chopped bell pepper
¼ cup chopped tomato
¼ cup chopped onion
1 teaspoon freshly squeezed lime juice

1.
Heat a griddle over medium-high heat.
2.
In a large bowl, combine the shrimp, olive oil, garlic powder, ¼ teaspoon of salt, and pepper. Mix until the shrimp are coated thoroughly.
3.
In a medium bowl, mix together the avocado, bell pepper, tomato, onion, and lime juice. Sprinkle with the remaining ¼ teaspoon of salt. Set aside in the refrigerator.
4.
Place the shrimp on the hot griddle, on their sides. Cook for 2 to 3 minutes. Flip, and cook for another 1 to 2 minutes. Remove the shrimp from the griddle.
5.
Plate with the avocado salad to serve.

Zucchini Noodles Shrimp

Ingredients:

2 tablespoons olive oil
1 tablespoon minced garlic
1 pound shrimp, peeled and deveined
¼ cup dry white wine
2 tablespoons freshly squeezed lemon juice
1 tablespoon butter

3 tablespoons heavy (whipping) cream

2½ cups zucchini noodles

¼ teaspoon salt

¼ teaspoon freshly ground black pepper

1 tablespoon chopped fresh parsley

1.

Heat a large skillet over medium heat. Add the olive oil and heat for about 1 minute. Add the garlic. Cook for 1 minute.

2.

Add the shrimp to the pan. Cook on all sides, turning, about 4 minutes. Remove the shrimp from the pan. Set aside, leaving the liquid in the pan.

3.

To the pan with the reserved liquid, add the white wine and lemon juice. Scrape the bottom of the pan to incorporate any solids with the liquid, stirring constantly for 2 minutes.

4.

Add the butter and heavy cream. Cook for 1 minute.

5.

Add the zucchini noodles to the pan. Cook, stirring occasionally, for about 2 minutes or until the zucchini is al dente (noodle-like) in texture.

6.

Return the shrimp to the pan. Season with the salt and pepper. Stir to incorporate all ingredients.

7.

Plate and garnish with fresh parsley. Serve immediately.

Bamboo Broccoli Shrimp Stir-fry

Ingredients:

2 tablespoons olive oil

¾ pound shrimp, peeled and deveined

1 tablespoon minced garlic

1 cup sliced bamboo shoots

¼ cup chopped onion

1 cup broccoli florets

½ teaspoon sesame oil

3 tablespoons soy sauce

½ teaspoon unsweetened rice wine vinegar

½ teaspoon Chinese five-spice powder

¼ teaspoon freshly ground black pepper

1.

Heat a large skillet over medium-high heat. Add the olive oil and heat for 1 minute.

2.

Add the shrimp and garlic to the skillet. Cook for 2 to 3 minutes, or until the shrimp are mostly cooked. Remove the shrimp from the skillet.

3.

Lower the heat to medium. Add the bamboo shoots, onion, and broccoli and sauté for 5 to 8 minutes, or until room temperature. Add the sesame oil, soy sauce, rice wine vinegar, Chinese five-spice powder, and black pepper. Mix to combine.

4.

Add the shrimp back to the skillet, and cook for another 1 to 2 minutes.

5.

Serve immediately.

Scallops Bacon Wrap

Ingredients:

5 bacon slices

1 pound scallops (about 10)

½ teaspoon salt, divided

¼ teaspoon freshly ground black pepper, divided

4 tablespoons (½ stick) butter, divided

15 broccolini pieces

1 teaspoon minced garlic

2 tablespoons dry white wine

2 teaspoons olive oil

1.

Cut the bacon slices in half crosswise, creating 10 small slices. Wrap one slice around each scallop, securing with a toothpick. Season with ¼ teaspoon of salt and ⅛ teaspoon of pepper.

2.

Heat a medium skillet over medium-high heat. Add 3 tablespoons of butter and heat for 2 minutes.

3.

Add the broccolini, garlic, and wine. Sauté for 2 minutes. Cover and reduce the heat to medium-low.

4.

Heat a large skillet over medium-high heat. Add the remaining tablespoon of butter and the olive oil and heat for 2 minutes.

5.

Increase the heat under the large skillet to high. Add the scallops. Sear for 1½ minutes per side. Roll the scallops onto their sides so the bacon crisps. Cook for about 1 minute on each side.

6.

Check the broccolini for doneness. Season with the remaining ¼ teaspoon of salt and ⅛ teaspoon of pepper.

7.

Plate immediately with the scallops, saucing with any excess garlic butter from the pan.

Spicy Pork Tenderloin

Ingredients
2 tablespoons chili powder
1 teaspoon salt
1/4 teaspoon ground ginger
1/4 teaspoon dried thyme
1/4 teaspoon ground black pepper
2 (1 pound) pork tenderloins

Directions
In a small bowl, mix together chili powder, salt, ginger, thyme, and black pepper. Rub spice mix into pork tenderloins. Place meat in a baking dish, cover, and refrigerator for 2 to 3 hours.
Preheat grill for medium heat.
Brush oil onto grill grate, and arrange meat on grill. Cook for 30 minutes, or to desired doneness, turning to cook evenly.

Steamed Corned Beef

Ingredients
1 (12 ounce) can corned beef
1/4 green bell pepper, chopped
1/4 onion, chopped
1 teaspoon vegetable oil
2 teaspoons tomato paste
1/4 cup water
1/4 teaspoon crushed red pepper flakes
1/4 teaspoon dried thyme
Salt and pepper to taste

Directions
Heat the oil in a skillet over medium heat. Add onion, green pepper, red pepper flakes and dried thyme; cook and stir until the onion is beginning to brown, about 7 minutes. Reduce the heat to low and stir in the tomato paste and season with salt and pepper. Simmer for 3 minutes then stir in the water. Mix in the corned beef and then let it simmer until most of the liquid has evaporated

Oven-Dried Beef Jerky

Ingredients
1 1/2 pounds beef round steak
1/4 cup soy sauce
1 tablespoon Worcestershire sauce
1/2 teaspoon onion salt
1/4 teaspoon garlic powder
1/4 teaspoon pepper

Directions
Trim and discard all fat from meat. Cut meat into 5-in. x 1/2-in. strips. In a large resealable plastic bag, combine the remaining ingredients; add meat. Seal bag and toss to coat. Refrigerate for 8 hours or overnight.

Place wire racks on foil-lined baking sheets. Drain and discard marinade. Place meat strips 1/4 in. apart on racks. Bake, uncovered, at 200 degrees F for 6-7 hours or until meat is dry and leathery. Remove from the oven; cool completely. Refrigerate or freeze in an airtight container.

Crab Cakes

Ingredients:

½ pound jumbo lump crabmeat

½ pound lump crabmeat

¼ cup mayonnaise

1 egg, beaten

¼ cup coconut flour

1 teaspoon mustard

1 teaspoon seafood seasoning

¼ teaspoon paprika

1 teaspoon minced garlic

¼ cup finely chopped onion

¼ cup finely chopped bell pepper

1 tablespoon finely chopped fresh parsley

¼ teaspoon salt

¼ teaspoon freshly ground black pepper

1 cup shredded Parmesan cheese

3 tablespoons butter

FOR THE AIOLI

2 teaspoons minced garlic

1 tablespoon freshly squeezed lemon juice

1 egg

½ teaspoon salt

⅛ teaspoon freshly ground black pepper

½ cup olive oil

To make the crab cakes

1.

In a large bowl, combine the jumbo lump crabmeat, lump crabmeat, mayonnaise, egg, coconut flour, mustard, seafood seasoning, paprika, garlic, onion, bell pepper, parsley, salt, and pepper. Mix well.

2.

Mix in the Parmesan cheese. Divide the crabmeat mixture into six equal portions. Form each into a patty. Refrigerate to firm up while making the aioli.

To make the aioli

1.

In a food processor, mix the garlic and lemon juice until smooth.

2.

Add the egg, salt, and pepper. Purée, while slowly adding the olive oil until the aioli forms. Set aside.

To finish the dish

1.

Heat a large skillet over medium-high heat. Add the butter. Cook for 1 minute.

2.

Gently add the crab cakes to the pan. Cook for 7 minutes, being careful not to burn the butter. Reduce the heat to medium. Flip the cakes. Cook for 5 to 7 minutes more, or until done. Transfer the crab cakes to paper towels to drain.

3.

Serve immediately with half of the aioli. Refrigerate the remaining aioli stored in an airtight container.

Beautiful Chicken Ginger Soup with Asparagus

Ingredients:

- ☐ 4 oz boneless, skinless chicken breast
- ☐ 1 cup Amy's Organic Chunky Vegetable soup
- ☐ 2 Tbsp dry quinoa
- ☐ 1 cup chopped kale
- ☐ 10 small asparagus spears
- ☐ 2 tsp soy sauce
- ☐ 1/8 tsp grated fresh ginger

Directions:
Heat chicken at 350°F for 25 minutes, then shred with a fork. Then, consolidate soup, quinoa, and kale in a pot, heat to the point of boiling, and stew until quinoa is done, around 15 minutes. Include chicken. Steam asparagus, then hurl with soy sauce and ginger. Serve asparagus as an afterthought.

Yummy Pork with Veggies

Ingredients:

- [ ] 1 pork tenderloin (4 oz)
- [ ] 1 cup steamed green beans
- [ ] 2 Tbsp sliced almonds
- [ ] 1 baked sweet potato

Directions:

Season pork with salt and pepper, singe in an ovenproof skillet covered with cooking shower, and exchange to a 450°F stove for 15 minutes, cut and present with green beans finished with almonds, and a sweet potato.

Healthy Pizza Party

Ingredients:
- [ ] 1 Amy's Light 'N Lean Italian Vegetable Pizza
- [ ] 3 oz broccoli slaw
- [ ] 1/4 cup black beans
- [ ] 1/4 cup sliced scallions
- [ ] 1 tsp olive oil

☐   1 oz lemon juice

Directions:
Bake pizza. Blend together slaw, beans, scallions, oil, and lemon juice, and serve on the side.

Garlic Chicken Bacon Stir-Fry

Ingredients:

2 tbsp. butter (salted)
1/2 tsp. pepper
2 tsp. garlic (minced)
1/2 tsp. red pepper flakes
1/2 cup parmesan cheese
3 cups broccoli florets
1/2 cup tomato sauce
3 cups spinach
1/4 cup red wine (merlot works well!)
1/2 tsp. salt
4 cheddar & bacon chicken sausages

Directions:
1. Slice your sausage into whatever sizes you wish.
2. Heat a pan on high, and toss in your sausage. Also bring a separate pot of water to boiling.
3. Throw your broccoli into the boiling water. Cook for about 5 minutes or until it reaches your desired consistency.
4. Continue to stir your sausages as they cook, until they are uniformly brown.
5. Nudge your sausages to one side of the pan and then drop the butter onto the other side.
6. Drop your garlic into the butter and cook for 1 to 2 minutes.
7. Now stir everything in your pan together and add your broccoli as well.
8. Pour in the red wine and tomato sauce. Sprinkle the pepper flakes in as well.
9. Mix everything together. Add the spinach, salt, and pepper. Continue to stir as it cooks down.
10. Simmer for 10 minutes
You're all set, enjoy!

Pork Rind Nachos

Ingredients:

1½ ounces pork rinds

⅓ cup shredded Mexican cheese blend

⅛ cup diced tomato

1 garlic clove, minced

¼ teaspoon cumin

⅛ cup sour cream

Fresh cilantro for garnish

1.

Arrange the pork rinds on a large microwaveable plate, being careful not to overlap them.

2.

Sprinkle the cheese evenly over all the pork rinds, covering each one to the edges.

3.

Top with the tomatoes and garlic. Season with the cumin.

4.

Place the plate in a microwave. Cook on high for 1 minute, 15 seconds. Check to see if the cheese has melted. If needed, cook for another 15 to 30 seconds, checking frequently. Make sure not to overcook, or the pork rinds will become soggy.

5.

Remove the plate from the microwave. Garnish the nachos with sour cream and cilantro. Serve.

Cauliflower Salmon Ginger

Ingredients:

1 tablespoon minced fresh ginger

½ teaspoon sesame oil

1 teaspoon olive oil

½ teaspoon rice wine vinegar

1 teaspoon soy sauce

2 (8-ounce) salmon fillets

1.

Preheat the oven to 400°F.

2.

In a medium bowl, mix together the ginger, sesame oil, olive oil, rice vinegar, and soy sauce.

3.

Add the salmon fillets. Cover completely with the sauce.

4.

Line a baking dish with aluminum foil. Place the fillets inside. Pour any remaining sauce over the fillets.

5.

Put the dish into the preheated oven. Bake for 15 to 20 minutes, depending on the thickness of the fillets.

6.

Remove the dish from the oven and check the fillets for doneness.

7.

Serve immediately with the Cauliflower Mash

Salmon Garlic Green Beans

FOR THE RUB

2 tablespoons stevia, or other sugar substitute

1 tablespoon chili powder

1 teaspoon freshly ground black pepper

½ tablespoon ground cumin

½ tablespoon paprika

½ tablespoon salt

¼ teaspoon dry mustard

Dash cinnamon

FOR THE SALMON

4 tablespoons coconut oil

4 (4- to 6-ounce) Alaskan salmon fillets

4 tablespoons Dijon mustard, divided
FOR THE GREEN BEANS
3 tablespoons butter
1 tablespoon olive oil
4 garlic cloves, minced
1 pound green beans
½ teaspoon salt
¼ teaspoon freshly ground black pepper
To make the rub
In a medium bowl, combine the stevia, chili powder, black pepper, cumin, paprika, salt, dry mustard, and cinnamon.
To prepare the salmon
1.
In a large skillet over medium heat, heat the coconut oil for about 5 minutes.
2.
Liberally coat each salmon fillet with 1 tablespoon of mustard.
3.
Season each fillet, on both sides, with an equal amount of the rub. Set aside.
4.
Once the coconut oil has heated, increase the heat to medium-high. Add the salmon and sear for about 2 minutes. Flip and reduce the heat to medium. Cook for 6 to 8 minutes more, until the fish is opaque.
To make the green beans
1.
In another large skillet over medium heat, heat the butter and olive oil. Add the garlic and cook until fragrant, about 1 minute.
2.
Add the green beans, salt, and pepper. Cover and reduce the heat to medium-low. Cook for 10 to 12 minutes, stirring occasionally.
3.
Serve immediately alongside the salmon.

Spicy Salmon Mayo & Asparagus

FOR THE SPICY MAYO

2 teaspoons minced garlic

1 tablespoon freshly squeezed lemon juice

1 egg

½ teaspoon salt

1 tablespoon cayenne pepper

⅛ teaspoon freshly ground black pepper

½ cup olive oil

FOR SALMON AND ASPARAGUS

12 asparagus spears

½ teaspoon minced fresh ginger

2 teaspoons olive oil, divided

½ teaspoon rice wine vinegar

¼ teaspoon freshly ground black pepper

4 tablespoons Teriyaki Sauce (see here), or purchased sugar-free teriyaki sauce (such as Seal Sama)

2 (8-ounce) salmon fillets

Sliced scallions, for garnish

To make the spicy mayo

1.

In a food processor, mix the garlic and lemon juice until smooth.

2.

Add the egg, salt, cayenne pepper, and black pepper to the garlic and lemon juice purée. While puréeing, slowly add the olive oil until the mayo forms. Set aside in the refrigerator while the fillets cook.

To make the salmon and asparagus

1.

Preheat the oven to 400°F.

2.

Remove the woody ends from the asparagus, leaving only the tender portion of the stalk.

3.

In a medium bowl, mix together the ginger, 1 teaspoon of olive oil, rice wine vinegar, pepper, and the Teriyaki Sauce (see here).

4.

Add the salmon and cover completely with the sauce.

5.

Line a baking dish with aluminum foil. Transfer the salmon from the sauce to the dish. Pour any remaining sauce over the fillets. Tuck the asparagus around the fillets and drizzle them with the remaining teaspoon of olive oil.

6.

Put the dish in the preheated oven. Bake for 15 to 20 minutes, depending on the thickness of the fillets.

7.

Remove the dish from the oven and check the fillets for doneness.

8.

Serve immediately with half of the spicy mayo. Garnish with the scallions. Refrigerate the remaining mayo in an airtight container.

Hot Dog Rolls

Ingredients:

1½ cups shredded mozzarella cheese

2 tablespoons cream cheese, at room temperature

¾ cup almond flour

1 egg

1 teaspoon minced garlic

1 teaspoon Italian seasoning

4 hot dogs

1.

Preheat the oven to 425°F.

2.

In a large microwaveable bowl, combine the mozzarella cheese and cream cheese. Microwave on high for 1 minute. Remove, stir, and microwave again for 30 seconds more. The mixture will be very hot.

3.

Add the almond flour, egg, garlic, and Italian seasoning to the cheese mixture. Stir to incorporate fully.

4.

With wet hands, divide the dough into four equal pieces. Shape one piece of dough around each hot dog, encasing the hot dog completely.

5.

Place the dough-wrapped hot dogs onto a parchment-lined baking sheet. Use a fork to poke holes into each piece of dough so it doesn't bubble up during cooking.

6.

Put the baking sheet into the preheated oven. Bake for 7 to 8 minutes.

7.

Remove the tray from the oven. Check for bubbles (prick with a fork, if formed). Turn the dogs over. Return to the oven for another 6 to 7 minutes.

8.

Remove the sheet from the oven. Cool the hot dog rolls for 3 to 5 minutes before serving.

Bacon Wrap Sticks

Ingredients:

Oil for frying
2 mozzarella string cheese pieces
4 bacon slices
1.
In a large saucepan, heat 2 inches of oil to 350°F.
2.
Cut each string cheese stick in half widthwise.
3.
Wrap each half of string cheese in one slice of bacon. Secure with a toothpick. Keep the ends of the cheese stick exposed for better cooking.
4.
Once the oil is hot, drop the bacon-wrapped cheese pieces into the oil. Cook for 2 to 3 minutes, or until the bacon is thoroughly browned. Transfer to paper towels to drain.
5.
Serve alone or with sugar-free marinara sauce.

Soy Sauce Beef Stuffed Peppers

Ingredients:

1 tsp. hot sauce
1 tbsp. garlic (minced)
1 tsp. liquid smoke
3 tbsp. olive oil
1 1/2 tsp. Worcestershire sauce
1 tbsp. soy sauce
2 tsp. oregano
1/2 tsp. black pepper
2 tbsp. ketchup (sugar free)
4 bell peppers
1 1/2 lbs. ground beef
4 slices bacon (thick cut)

Directions:

1. Break out a Ziploc bag, and toss in your beef, spices, and oil. Seal the bag, and mix all the contents thoroughly.

2. Allow this bag to sit in the fridge for at least 3 hours.

3. Preheat your oven to 350☐F, and bring a pot of salted water to a boil on the stove.

4. Blanch the peppers in the boiling water for 3 minutes, and then immediately remove and dry them.

5. Finely chop your bacon and give it a light fry, don't cook it all the way. Add this bacon to the beef mixture.

6. Now stuff the peppers with the bacon and beef mixture.

7. Bake the peppers for 55 minutes. If you have a meat thermometer, cook until the filling is at medium for beef.

8. Sprinkle some cheese on top, and broil until the cheese is bubbling.

Serve and enjoy!

Chili Cheddar Meatballs

Ingredients:

1 tsp. cumin
1 cup cheddar cheese
1 cup tomato sauce
1/3 pork rinds (crushed)
2 large eggs
1 tsp. chili powder
1 1/2 chorizo sausage
1 1/2 lbs. ground beef
1 tsp. salt
Directions:

1. Preheat your oven to 350☐F.

2. Break up your sausage and mix it with the ground beef. You want a fairly uniform mixture here.

3. Now add your pork rinds, spices, cheese, and eggs to the beef mixture. Combine well.

4. Form your meatballs and lay them on a foiled baking sheet.

5. Bake for about 35 minutes, or until fully cooked.

6. Drizzle the tomato sauce over the meatballs and serve.
Enjoy!

Smoked Salmon Avocado Shushi Roll

Ingredients:

14 ounces smoked salmon
1 tablespoon wasabi paste (optional)
¾ cup cream cheese, at room temperature
½ avocado, sliced
1 tablespoon sesame seeds

1.
On a cutting board, lay out a large piece of plastic wrap.
2.
Place the salmon pieces on the plastic wrap, overlapping, to create a large rectangle 6 to 7 inches long and 4 inches wide.
3.
In a small bowl, mix together the wasabi paste (if using) and the cream cheese.
4.
Spread the cream cheese evenly over the entire smoked salmon rectangle.
5.
Arrange the avocado over the cream cheese, in the center of the rectangle.
6.
Grabbing the plastic wrap at one end, lift and carefully begin to roll the salmon. Hold the plastic wrap tightly over the roll as you go to apply pressure to hold it together.
7.
Unwrap the plastic wrap from the sushi roll.
8.
Cover the sushi roll in sesame seeds, patting them into the outer layer.
9.
Refrigerate the roll for 15 to 20 minutes.

10.
 With a very sharp knife, slice into pieces and serve.

Garlic Roasted Cod With Bok Choy

Ingredients:

2 (8-ounce) cod fillets
¼ cup (½ stick) butter, thinly sliced
1 tablespoon minced garlic
½ pound baby bok choy, halved lengthwise
¼ teaspoon salt
¼ teaspoon freshly ground black pepper
1.
Preheat the oven to 400°F.
2.
Make a large pouch from aluminum foil and place the cod inside. Top with slices of butter and the garlic, evenly divided.
3.
Tuck the bok choy around the fillets. Season with the salt and pepper.
4.
Close the pouch with the two ends of the foil meeting at the top, so the butter remains in the pouch.
5.
Place the sealed pouches in a baking dish. Put the dish in the preheated oven, and bake for 15 to 20 minutes, depending on the thickness of the fillets.
6.
Remove the dish from the oven and check the fillets for doneness.
7.
Serve immediately.

Beef Kelaguen

Ingredients
1 1/2 cups lemon juice
2 tablespoons soy sauce
Tabasco to taste
1 bunch green onions, thinly sliced
2 pounds beef flank steak, very thinly sliced against the grain

Directions
Pour lemon juice, soy sauce, and Tabasco in a large, glass bowl. Stir in the green onions and beef. Add additional lemon juice if needed to cover the beef.
Cover the bowl with plastic wrap, and allow to rest at room temperature for one hour, until the meat turns a grayish-brown color and appears cooked.

Delight American Roast Beef

Ingredients
3 pounds beef eye of round roast
1/2 teaspoon kosher salt
1/2 teaspoon garlic powder
1/4 teaspoon freshly ground black pepper

Directions
Preheat oven to 375 degrees F (190 degrees C). If roast is untied, tie at 3 inch intervals with cotton twine. Place roast in pan, and season with salt, garlic powder, and pepper. Add more or less seasonings to taste.
Roast in oven for 60 minutes (20 minutes per pound). Remove from oven, cover loosely with foil, and let rest for 15 to 20 minutes.

Butter Beef Bacon Rolls

Ingredients
1 1/2 pounds top sirloin, lean
1 pound bacon
1 cup chopped onion
1 1/3 cups butter

Directions

Cut the beef into strips that are approximately 1 inch wide and the same length or close to the length of the bacon strip, about 1/8 inch thick. Serve hot.

Make the beef bacon rolls by laying a strip of bacon on a strip of beef and rolling the two meats together so that the beef is on the outside when you finish rolling. Insert a toothpick so that it goes in on the bottom left side and comes out the top right side when looked at vertically.

In large skillet, saute onions and butter until onions are tender. Lay a single layer of beef bacon rolls in the skillet. Brown them on medium heat, turning once or twice. Cover the skillet and simmer about 2 hours.

Spicy Ground Beef Stew

Ingredients
1 pound ground beef
2 (10.75 ounce) cans condensed vegetable beef soup
1 (10 ounce) can diced tomatoes and green chilies, undrained

Directions
In a large saucepan, cook the beef over medium heat until no longer pink; drain. Stir in soup and tomatoes; heat through.

Oriental Beef Ribbons

Ingredients
3/4 pound beef flank steak
2 tablespoons teriyaki sauce
1 1/2 teaspoons vegetable oil
1 garlic clove, minced
1/4 teaspoon ground ginger
1/8 teaspoon crushed red pepper flakes
1/2 teaspoon toasted sesame seeds

Directions
Slice meat across the grain into 1/4-in. strips. In a resealable plastic bag, combine the teriyaki sauce, oil, garlic, ginger and red pepper flakes; add meat. Seal bag and turn to coat; refrigerate for 8 hours or overnight, turning several times.

Drain and discard marinade. Weave meat onto metal or soaked wooden skewers. Grill, covered, over medium heat or broil 4 in. from heat for 2-4 minutes on each side or until desired doneness. Remove from grill or broiler and sprinkle with sesame seeds.

Yummy Skillet Lamb Chops

Ingredients
2 (8 ounce) lamb shoulder blade chops
2 tablespoons vegetable oil
1/2 cup warm water
1 teaspoon lemon juice
1 teaspoon dried minced onion
1/2 teaspoon dried oregano
1/4 teaspoon salt
1/8 teaspoon pepper

Directions
In a large skillet, brown lamb chops in oil. Add the remaining ingredients; bring to a boil. Reduce heat; cover and simmer for 30 -35 minutes or until meat juices run clear.

Braised Lamb Shanks

Ingredients
2 large white onions, chopped
4 lamb shanks
2 cups dry red wine
1 cup balsamic vinegar
1/3 cup olive oil

4 cloves garlic, pressed
2 lemons, quartered
2 (14.5 ounce) cans diced tomatoes
1 bunch fresh basil, chopped
1 tablespoon kosher salt
1 tablespoon cracked black pepper

Directions
Preheat the oven to 350 degrees F (175 degrees C).
Place the onions in a layer in the bottom of a Dutch oven or medium roasting pan with a lid.
Arrange the lamb shanks on top of the onions. Pour the wine, balsamic vinegar and olive oil over the lamb. Place a clove of pressed garlic next to each shank, and a quarter of a lemon on each side. Pour the tomatoes over everything, then season with salt, pepper and basil.
Cover and place in the preheated oven. Cook for 3 hours. Use juices from the pan to make a nice flavorful gravy.

Lemon and Thyme Lamb Chops

Ingredients
1/2 cup olive oil
1/4 cup lemon juice
1 tablespoon chopped fresh thyme
Salt and pepper to taste
12 lamb chops

Directions
Stir together olive oil, lemon juice, and thyme in a small bowl. Season with salt and pepper to taste. Place lamb chops in a shallow dish, and brush with the olive oil mixture. Marinate in the refrigerator for 1 hour.
Preheat grill for high heat.
Lightly oil grill grate. Place lamb chops on grill, and discard marinade. Cook for 10 minutes, turning once, or to desired doneness.
66   Baked Chickens with Mushrooms and Sweet Potato

Ingredients:

- [ ] 1/2 skinless chicken breast
- [ ] 1 cup baby portobello mushrooms, sliced
- [ ] 1 Tbsp chives
- [ ] 1 Tbsp olive oil
- [ ] 1 medium sweet potato

Directions:

In a 350°F stove, prepare chicken, finished with mushrooms, chives, and oil, for 15 minutes. Microwave sweet potato for five to seven minutes.

Jicama Shrimp Ceviche

Ingredients:

- [ ] 1/2 cup chopped cucumber
- [ ] 1/3 cup chopped jicama
- [ ] 1/3 cup chopped mango
- [ ] 1 Tbsp chopped onion
- [ ] 1/4 cup sliced avocado
- [ ] 1 tomato, sliced
- [ ] 1 cup cooked shrimp
- [ ] 1/4 cup lemon juice
- [ ] 1 tsp red pepper

Directions:

Toss all together, and dress with lemon juice.

Tasty Light Lasagna

Ingredients:
- 1/2 cup cooked whole-wheat spaghetti
- 1/4 cup part-skim ricotta
- 1/3 cup prepared tomato sauce
- 1/2 tsp crushed red chili flakes
- 1 Coleman Natural Mild Italian Chicken Sausage link, cooked
- 2 cups spinach

Directions:
Combine pasta, ricotta, sauce, and chili flakes, and then crumble sausage on top. Also include spinach, and let wilt.

Mustard Shallot Chicken Drumsticks

Ingredients:
1½ pounds chicken drumsticks

¼ teaspoon salt

¼ teaspoon freshly ground black pepper

2 tablespoons butter

3 tablespoons finely chopped shallots

2 fresh thyme sprigs

1 tablespoon balsamic vinegar

¼ cup dry white wine

1 teaspoon Worcestershire sauce

½ cup chicken broth

2 teaspoons tomato paste

½ cup heavy (whipping) cream

1 tablespoon Dijon mustard

2 tablespoons finely chopped fresh parsley

1.

Season the drumsticks with the salt and pepper. Set aside.

2.

In a large skillet over medium-high heat, melt the butter. Add the drumsticks, skin-side down. Cook for 6 to 7 minutes, until browned. Turn the drumsticks on their sides. Cook for 2 minutes more. Turn the drumsticks again to the remaining uncooked side. Cook for 3 to 4 minutes more. With a meat thermometer, check the internal temperature. The chicken should reach 165°F before it is removed from the skillet.

3.

Transfer the cooked chicken to a serving dish. Keep warm.

4.

To any butter remaining in the skillet, add the shallots and thyme. Cook for 1 minute, until the shallots are tender.

5.

Add the vinegar, white wine, and Worcestershire sauce. Bring the mixture to a boil.

6.

Stir in the chicken broth. Return the mixture to a boil.

7.

Add the tomato paste. Stir to combine. Cook for 5 to 6 minutes, or until the mixture reduces by half.

8.

Once reduced, add the heavy cream. Bring to a boil again. Whisk in the mustard. You will have about 1 cup of sauce.

9.

Pour the sauce over the drumsticks. Allow the drumsticks to rest for 2 minutes.

10.

Garnish with the chopped parsley, and serve.

Whole Chicken Herb Roast

Ingredients:

1 shallot, minced
2 fresh thyme sprigs, chopped
2 fresh rosemary sprigs, chopped
2 garlic cloves, minced
2 fresh sage sprigs, chopped
2 tablespoons chopped fresh parsley
1 (5-pound) whole roasting chicken
¼ cup olive oil
1 cup roughly chopped jicama
½ teaspoon salt

¼ teaspoon freshly ground black pepper

1.

Preheat the oven to 425°F.

2.

To a food processor or blender, add the shallot, thyme, rosemary, and garlic. Pulse to chop. Add the sage and parsley. Pulse lightly until mixed.

3.

On a flat surface, place the chicken breast-side up. Carefully slide your fingers under the skin of each breast to separate the skin from the meat, creating a pocket. Do not remove the skin from the chicken.

4.

Turn the chicken onto its side. Repeat the process of lifting up the skin on the thighs.

5.

Stuff an equal amount of the herb mixture under the skin of the breasts and thighs. Place the chicken into a baking dish.

6.

Pour the olive oil over the herbed chicken. Massage it into the skin. If any herb mixture is left, spread it over the outside of the chicken.

7.

Place the baking dish in the preheated oven. Bake for 15 minutes. Remove the pan from the oven.

8.

Arrange the jicama around the chicken, and season with salt and pepper. Return the pan to the oven. Reduce the heat to 375°F. Cook the chicken for 1 hour, or until the internal temperature reaches 165°F.

9.

Remove the chicken from the oven. Allow the chicken to rest for at least 15 minutes before carving.

Spicy Lamb Patties

Ingredients
1 pound ground lamb
3 green onions, minced

4 cloves garlic, minced
1 tablespoon curry powder
1 teaspoon ground cumin
1/4 teaspoon dried red pepper flakes
Salt and pepper to taste

Directions
Preheat the grill for high heat.
In a bowl, mix the lamb, green onions, garlic, curry powder, cumin, red pepper, salt and pepper.
Form into 4 patties.
Lightly oil grill grate. Grill patties 5 minutes on each side, or until done.

Yummy Chickens with Cheesy Broccoli Soup

Ingredients:

- 1 cup chopped broccoli
- 1 cup chopped parsnips
- 3/4 cup nonfat chicken stock
- 1/4 cup low-fat shredded cheddar cheese
- 1 Tbsp sliced almonds
- 4 oz chicken breast
- 1 tsp lemon juice
- Salt and pepper, to taste

Directions:
Steam broccoli & parsnips, and then puree with stock & cheddar; also sprinkle with nuts. Bake chicken, top with lemon juice, as well as season.

Tomatoes with Seafood Dressing

Ingredients
1 cup canned shrimp
2 hard-cooked eggs, chopped
1 1/2 cups finely grated carrots
1 tablespoon minced onion
1/2 teaspoon salt
1/8 teaspoon ground black pepper
1/2 cup mayonnaise
2 tablespoons lemon juice
1/2 teaspoon prepared mustard
4 medium tomatoes
4 leaves of lettuce

Directions
Add shrimp, eggs, carrots, onion, salt, and pepper to the bowl of a food processor. Pulse until just combined. Blend mayonnaise with lemon juice and mustard; mix into shrimp mixture with a fork.
Core tomatoes. Cut into quarters without cutting all the way to the bottom. Place each tomato on a lettuce leaf, and open. Spoon shrimp mixture into the center. Serve

Scallions Asian Turkey Lettuce Cups

Ingredients:

- 4 oz ground lean turkey
- 1/2 cup white mushrooms, chopped
- 1 tsp minced garlic
- 1/4 cup shelled and cooked edamame
- 2 Boston lettuce leaves
- 2 Tbsp sliced scallion

Sauce

- 1/2 Tbsp hoisin sauce
- 1 tsp low-sodium soy sauce
- 1/2 tsp rice vinegar

Asian Slaw

- 1/2 cup shredded red cabbage and green cabbage
- 1/4 cup sliced jicama
- 1/4 cup grated carrot
- 1 tsp olive oil
- 1/2 tsp rice vinegar

Directions:

In a nonstick skillet covered with a cooking splash, sauté initial three elements for five minutes. Include edamame, scoop blend onto lettuce, best with scallion, and wrap up. Sprinkle with sauce, and serve slaw as an afterthought.

Tasty Pork with Roasted Vegetables

Ingredients:

- 3 oz pork tenderloin
- 1 cup baked cubed butternut squash
- 2 cups brussels sprouts cooked in 1 Tbsp olive oil
- 1/2 tsp salt
- 1 tsp black pepper

Directions:

Roast pork tenderloin at 425°F, and then serve with hot vegetables.

Onion Mushroom Bison Burger

Ingredients:
- ☐ 4 oz grass-fed bison burger
- ☐ 1 portobello mushroom, grilled
- ☐ 1 slice red onion
- ☐ 2 slices tomato
- ☐ 2 lettuce leaves
- ☐ 1 Arnold Artisan Ovens Multi-Grain Flatbreat

Directions:
Grill mushroom & burger, & also top with onion, tomato, & lettuce on flatbread.

Parsmo[Salmon with Lemon and Dill

Ingredients:
- ☐ 5 oz wild Atlantic salmon
- ☐ 1 Tbsp lemon juice
- ☐ 1 tsp dill
- ☐ 2/3 cup parsnips
- ☐ 1 1/2 cup chopped broccoli, steamed

Directions:
Sprinkle salmon with lemon juice & dill & bake for 14 minutes at 220°F.

Shrimp Pasta with Salad

Ingredients:

- ☐ 1/2 cup dry rigatoni, cooked
- ☐ 3 oz shrimp, poached
- ☐ 1/2 cup oil-packed sun-dried tomatoes, drained and pureed
- ☐ 3 large black olives, sliced
- ☐ 1/2 Tbsp pine nuts
- ☐ 2 tsp grated Parmesan

Salad

- ☐ 1 cup romaine lettuce
- ☐ 1/4 cup chopped tomato
- ☐ 1/2 cup sliced cucumber
- ☐ 1/2 Tbsp balsamic vinegar
- ☐
- ☐

Directions:

Toss pasta by adding shrimp, sun-dried tomatoes or with oven, olives, & pine nuts. Top with Parmesan. Serve alongside the salad.

Scallops with Lemon Juice and Sage

Ingredients:

- ☐ 2 tsp canola oil
- ☐ 3 oz sea scallops
- ☐ 2 tsp lemon juice

- 1/2 tsp ground sage
- 1 1/2 cups cubed roasted acorn squash
- 2 cups kale sautéed in 2 tsp olive oil

Directions:

Warm canola oil in a huge nonstick skillet over high warmth
Include scallops and cook without mixing until all around seared, around two minutes. Flip scallops and cook until the sides are firm and focuses misty, 30 to 90 seconds. Shower with lemon squeeze, and sprinkle sage on top. Present with squash and kale.

Delight Cheesy Veggie Pasta

Ingredients:
- 1/2 cup whole-wheat macaroni
- 1 cup crushed whole, peeled canned tomatoes
- 1/2 cup low-fat ricotta cheese
- 3/4 cup chopped spinach
- 1 cup zucchini wedges
- 2 tsp olive oil

Directions:
Cook vegetables over medium-high heat and combine with cooked macaroni & cheese.

Cheesy Bacon Wrap Chicken

Ingredients:
4 (4-ounce) boneless chicken breasts
¾ cup cream cheese, at room temperature

4 jalapeño peppers, halved

1 teaspoon onion powder

2 garlic cloves, minced

8 bacon slices

¼ teaspoon salt

⅛ teaspoon freshly ground black pepper

2 tablespoons olive oil

1.

Preheat the oven to 400°F.

2.

On a flat surface, cut each chicken breast in half horizontally. Do not cut all the way through the other side. Open the breasts flat.

3.

Spread an equal amount of cream cheese over each of the butterflied breasts.

4.

Top each with two jalapeño halves. Sprinkle with onion powder and garlic. Fold the breasts closed. Wrap each breast with two bacon slices. Secure with toothpicks. Season the outside of the breasts with the salt and pepper.

5.

Place the bacon-wrapped chicken in a baking pan. Drizzle with the olive oil.

6.

Put the pan into the preheated oven. Bake the chicken for 20 minutes, or until the internal temperature is 165°F.

7.

Remove the pan from the oven. Allow the chicken to rest for 2 to 3 minutes. Remove the toothpicks from the meat and serve.

Olive Garlic Stuffed Chicken

Ingredients:

1 cup crumbled feta cheese

¼ cup shredded Swiss cheese

1 teaspoon minced garlic

1 tablespoon olive oil

¼ cup olives, chopped

1 pound boneless chicken thighs

¼ teaspoon salt

¼ teaspoon freshly ground black pepper

1.

Preheat the oven to 425°F.

2.

In a large bowl, mix together the feta cheese, Swiss cheese, garlic, olive oil, and olives.

3.

On a flat surface, lay out the chicken thighs. Spread the meat open so the thighs lay flat. Place an equal portion of the feta mixture on each piece of chicken. Close the thighs. Secure with toothpicks. Season with the salt and pepper.

4.

Place the chicken in a baking dish. Put the dish into the preheated oven and bake for about 18 minutes. With a meat thermometer, check the internal temperature. It should reach 165°F before serving.

Creamy Lemon Chicken Thighs

Ingredients:

1 tablespoon butter
1 tablespoon minced shallots
1 cup sour cream
2 tablespoons freshly squeezed lemon juice
½ teaspoon salt, divided
¼ teaspoon freshly ground black pepper, divided
1 pound bone-in chicken thighs

1.

Preheat the oven to 425°F.

2.

In a large skillet over medium-low heat, melt the butter. Add the shallots. Cook for 3 to 4 minutes, or until tender. Decrease the heat to low. Add the sour cream, lemon juice, ¼ teaspoon of salt, and ⅛ teaspoon of pepper. Mix well to combine. Refrigerate until ready to serve.

3.

Season the chicken with the remaining ¼ teaspoon of salt and ⅛ teaspoon of pepper.

4.

Place the chicken into a baking dish and into the preheated oven. Bake for about 18 minutes. With a meat thermometer, check the internal temperature. It should reach 165°F.

5.

Plate the chicken, spooning an equal amount of lemon cream sauce on each thigh.

Parsley Chicken Piccata

Ingredients:

1 pound boneless chicken thighs

¼ teaspoon salt

⅛ teaspoon freshly ground black pepper

¼ cup olive oil

½ cup dry white wine

1 tablespoon freshly squeezed lemon juice

1 garlic clove, minced

1 tablespoon capers, chopped

3 tablespoons chopped fresh parsley

1.

On a flat surface, flatten the chicken thighs with a meat tenderizer until they are ¼ inch thick. Season with the salt and pepper.

2.

In a large skillet over medium heat, heat the olive oil for about 1 minute. Place two chicken thighs in the pan. Cook for about 4 minutes per side. Remove to a plate. Repeat, two at a time, with the remaining thighs. Set aside.

3.

Using the same skillet, increase the heat to high. Add the white wine, lemon juice, garlic, and capers. Stir the sauce, scraping any browned bits from the bottom of the pan. Bring to a boil. Cook for 1 minute.

4.

Add the chicken back into the pan. Heat in the sauce for 1 minute.

5.

Add the parsley and stir to incorporate before serving.

Chili Cilantro Chicken Skewers

Ingredients:

1 cup fresh cilantro, chopped
2 tablespoons olive oil
¼ cup red chili paste
2 tablespoons soy sauce
2 garlic cloves, minced
1 teaspoon onion powder
1 teaspoon minced fresh ginger
¼ teaspoon freshly ground black pepper
1 pound boneless chicken thighs cut into 1-inch cubes
1 onion, roughly chopped
2 red bell peppers, roughly chopped

1.
Preheat the oven to broil.

2.
In a large bowl, combine the cilantro, olive oil, red chili paste, soy sauce, garlic, onion powder, ginger, and black pepper.

3.
Add the thigh meat. Toss to coat. Refrigerate for 15 minutes to marinate.

4.
Remove the chicken from the refrigerator. Skewer the chicken cubes, alternating with the onions and peppers between each piece.

5.
Place a foil-lined baking sheet on the lowest oven rack.

6.
Lay the chicken skewers directly on the middle rack above the baking sheet, perpendicular to the rack. Cook for 3 minutes. Turn the skewers over and cook for 3 minutes more. Turn the skewers again, and cook for 4 minutes more. With a meat thermometer, check the internal temperature. When it reaches 165°F, remove from the oven to cool.

7.
Serve on the skewers or remove the meat and vegetables from the skewers prior to plating.

Almond Avocado Chicken Burger

Ingredients:

1 pound ground chicken
½ cup almond flour
2 garlic cloves, minced
1 teaspoon onion powder
¼ teaspoon salt
⅛ teaspoon freshly ground black pepper
1 avocado, diced
2 tablespoons olive oil
4 low-carb buns or lettuce wraps (optional)

1.
In a large bowl, mix together the ground chicken, almond flour, garlic, onion powder, salt, and pepper.
2.
Add the avocado, gently incorporating into the meat while forming four patties. Set aside.
3.
In a large skillet over medium heat, heat the olive oil for about 1 minute. Add the patties to the skillet. Cook for about 8 minutes per side, or until golden brown and cooked through.
4.
Serve on a low-carb bun, in a lettuce wrap (if using), or on its own.

Beef Stir-Fry with Butternut Squash Soup

Ingredients:
- 3 oz steak tenderloin fillet, sliced thin
- 1/2 cup sliced shiitake mushrooms
- 1/2 onion, sliced

- [ ] 2 tsp olive oil
- [ ] 1/3 cup cooked bulgur

Butternut Squash Soup
- [ ] 1/2 cup Pacific Natural Foods organic light-sodium
- [ ] Stir-fry beef, onion, & mushroom.
- [ ] Asian Snapper
- [ ] 1/4 cup raw pistachios
- [ ] 1/2 cup cooked millet
- [ ] 1/2 cup bok choy
- [ ] 6 oz cooked snapper
- [ ] 4 tsp low-sodium soy sauce
- [ ] 2 tsp sesame seeds
- [ ] 1/2 cup sugar snap peas, cooked

Directions:

Blend pistachios into millet. Beat millet with bok choy and after that snapper. Shower snapper with soy sauce, and sprinkle with sesame seeds. Serve sugar snap peas as an afterthought.

Grilled Chickens and Pineapple Sandwich

Ingredients:

- [ ] 1 boneless, skinless chicken breast
- [ ] 1 Tbsp Teriyaki sauce
- [ ] 1 slice Swiss cheese
- [ ] 1 slice pineapple (1/2" thick)
- [ ] 1 whole-wheat kaiser roll
- [ ] Red onion, thinly sliced (to taste)
- [ ] Pickled jalapeno slices (to taste)

Directions:

Marinate chicken in Teriyaki sauce in re-sealable sack in ice chest. Barbecue chicken for four to five minutes, flip, and promptly add the cheddar to bosom. Keep cooking until the cheddar is softened and the chicken is gently singed and feels firm to the touch. Evacuate, and put aside. While the chicken is resting, put the pineapple cuts and moves on the flame broil. Toast the moves daintily, and cook the pineapple until it's delicate and caramelized, around two minutes on each side. Best each move with chicken, pineapple, onion, and jalapeno.

Delicious Chicken Goat-Cheese

Ingredients:

- 3/4 oz goat cheese, softened to room temperature
- 1 Tbsp shredded Monterey jack cheese
- 1/4 tsp virgin olive oil
- 2 Tbsp chopped Vidalia onion
- 1/4 cup frozen corn kernels, thawed
- Pinch ground black pepper
- 1/4 cup diced cooked skinless white-meat chicken
- 1/2 Tbsp chopped fresh cilantro
- 2 six-inch corn tortillas

Directions:

Consolidate cheeses in a little bowl. Put aside. Warm olive oil in a medium sauté skillet over medium-low warmth. Include onion, and sauté for two minutes. Include corn and pepper; sauté for one moment. Include chicken and sauté for one moment. Expel from warmth, then mix in cilantro. Separate cheddar blend, and spread more than two tortillas. Layer every tortilla with a large portion of the chicken blend, and top with residual tortillas. Shower an extensive skillet or frying pan with cooking splash. Warm quesadillas over medium warmth for five to six minutes, flipping part of the way through.

Cooked Rice Blend with Veggies

Ingredients:

- 1 veggie burger
- 1/2 cup cooked brown rice
- 2 Tbsp corn
- 2 Tbsp salsa
- 1/2 cup chopped red, green, or yellow bell peppers
- 3/4 cup diced squash
- 3/4 cup diced zucchini
- 1/4 cup chopped red onion
- 1 tsp olive oil
- Salt, to taste

Directions:

Cook burger in skillet spritzed with cooking shower, then cleave burger and consolidate with rice, corn, and salsa. Hurl veggies with oil and salt, broil for 15 to 20 minutes, and serve as an afterthought.

Salmon rolls

Ingredients:
- 10 oz smoked salmon, sliced
- ½ cup cream cheese
- 1 tablespoon butter
- 1 tablespoon dill
- 1 teaspoon cilantro
- ½ teaspoon minced garlic
- 1 oz walnuts
- 1 teaspoon salt
- 1 tablespoon oregano
- 1 teaspoon nutmeg

Directions:
1. Take the mixing bowl and combine the cream cheese and butter together.
2. Take the hand mixer and mix the mixture carefully till you get smooth and fluffy mass.

3.	Then sprinkle the mixture with the dill, cilantro, minced garlic, salt, oregano, and walnuts.
4.	Stir the cream mixture very carefully with the help of the spoon.
5.	After this, crush the walnuts and sprinkle the cream mixture.
6.	Stir it again until homogenous.
7.	Then take the sliced salmon and cover every slice with the cream mixture.
8.	Roll the salmon slices.
9.	Transfer the salmon rolls in the fridge and keep them for 10 minutes there.
10.	Remove the dish from the fridge and serve it immediately.

Nutritional value: calories: 350, fat: 27.4g, total carbs: 4.0g, sugars: 0g, protein: 22.9g

Almond Crab rissoles

Ingredients:
- 12 oz crab meat
- 1 tablespoon flax meal
- 1 tablespoon almond flour
- 1 tablespoon coconut flour
- 1 teaspoon ground black pepper
- 1 teaspoon salt
- ¼ cup almond milk
- 1 tablespoon coconut oil
- 2 tablespoon butter
- 2 eggs
- 1 teaspoon nutmeg
- 1 teaspoon chives
- 1 teaspoon onion powder

Directions:
1.	Chop the crab meat into the tiny pieces and combine it with eggs.
2.	Stir the mixture carefully until homogenous.
3.	After this, sprinkle it with the flax meal, ground black pepper, and salt.
4.	Add butter and onion powder.
5.	After this, add nutmeg and chives. Stir the mixture carefully.
6.	Make the medium rissoles and deep the rissoles in the almond milk.

7.   Then combine the almond flour and coconut flour together and sprinkle the rissoles with this mixture.

8.   Preheat the skillet and pour coconut oil.

9.   Then transfer the rissoles in the skillet and fry them for 4 minutes from the both sides.

10.   When the rissoles are cooked - chill them for 2 minutes and serve.

11.   Enjoy!

Delight Seafood Stuffed Avocados

Ingredients
1/2 cup flaked cooked crabmeat
1/2 cup cooked small shrimp
2 tablespoons peeled and diced cucumber
1 tablespoon mayonnaise
1 teaspoon chopped fresh parsley
1 pinch salt
1 pinch ground black pepper
1 pinch paprika
1 avocado

Directions
In a bowl, mix the crab, shrimp, cucumber, mayonnaise, and parsley. Season with salt, and pepper. Cover, and chill until serving.
Slice the avocados lengthwise, and remove the pit. Scoop out the flesh of the avocado, leaving about 1/2 inch on the peel. Spoon the seafood mixture into the hollowed centers of the avocado halves. Sprinkle the tops with paprika.

Lemon Seafood Melange

Ingredients
4 sole, patted dry
10 bay scallops, raw

3/4 cup crabmeat
3/4 cup cooked shrimp
1/2 cup shredded Monterey Jack cheese
1/2 cup butter 2 egg yolks
1 tablespoon lemon juice
1/2 teaspoon mustard powder
1/8 teaspoon salt
2 tablespoons chopped fresh parsley
1/4 teaspoon paprika

Directions
Butter two 2-cup au gratin dishes. Place 1 fillet on bottom of each, then layer with scallops, crabmeat, shrimp, cheese and a second fillet; set aside.
Preheat oven to 450 degrees F (230 degrees C).
Melt butter. In a medium mixing bowl, combine yolks, lemon juice, mustard and salt; mix on high and slowly add butter in a steady stream until sauce is thick and creamy. Pour sauce over fillets.
Bake in preheated oven for 10 to 15 minutes; sprinkle with parsley and paprika. Serve.

Cilantro Shrimp with Squash, Chard, and Wild Rice

Ingredients:

- [ ] 8 large shrimp
- [ ] 1 Tbsp olive oil
- [ ] 2 tsp fresh cilantro
- [ ] 2 tsp fresh lime juice
- [ ] 1 yellow squash, sliced
- [ ] 1 cup Swiss chard
- [ ] 1/4 cup dry wild rice blend

Directions:
Singe shrimp in olive oil over medium warmth for three to four minutes, flavoring with cilantro and lime juice. Steam squash and chard for five to seven minutes, and cook rice as per package directions.

Lamb Chops in Duck Sauce

Ingredients
3 pounds lamb chops
2 tablespoons Worcestershire sauce
1 tablespoon adobo seasoning cayenne pepper to taste
Salt and pepper to taste
1 1/2 cups duck sauce

Directions
Preheat oven to 350 degrees F (175 degrees C).
Arrange lamb chops in a medium baking dish, and evenly coat with Worcestershire sauce, adobo seasoning, and cayenne pepper. Season with salt and pepper.
Bake 1 hour in the preheated oven.
Cover lamb chops with duck sauce, and continue baking 15 to 20 minutes, to an internal temperature of 145 degrees F (65 degrees C).

Butter Roasted Trout

Ingredients:

1 teaspoon salt, divided

½ teaspoon freshly ground black pepper, divided

4 (8-ounce) trout, cleaned

4 fresh dill sprigs

4 fresh fennel sprigs

2 pounds Swiss chard, cleaned and leaves separated from stems

4 tablespoons olive oil, divided

4 tablespoons butter, divided

1 lemon, quartered

4 tablespoons dry vermouth, or white wine, divided

1.

Preheat the oven to 450°F.

2.

Using ½ teaspoon of salt and ¼ teaspoon of pepper, season the insides of the trout. Place 1 dill sprig and 1 fennel sprig inside each trout.

3.

Cut the Swiss chard stems into 2-inch pieces. Cut the leaves crosswise into 1½-inch strips. Set aside.

4.

Cut four large pieces of aluminum foil into oval shapes large enough to fit one trout and one-quarter of the Swiss chard, with room enough to be sealed.

5.

Using ¾ tablespoon of olive oil, brush the trout. Place one trout in the center of each piece of foil. Top each trout with one-quarter of the Swiss chard.

6.

Season the trout with the remaining ½ teaspoon of salt, ¼ teaspoon of pepper, and 3¼ tablespoons of olive oil. Top each trout with 1 tablespoon of butter.

7.

Squeeze a lemon quarter over each Swiss chard and trout bundle. Spoon 1 tablespoon of vermouth over each, as well. Close and seal the foil pouches tightly.

8.

Place the foil packets on a baking sheet. Bake in the preheated oven for 10 to 12 minutes, depending on the thickness of the fish.

9.

Remove from the oven and allow the packets to cool for 1 to 2 minutes before opening. Serve in the foil packet.

Garlic Roasted Butterfish

Fat Ingredients:

Four giant butterfish fillets
8 tablespoon butter or ghee
Other Ingredients:
4 cloves garlic
4 teaspoon freshly chopped thyme
Pinch sea salt
Juice from 1 lemon

Directions:

1. Begin by seasoning the butterfish fillets with a little bit of salt and place them on a plate.
2. Soften the butter, add the herbs and crushed garlic and blend all the pieces collectively in a small bowl.
3. Pour the butter combination over the fish.
4. Warm a non-stick pan over medium heat and add the fish.
5. Roast for about 2 to 3 minutes on both sides until cooked and the fish will get a crispy golden texture. Be certain that the fillet is totally cooked by slicing into it. Cooked flesh will look opaque.
6. Place the fish onto a serving plate and squeeze a little bit of lemon over it. Serve sizzling.

Creamy Broccoli and Ham Quiche

Fat Ingredients:

10 large organic eggs or 12 medium eggs
2 cups of thinly sliced ham
1 cup of grated cheddar cheese
1 ½ cups of heavy cream
3 tablespoons of olive oil
Other Ingredients:
12 cups of cubed broccoli flowerets
2 teaspoons of chili flakes

Directions:

1. Preheat the oven to 350F.
2. Take 2 deep 10 inch quiche pans. Grease them with a bit of olive oil and keep aside.
3. Take a large mixing bowl. Crack all the eggs and pour into the bowl. Then add the heavy cream, chili flakes, and beat well until it has all been mixed well.
4. Take each quiche pan and place the ham slices and broccoli flowerets evenly in each pan. Then sprinkle the cheese over them and finally pour the egg and cream mixture over it.
5. Bake for 20 minutes until the top is golden brown in color. Prick with a fork till the bottom of quiche to check if done. If it is clean, then the quiche is ready to enjoy.

5. Baked Salmon (Serves 4)
Fat Ingredients:
4 6-ounce salmon fillets
3 tbsp. olive oil
Other Ingredients:
2 tablespoons of lemon juice
1 tablespoon each of minced parsley, mint, garlic, paprika, sunflower seeds (slightly crushed)
How to Prepare:
1. Clean the fillet and put aside.
2. Place all the other ingredients in another bowl, and mix well and pour onto the fish. Marinate the fillet for 6 hours.
3. After 6 hours, place in a baking dish and bake for 1 hour at 250F until flaky and cooked.
4. Serve with sour cream, green beans and apricots.

Fried Chicken

Fat Ingredients:
1 pound or 4 (4-ounce) boneless, skinless chicken breasts
1/2 cup crushed pork rinds
1/2 cup grated Parmesan cheese
2 large eggs
2 tablespoons coconut oil
Other Ingredients:
1/2 teaspoon garlic powder
1/4 teaspoon onion powder

1/4 teaspoon dried minced onion

1/4 teaspoon salt

1/4 teaspoon black pepper

How to Prepare:

1. Put pork rinds, Parmesan cheese, garlic powder, onion powder, minced onion, salt, and black pepper in a large mixing bowl and stir until well mixed.

2. Crack eggs into a separate bowl and whisk.

3. Dip each chicken breast into eggs and then coat in pork rind mixture, making sure the chicken is completely covered.

4. Heat coconut oil in a skillet over medium-high heat. Place the chicken breasts into the pan. Let them cook for 5–7 minutes or until pork rind crust is browned. Flip chicken over and let them cook for another 5–7 minutes until cooked through.

5. Serve hot.

Ginger Baked Chicken Thighs

Ingredients:

4 chicken thighs (deboned, skin on)

1/4 cup olive oil

Other Ingredients:

2 zucchinis

1/2 cup carrot (sliced)

2 tablespoon balsamic vinegar

1 cup daikon radish

1 inch length of cube ginger, minced

Directions:

1. Pre-heat an oven to 350 degrees.

2. Use a paper towel, and pat the chicken thighs dry.

3. Wrap the skins around the chicken thighs, and place these on a buttered or greased baking sheet.

4. Slice the radish and zucchinis, and with the carrots, place them around the thigh pieces.

5. Using a small bowl mix the vinegar, oil, and ginger – this is your sauce. Pour the mix over the chicken.

5. Season with salt and pepper and bake the chicken thighs for 30 minutes.

Garlic Pork Roast

Ingredients
1 tablespoon vegetable oil
1 (2 pound) boneless pork roast
Salt and pepper to taste
4 sweet potatoes, quartered
1 onion, quartered
6 cloves garlic
1 (14.5 ounce) can chicken broth

Directions
Heat oil in large heavy skillet. Season meat with salt and pepper, and brown in oil.
In a slow cooker, layer sweet potatoes, onion and garlic. Place browned roast on top of vegetables, and pour in chicken broth.
Cover, and cook on low setting for 6 hours.

Baked Peanut Chicken

Ingredients
1/2 cup crushed dry-roasted, salted peanuts
1/2 teaspoon garlic powder
1/2 teaspoon onion powder
1 teaspoon salt-free herb seasoning blend
6 chicken thighs, skinned
1/2 cup melted butter

Directions
Preheat oven to 375 degrees F (190 degrees C).
In a shallow bowl, mix the peanuts, garlic powder, onion powder, and salt-free herb seasoning blend.
Dip the chicken thighs in the melted butter, then press into the peanuts to coat. Arrange on a baking sheet.

Bake 45 minutes in the preheated oven, or until chicken juices run clear.

Mayonnaise Broiled Ginger Chicken

Ingredients
4 pounds skinless, boneless chicken breast halves
1/2 cup mayonnaise
1 tablespoon soy sauce
1/4 teaspoon ground ginger
1/8 teaspoon cayenne pepper

Directions
Flatten the chicken to 1/4-in. thickness. Place on a broiler pan rack. Broil for 3 minutes on each side. Combine mayonnaise, soy sauce, ginger and cayenne; brush over chicken. Broil 2-3 minutes longer on each side or until juices run clear.

Kentucky Grilled Chicken

Ingredients
1 cup cider vinegar
1/2 cup vegetable or canola oil
5 teaspoons Worcestershire sauce
4 teaspoons hot pepper sauce
2 teaspoons salt
10 bone-in chicken breast halves

Directions

In a bowl, combine the first five ingredients; mix well. Pour 1 cup marinade into a large resealable plastic bag; add the chicken. Seal bag and turn to coat; refrigerate for at least 4 hours. Cover and refrigerate the remaining marinade for basting.

Coat grill rack with nonstick cooking spray before starting the grill. Drain and discard marinade from chicken. Grill bone side down, covered, over indirect medium heat for 20 minutes. Turn; grill 20-30 minutes longer or until juices run clear, basting occasionally with reserved marinade.

Dijon Bacon-Flavored Mayo

Ingredients:

1 free range egg yolk
½ cup of crispy bacon (crumbled)
¾ teaspoon of strong Dijon mustard
1 teaspoon of freshly squeezed lemon juice
Season to taste

Mix together the egg yolk and lemon juice slowly until completely incorporated. Add the rest of the ingredients. If you feel that the mayo is not runny enough, you can water it down a little. Store in the refrigerator – it will keep for about 2 – 3 days.

Mozzarella and Cilantro Topping
Serves 4
5 cloves of crushed garlic
4 cups of freshly picked cilantro leaves
2/3 cup of raw cashew nuts (crushed)
4 ounces of mozzarella (shredded)
½ cup of good quality olive oil
Salt and pepper to taste

Mix together all the ingredients until completely combined. Serve over food.

Shrimp with Garlic Sauce

Ingredients
- ½ lb. of large shrimp
- 2 cloves of garlic, minced

- ¼ tsp. of cayenne
- ¼ cup of olive oil
- 1 wedge of lemon
- Salt & pepper to taste

Instructions

1.   Pour some olive oil in a small-sized pan. Set heat to medium-low. Add the cayenne and garlic, and cook until the fragrance pervades the air.

2.   Peel the shrimp and devein as necessary. Cook each side for 2 to 3 minutes.

3.   Drizzle with salt & pepper. Squeeze the lemon wedge on the shrimp.

4.   The dish is best served warm. You can use the remaining garlic oil as dipping sauce served separate from the dish.

Mozzarella Pepperoni Bake

Ingredients:

6 cups of cauliflower (broken into small bits)
1/4 cup of double cream
2 tablespoons of farm butter
2 tablespoons of parmesan (shredded)
1/2 cup of keto-friendly Marinara Sauce
1 cup of mozzarella
1 teaspoon of dried Italian seasoning
12 slices of pepperoni

Directions:

Set your oven to 375°F. Put a pot of water on the stove and bring it to a boil. Boil the cauliflower until tender, and strain. Place in the food processor and quickly add the cream and butter. Process till smooth. Add the parmesan, half the mozzarella, and seasoning. Pour into an oven-proof dish and top with the marinara sauce and the remaining cheese.
Bake for about half an hour or until the cheese is golden.

Zesty Cheese and Turkey

Ingredients:

12 ounces of turkey breast (sliced)
12 slices of cheese – swiss or cheddar
1 big avocado (sliced into 12 pieces)
3 cups freshly picked baby spinach
1/2 cup of keto-friendly mayo
Salt to taste
1/4 teaspoon of lemon pepper

Directions:

Layer each piece of turkey with a slice of cheese. Top this with three pieces of the avocado and finish it off with some spinach.
Drizzle some mayo over the top and season to taste. Add a bit of lemon pepper over each.
Roll everything up and serve.

Garlic Steak Salad

Ingredients:

1 1/2 lbs. Flat Iron Steak
1/4 Cup Balsamic Vinegar
3 Tbs. Olive Oil
6 oz. Sliced Sweet Onion
4 oz. Sliced Cremini Mushrooms
2 minced Cloves Garlic
1 Large Head Romaine lettuce

1 Avocado
1 Orange Bell Pepper
1 Yellow Bell Pepper
3 oz. Sun-Dried Tomatoes
1 tsp. Garlic Salt
1 tsp. Onion Powder
1 tsp. Italian Seasoning
1 tsp. Red Pepper Flakes

Directions:
Cut flat iron steak into ½ inch thick slices. Marinate meat in large mixing bowl with balsamic vinegar. Toss to coat.
In medium heat sauté pan, heat olive oil and mushrooms, onions, garlic and a dash of salt and pepper. Saute until mushrooms and onion brown and caramelize – About 20 minutes.
In a mixing bowl, mix chopped Romaine, bell peppers, tomatoes and avocado
In a broiling pan, line strips of meat in a single layer and adds garlic salt, onion powder, Italian seasoning, and red pepper flakes.
Broil meat on high on top rack for 5 minutes for medium rare and cook longer for well done on both sides.
Plate your salad mixture meat first and then adding the caramelized onions and mushrooms.

Cordon Bleu Chicken

Ingredients:

1 cup of baked ham
1 cup of cheese that you like
1/2 cup of double cream
1/2 cup of plain cream cheese
1/2 cup of sour cream
1/2 teaspoon of onion flakes
1/2 teaspoon of garlic flakes
1/2 cup of pork rinds (crushed)
Salt and pepper to taste

Directions:

Set your oven to 350°F. Mix together the meats and place them at the bottom of an oven-proof dish.

Layer the solid cheese over this and set aside. Mix together the creams and cream cheese. Set your stove to medium and put the mixture in a pot. Heat; stirring often until thoroughly smooth and combined.

Add in the seasoning, and then pour over the meat/cheese in the dish. Top with the pork rinds and bake for about half an hour.

Rosemary Lamb Burger

Ingredients
1 pound ground lamb
1 tsp sea salt
1 TBS fresh rosemary, minced
1 TBS coconut oil
FOR PESTO
1 bunch fresh basil leaves
¼ cup olive oil
1 tsp fresh lemon juice
1 clove of garlic, minced
¼ teaspoon sea salt
¼ cup hemp seeds or raw pumpkin seeds
GARNISH
arugula
olive oil
white wine vinegar
salt and pepper

Directions:

In a bowl, mix ground lamb, rosemary, and salt until thoroughly combined using your hands. Form into 1 inch think patties.

Melt coconut oil in skillet and cook patties over medium high heat. Brown on both sides to desired doneness, about 4 -5 minutes.

In a food processor, blend olive oil, lemon, garlic and basil and salt until smooth paste. Add in hemp seeds and pulse again to desired consistency. Adjust seasoning with salt and lemon.

Toss arugula with olive oil, white wine vinegar and season with salt and pepper.

Assemble by placing lamb burgers on top of greens and tablespoon (or more) of pesto to enjoy!

Tasty Spicy Sausage Soup

Ingredients:
450 grams sausage
140 grams spinach, raw
2 cups beef stock
½ can spicy tomatoes
½ sweet pepper, sliced
½ tablespoon chili powder
½ tablespoon cumin
½ tablespoon extra-virgin olive oil
½ teaspoon garlic powder
½ teaspoon onion powder
½ teaspoon crushed, dried basil
Dash of salt

Directions:
1.   Put large pot with olive oil over stove on medium heat.
2.   Once oil is hot, put sausage in the pot.
3.   Allow sausage to brown on one side before breaking it up and mixing it around a bit.
4.   Allow it to cook a little.
5.   Add sweet pepper, salt, and pepper and stir to thoroughly incorporate.
6.   Pour in spicy tomatoes and again stir to incorporate.
7.   Add the spinach on top, just the way it is. Cover with a lid and let sit until spinach wilts. This step should take about 8 minutes.
8.   Once spinach has wilted, stir into the sausage mixture.
9.   Mix chili powder, cumin, garlic powder, onion powder, and basil in a small bowl. Once well-mixed, add the spices to the sausage mixture and stir until well incorporated.
10.   Add the beef stock and stir again.
11.   Reduce heat to medium-low and put the lid back on the pot. Let simmer for 30 minutes.
12.   Take the lid off and let the soup simmer for another 15 minutes.
13.   Portion, serve, and enjoy!

Delight Grilled Cheese

Bread Ingredients:
4 eggs
4 tablespoons almond flour
4 tablespoons butter, softened
3 tablespoons psyllium husk powder
1 teaspoon baking powder

On the inside:
115 grams cheese of your choice
2 tablespoons butter

Directions:
1.   Mix almond flour, butter, psyllium husk powder, and baking powder in a small bowl until a dough-like substance appears.
2.   Crack the eggs into the dough-like mixture and mix again. Keep mixing until dough is thick.
3.   Take half of the mixture and mold it into a square using a square dish or pan. Keep in mind while trying to size it that this will be the shape of your bread slices.
4.   Squish the dough into the dish to make it as level as possible.
5.   Put the dish with the dough into the microwave for about 1 minute 30 seconds, or until texture is cooked through and bread-like.
6.   Get the dough out of the dish by flipping the dish upside-down and lightly tapping it against a hard surface.
7.   Cut the bread in half.
8.   Repeat steps 3-7 with the other half of the dough.
9.   Divide the cheese into two even portions and place each portion between two slices of the bread.
10.   Put pan with the butter over a stove on medium heat.
11.   Once butter has melted, put the sandwiches into the pan.
12.   Let the first side brown for about 2 minutes and then flip the sandwiches to brown the other side.
13.   Once bread is crispy and cheese has melted, plate and enjoy!

Almond Spicy Sour Meatballs

Ingredients:

16 ounces ground beef
16 ounces ground pork
4 green onions, chopped
3 chili peppers, chopped
¼ cup almond flour
6 tablespoons sesame seeds
2 tablespoons soy sauce
1 ½ tablespoons sesame oil
1 ½ tablespoons extra-virgin olive oil
1 teaspoon ginger powder
1 teaspoon salt
1 teaspoon garlic powder

Directions:
1. Put the ground beef, ground pork, green onion, and chili peppers into a large bowl.
2. Mix until well incorporated.
3. Add soy sauce, ginger powder, salt, and garlic powder to the bowl.
4. Mix until well incorporated.
5. Sift in the almond flour.
6. Mix until well incorporated and flour has been thoroughly absorbed.
7. Divide the mixture into 20 meatballs, rolling them as you go.
8. Put a large pan with the sesame oil and extra-virgin olive oil over medium-high heat.
9. When the oil begins to sizzle, place about 10 meatballs in the pan.
10. Cover with a lid and let the meatballs sizzle for 4 minutes.
11. Uncover and roll the meatballs over to the un-cooked side.
12. Re-cover pan and let sizzle again until cooked all the way through.
13. Repeat steps 9-12 with the remaining ten meatballs.
14. Roll meatballs in sesame seeds.
15. Plate and serve with your favorite keto-friendly dipping sauce!

Stuffed Avocados

Ingredients:

2 (6-ounce) cans tuna in oil
4 tablespoons mayonnaise
2 large avocados
Other Ingredients:
1 medium green bell pepper, chopped
1 teaspoon dried minced onion
1 teaspoon garlic salt
1 teaspoon black pepper
How to Prepare:
1. Cut avocado in half lengthwise and remove the pit. Set aside.
2. Put tuna, mayonnaise, bell pepper, dried onion, garlic, salt, and black pepper in a medium mixing bowl and mash together with a fork until combined.
3. Scoop half of the mixture into each half of the avocado.

Goat Cheese Pork Tacos

Ingredients:
25 oz. pork mince
½ cup of goat cheese
½ cup of mayonnaise
Other Ingredients:
3 teaspoons Taco Seasoning
4 Romaine Lettuce Leaves

Directions:
1. Place the pork mince in a skillet and cook it for 20 minutes until nice and brown. Leave to cool.
2. Place the pork mince on the lettuce leaves.
3. Add the seasoning, goat cheese and a dollop of mayonnaise.
4. Wrap securely.

Chicken Kebabs

Ingredients:

1.5 lbs. chicken tenderloins (approx. 10)
1/2 tbsp. rosemary olive oil (or regular)
Other Ingredients:
10 6" rosemary skewers (soaked in water for at least 1 hour)

A few sprigs of fresh thyme
1/2 tbsp. garlic salt
1/2 tbsp. lemon pepper seasoning

Directions:

1. Preheat oven to 350 degrees.
2. Soak the rosemary skewers for at least 1 hour in water.
3. Use a short sharp knife to twiddle a point on the end of each stick.
4. Toss chicken with ingredients. Slide the leaves off the thyme sprigs and sprinkle them in.
5. Skewer the tenderloin with a rosemary stick.
6. Bake at 350 F for 40 minutes.

Chili Sausage Balls

Ingredients:

2 cups of sausages shredded
½ cup of cheddar cheese
½ cup of cottage cheese
1 egg
1 tablespoon butter
Other Ingredients:
1 teaspoon of chili flakes
½ cup of red peppers
¼ teaspoon of mustard powder

Directions:
1. Preheat an oven to 350 degrees.
2. Add the egg, chili, and red peppers in a bowl and mix/whisk until the ingredients are mixed completely.
3. Mix in the remaining ingredients.
4. Using a wooden baking spoon, or cookie scoop, remove the mixture, and hand-roll the sausage into about two dozen sausage balls.
5. Place the formed balls on a buttered baking pan, or cookie sheet.
6. Bake for about 15 minutes. Serve.

7. You may also store the cooked sausage bags in a covered bowl, or sandwich bags in the refrigerator for later use.

Mayonnaise Tarragon Tuna

Ingredients:

Two 6-ounce tuna steaks, 1 inch thick
2 teaspoons mayonnaise
1 teaspoon olive oil
Other Ingredients:
2 tablespoons minced fresh or 2 teaspoons dried tarragon plus tarragon sprigs for garnish
Salt and cracked pepper to taste

Directions:

1. Stir together the mayo and tarragon in a small bowl. Cover and set aside.
2. Heat a heavy skillet or ridged grill pan over medium-high heat.
3. Pat the tuna dry with paper towels, then season to taste with salt and cracked pepper. Dab olive oil over the surfaces of the fish.
4. Pan grilled the fish for about 3 minutes per side for medium. Transfer to warmed dinner plates.
5. Top each steak with a dollop of tarragon mayonnaise, and garnish with tarragon sprigs. Place a mound of squash beside the tuna.

Onion Tuna and Egg Salad

Ingredients:

2 large hard-boiled eggs
2 (6-ounce) cans tuna (try to get those packed in oil

½ cup mayonnaise

Other Ingredients:

¼ cup diced white onion

¼ cup sugar-free relish

½ teaspoon salt

½ teaspoon black pepper

Directions:

1. Put eggs in a medium mixing bowl and mash with a fork. Add tuna and mayonnaise and mash together until ingredients are combined.

2. Stir in onion, relish, salt, and pepper.

Black Olive Chicken Avocado Salad

Fat Ingredients:

1 (12.5-ounce) can shredded chicken breast

½ cup Homemade Mayonnaise

1 teaspoon olive oil

1 medium avocado, cubed

Other Ingredients:

2 tablespoons sliced black olives

½ teaspoon garlic salt

½ teaspoon black pepper

¼ teaspoon paprika

1 teaspoon fresh lemon juice

Directions:

Put all ingredients in a medium mixing bowl and mash with a fork until combined.

Chapter 3 KETOGENIC DINNER

Blackberries Sweet & Spicy Wings

Ingredients:
10 chicken wings
½ cup water
¼ cup blackberries
3 tablespoons Sriracha
Dash of salt and pepper

Directions:
1.   Preheat oven to 400 degrees Fahrenheit.
2.   Pulse blackberries in a blender or food processor until thoroughly mashed.
3.   Add water, Sriracha, salt, and pepper to blender and pulse until all ingredients are thoroughly incorporated.
4.   Pour mixture into a large freezer bag and add wings.
5.   Seal bag and shake until wings are thoroughly coated with sauce.
6.   Place a wire rack over a cookie sheet.
7.   Place wings on top of wire rack.
8.   Pour half of the leftover sauce over the wings.
9.   Bake wings for 15 minutes.
10.   After 15 minutes, take the wings out and flip them, brushing with leftover half of sauce.
11.   Bake for another 45 minutes, or until wings are golden and crispy.
12.   Plate and enjoy!

Mushroom Burgers

Ingredients:

340 grams ground beef
½ cup cheese of your choice

2 tablespoons mustard

2 teaspoons pepper

2 teaspoons salt

Bun Ingredients:

4 Portobello mushroom caps

1 tablespoon coconut oil

2 garlic cloves

1 teaspoon oregano

Dash of salt and pepper

Directions:

1.   Remove the insides, or "gills", from the Portobello mushrooms.
2.   Mix coconut oil, garlic, oregano, salt, and pepper together in a bowl.
3.   Put Portobello caps into marinade mixture and let sit.
4.   Mix beef, cheese, mustard, salt, and pepper in another bowl until well combined.
5.   Once thoroughly combined, squish meat into two separate patties.
6.   Put a pan over high heat. Once hot, put marinaded mushroom caps on pan.
7.   Let sit until heated.
8.   Once thoroughly heated, remove from heat and set aside.
9.   Place patties in pan. Let cook for 5 minutes on one side, then flip and let cook for 5 minutes on the other side.
10.   Place each patty between two mushroom caps, dress with keto-friendly toppings, and enjoy!

Parmesan Chicken Parmigiana

Ingredients:

☐   4 oz grilled chicken, diced

- ☐ 1/2 cup tomato sauce
- ☐ 1 cup spinach
- ☐ 1/2 cup whole-wheat penne
- ☐ 1 1/2 Tbsp grated Parmesan

Directions:
Sauté spinach in one teaspoon olive oil, & hurl with chicken, penne, & tomato sauce. Beat with Parmesan.

Butternut Squash Soup

- ☐ 1/2 cup Pacific Natural Foods organic light-sodium
- ☐ Stir-fry beef, onion, & mushroom.
- ☐ Asian Snapper
- ☐ 1/4 cup raw pistachios
- ☐ 1/2 cup cooked millet
- ☐ 1/2 cup bok choy
- ☐ 6 oz cooked snapper
- ☐ 4 tsp low-sodium soy sauce
- ☐ 2 tsp sesame seeds
- ☐ 1/2 cup sugar snap peas, cooked

Directions:
Blend pistachios into millet. Beat millet with bok choy and after that snapper. Shower snapper with soy sauce, and sprinkle with sesame seeds. Serve sugar snap peas as an afterthought.

Jambalaya Blend with Veggies

Ingredients:

- 1 veggie burger
- 1/2 cup cooked brown rice
- 2 Tbsp corn
- 2 Tbsp salsa
- 1/2 cup chopped red, green, or yellow bell peppers
- 3/4 cup diced squash
- 3/4 cup diced zucchini
- 1/4 cup chopped red onion
- 1 tsp olive oil
- Salt, to taste

Directions:

Cook burger in skillet spritzed with cooking shower, then cleave burger and consolidate with rice, corn, and salsa. Hurl veggies with oil and salt, broil for 15 to 20 minutes, and serve as an afterthought.

Yummy Cod with Rosemary Polenta and Beans

Ingredients:

- 3 oz cod
- 1 tsp chopped fresh parsley
- Dash of salt
- Dash of pepper
- 1/4 cup dry polenta
- 1/2 cup 1 percent milk
- 1 Tbsp pine nuts
- 1/2 tsp rosemary
- 1/2 cup cooked green beans

Directions:

Season cod with parsley, salt, and pepper, then steam for eight minutes. Cook polenta with drain, per bundle guidelines, and after that top with pine nuts and rosemary. Present with green beans.

Roast Beef and Horseradish Wrap

Ingredients:

- [ ] 2 Tbsp 2% plain Greek yogurt
- [ ] 1 Tbsp horseradish sauce
- [ ] 2 leaves Bibb lettuce
- [ ] 4 slices lean deli-style roast beef
- [ ] 4 slices tomato
- [ ] 1 cup fresh raspberries

Directions:
Join yogurt and horseradish, and spread on lettuce. Best with dish meat and tomato, and move into a wrap. Present with raspberries.

Tasty Tuna-Avocado Sandwich

Ingredients:

- [ ] 1/3 avocado, mashed
- [ ] 1/2 Tbsp lemon juice
- [ ] 4 oz white albacore tuna, drained
- [ ] 1 thick slice tomato
- [ ] 1 piece butter lettuce
- [ ] 1 slice red onion
- [ ] 1 slice whole-grain bread

Directions:

Join avocado with lemon squeeze, and overlay in fish. Stack tomato, lettuce, onion, and avocado and fish blend on bread for an open-confront sandwich.

Sesame Tofu Salads

Ingredients:

- [ ] 1 Tbsp soy sauce
- [ ] 1 Tbsp almond butter
- [ ] 1/8 tsp minced garlic
- [ ] 4 oz tofu, extra firm, thinly sliced
- [ ] 1 cup snow peas, slivered
- [ ] 1/2 tsp sesame seeds
- [ ] 2 Scandinavian crispbread crackers

Directions:

Whisk soy sauce, almond spread, and garlic. Hurl with tofu and snow peas. Beat with sesame seeds, and present with wafers.

Spicy Chicken Salad

Ingredients:

- [ ] 1 cup roasted skinless chicken breast, cubed
- [ ] 1 Tbsp fresh lemon juice
- [ ] 4 tsp Dijon mustard
- [ ] 1/2 jalapeno, diced
- [ ] 1/2 medium celery stalk, chopped
- [ ] Dash of black pepper
- [ ] 1 cup baby spinach

Directions:

Combine the first six ingredients, & serve on a bed of spinach.

Smoked Salmon Sandwich

Ingredients:

- ☐   1 slice pumpernickel bread
- ☐   2 Tbsp part-skim ricotta
- ☐   4 oz smoked salmon
- ☐   2 Tbsp capers
- ☐   1 1/2 Tbsp minced onions

Directions:
Layer in the order listed above.

Dijon Mustard Egg Salad Sandwich

Ingredients:
- ☐   1 tsp Dijon mustard
- ☐   2 slices multigrain bread
- ☐   1 hard-boiled egg, sliced
- ☐   2 Tbsp shredded cheddar cheese
- ☐   1/4 cup chopped scallion
- ☐   1/4 cup raw spinach
- ☐   Juice of 1/4 lemon

Directions:
Spread mustard onto bread slices, and then layer egg, cheese, scallion, & spinach on top. Drizzle with lemon juice.

Yummy Salmon Cucumber Boats

Ingredients:

- [ ] 3 oz canned pink salmon, drained
- [ ] 1 Tbsp capers
- [ ] 1 tsp yellow mustard
- [ ] 2 Tbsp plain low-fat yogurt
- [ ] Dash salt
- [ ] Dash pepper
- [ ] 1 cucumber

Directions:

Consolidate the initial six fixings. Split cucumber the long way, burrow out every half, and stuff with salmon blend.

Healthy Side Salad

Ingredients:

- [ ] 3/4 cup romaine lettuce
- [ ] 2 Tbsp chopped macadamia nuts
- [ ] 1 clementine
- [ ] 2 tsp olive oil
- [ ] 1/2 Tbsp cider vinegar
- [ ] Dash salt
- [ ] Dash pepper

Direction:

Capers add a salty zing with just two calories per tablespoon. Pile them on.

Brussels Sprouts Pumpkin Mix

Ingredients:

- [ ] 3/4 cup Brussels sprouts
- [ ] 1 cup cubed pumpkin
- [ ] 2 tsp olive oil
- [ ] 1 oz crumbled goat cheese
- [ ] 2 Tbsp pistachios
- [ ] 1/2 medium pear, sliced
- [ ] 2 Tbsp balsamic vinegar
- [ ] 2 tsp yellow mustard

Directions:

Hurl Brussels sprouts and pumpkin with oil, and dish for 30 minutes at 350°F, turning part of the way through. Expel from broiler, and hurl with outstanding fixings.

Coconut Chicken Tenders

\
Ingredients

1 pound boneless and skinless chicken tenders
1 egg
½ cup cashew flour
1 cup shredded coconut
¼ teaspoon salt
¼ teaspoon pepper
¼ teaspoon garlic powder
1/8 teaspoon cinnamon

Directions:

- [ ] Preheat the oven to 375°F.

- Beat the egg and set aside.
- In a separate bowl, combine the cashew flour, the coconut and the spices.
- Dip each chicken tender, first in the egg, and then the coconut spice batter.
- Place each tender on a pan lined with baking parchment.
- Bake in the oven for around 20 minutes, or until cooked.

Tasty Tuna on Greens

Ingredients:
- 3 oz canned water-packed light tuna, drained
- 1 1/2 cups red leaf lettuce
- 1 cup romaine lettuce
- 1 medium carrot, shredded
- 1 4-inch whole-wheat pita

Tabbouleh

- 1/2 cup cooked bulgur
- 3 Tbsp finely chopped fresh parsley
- 1/2 medium tomato, chopped
- 1/2 Tbsp olive oil
- 1 Tbsp fresh lemon juice
- 2 Tbsp chopped scallions
- 1/2 clove garlic, minced

Directions:
Combine all tabbouleh ingredients, and then use to top lettuce with tuna & carrot.

Marinara Sauce Chicken Panini

Ingredients:

- [ ] 1 1/2 oz sliced low-fat Swiss
- [ ] 1 oz sliced reduced-sodium Black Forest deli ham
- [ ] 1 oz sliced reduced-sodium deli chicken breast
- [ ] 1 whole-wheat roll (12 oz total), sliced and gutted
- [ ] 1/4 cup marinara sauce, heated

Directions:

Warm softly oiled flame broil or panini press to medium warmth (or utilize a barbecue skillet). Put cheddar, ham, and chicken on the move, beginning and closure with cheddar. Close sandwich, and barbecue, flipping and squeezing with spatula if vital, until brilliant chestnut on both sides and cheddar is softened, around five minutes add up to. Divide sandwich, and present with marinara sauce for dipping.

Juicy Asian Style Ribs

Ingredients:

Ribs and Marinade:
2 tbsp. rice vinegar
1/4 cup soy sauce
2 tbsp. fish sauce
6 large short ribs, flank cut (about 1.5 lbs.)
Asian Spice:
1/2 tsp. red pepper flakes
1/2 tsp. garlic (minced)
1/2 tsp. onion powder
1 tsp. ginger (ground)
1/2 tsp. sesame seed
1 tbsp. salt
1/4 tsp. cardamom

Directions:
1. For the ribs, mix all of the marinade ingredients. Marinade the ribs for at least an hour.
2. Mix together all of the ingredients for the spice rub.
3. Remove the ribs from the marinade and rub with the spices from the previous step.
4. Heat your grill, and grill for approximately 5 minutes per side.

Weekend Quick Healthy Pizza

Ingredients:

Crust:
1/2 tsp. Italian seasoning
1 tbsp. psyllium husk powder
2 large eggs
2 tsp. frying oil of choice
2 tbsp. parmesan cheese
Salt to taste
Toppings:
3 tbsp. tomato sauce
1 tbsp. basil (chopped)
1.5 oz. mozzarella cheese

Directions:
1. Use a food processor, or blender, or immersion blender to combine all of the pizza crust ingredients.
2. Heat the oil in a frying pan, and add the crust mixture to the pan when hot. Spread into a circle.
3. Once the edges of the crust begin to brown, flip and cook for an additional 60 seconds.
4. Now top the crust with the cheese and tomato sauce, and broil for 2 minutes until the cheese begins to bubble.
Top with basil and enjoy!

Favorite Seared Ribeye

Ingredients:

3 tbsp. bacon fat
salt and pepper to taste
2 medium ribeye steaks (about 1.25 lbs.)
Directions:
1. Preheat your oven to 250□F.
2. Season the steaks with salt and pepper, then place on wire racks for baking.

3. Insert a meat thermometer into the streak.

4. Bake until the thermometer shows a temperature of 124□F.

5. Now heat a cast iron skillet on the stove and add your bacon grease. When very hot, sear your steaks for about 40 seconds per side. Enjoy

Custard Paprika Seafood Melange

Ingredients
4 sole, patted dry
10 bay scallops, raw
3/4 cup crabmeat
3/4 cup cooked shrimp
1/2 cup shredded Monterey Jack cheese
1/2 cup butter 2 egg yolks
1 tablespoon lemon juice
1/2 teaspoon mustard powder
1/8 teaspoon salt
2 tablespoons chopped fresh parsley
1/4 teaspoon paprika

Directions
Butter two 2-cup au gratin dishes. Place 1 fillet on bottom of each, then layer with scallops, crabmeat, shrimp, cheese and a second fillet; set aside.
Preheat oven to 450 degrees F (230 degrees C).
Melt butter. In a medium mixing bowl, combine yolks, lemon juice, mustard and salt; mix on high and slowly add butter in a steady stream until sauce is thick and creamy. Pour sauce over fillets.
Bake in preheated oven for 10 to 15 minutes; sprinkle with parsley and paprika. Serve.

Cheddar Broccoli Salad

Ingredients
1 1/2 cups fresh broccoli florets
3/4 cup shredded Cheddar cheese
4 bacon strips, cooked and crumbled
1/4 cup finely chopped onion
3 tablespoons mayonnaise
2 tablespoons white vinegar

Directions
In a bowl, combine the broccoli, cheese, bacon and onion. In another bowl, whisk the mayonnaise, vinegar. Pour over broccoli mixture and toss to coat. Cover and refrigerate for at least 1 hour before serving.

Yummy Summer Vegetable Salad

Ingredients
1/2 cup red wine vinegar
1/3 cup vegetable oil
3 garlic cloves, minced
1/2 teaspoon salt
1/8 teaspoon pepper
1/2 pint cherry tomatoes, halved
1 small cucumber, peeled and thinly sliced
1 small green pepper, julienned
1 small red onion, sliced into rings
1 tablespoon chopped fresh basil

Directions

In a large bowl, combine vinegar, oil, garlic, salt, pepper and sugar if desired; mix well. Add remaining ingredients and toss gently. Cover and chill for at least 1 hour.

Dijon Asparagus Ham Salad

Ingredients
1 pound fresh asparagus, trimmed
1/2 cup olive or vegetable oil
1/4 cup cider or white wine vinegar
1 tablespoon Dijon mustard
1/2 teaspoon salt
1/4 teaspoon pepper
1 cup diced fully cooked ham
2 green onions, thinly sliced

Directions
In a skillet, cook asparagus in a small amount of water until crisp-tender, about 6-8 minutes; drain well. Cover and refrigerate for at least 1 hour.
Meanwhile, in a jar with tight-fitting lid, combine the oil, vinegar, mustard, salt, pepper and sugar if desired; shake well. Cover and refrigerate at least 1 hour. Place asparagus in a serving bowl. Top with ham, onions and dressing. Serve with a slotted spoon.

Broccoli Stir-Fry Salmon

Ingredients:
- 1 pound fresh broccoli (cut into florets)
- 2 pounds fresh salmon fillets (cut into cubes)
- 1 tablespoon olive oil
- 3 garlic cloves (minced)
- 2 medium onions (halved and thinly sliced)

- 1/4 pound frozen peas
- 1 tablespoon sesame seeds
- 2 tablespoons soy sauce
- 1 tablespoon chopped parsley
- 1 teaspoon toasted sesame oil

Directions:

1.   Add the olive oil to a wok over high heat. Once the oil is hot, add the garlic and stir constantly for about 20 seconds. Add the salmon and cook until it changes color.
2.   Add onion, broccoli and peas to the wok and stir occasionally for 5 minutes or until the vegetables are soft.
3.   Add the soy sauce, sesame oil and chopped parsley. Stir these ingredients in and then gently toss to coat before removing the wok from the heat.
4.   Divide between six plates, sprinkle extra parsley and sesame seeds on top of each portion and add a lemon wedge right before serving (optional).

Coconut Parsley Tuna

Ingredients:

- 3 tablespoons coconut oil
- 2 cloves garlic (crushed)
- ½ pound fresh tuna fillets (cut into slices)
- 5 tablespoons coconut milk
- 1 tablespoon fish sauce
- Ground black pepper to taste
- Salt to taste
- Small bunch fresh parsley (chopped)

Directions:

1.   Add coconut oil to a skillet or frying pan over a medium heat. Once the oil is hot, add crushed garlic and sauté for about 2 minutes, until soft.
2.   Add the tuna slices and sauté for about 3 minutes, until the tuna is cooked.

3. Stirring carefully, add the coconut milk, fish sauce, ground black pepper and salt. Sauté for about 1 minute.

4. Divide the tuna between 2 plates or set out on a serving dish. Sprinkle chopped parsley.

5. Pour any remaining liquid from the skillet over the shrimp and sprinkle with chopped cilantro before serving.

Soy Sauce Shrimp Cucumber Noodles

Ingredients:

- 2 cucumbers (preferably seedless)
- ½ pound fresh shrimp (peeled and deveined)
- 1 tablespoon Thai red curry paste
- ½ scallion or spring onion (chopped)
- 2 garlic cloves (finely chopped)
- 1 ounce ginger (finely chopped)
- 1 tablespoon soy sauce
- 1 tablespoon olive oil
- 1 green chili (finely chopped)
- 1 bunch cilantro (finely chopped)
- 1 tablespoon chopped peanuts to decorate

Directions:

1. Use a spiralizer, mandolin or vegetable peeler to turn the cucumbers into spaghetti or tagliatelle noodles. Place the noodles in a small bowl and set aside.

2. Heat the olive oil over a medium heat and sauté the scallion, garlic, ginger and chili for about 2 minutes.

3. Stir in the curry paste, soy sauce and half the cilantro. Sauté for another 2 minutes.

4. Add the shrimp and cover evenly in the sauce. Cook for about 8 minutes.

5. Divide the noodles between 2 plates and then carefully add the shrimp to each plate. Decorate with chopped peanuts.

6. Sprinkle with remaining cilantro. Serve right away.

Lemon Shrimp Cucumber Noodles

Ingredients:
- 2 cucumbers
- 3 cups cauliflower (cut into small pieces)
- 1 small red onion (finely chopped)
- 3 ounces pitted olives (halved)
- 1 pound fresh shrimp (peeled and deveined)
- 1 ½ lemons (juice and zest)
- 1 tablespoon capers
- 3 tablespoons olive oil (plus extra for drizzling)
- Salt to taste
- Black pepper to taste

Directions:

1.   Spiralize the cucumber (or cut into strips) and place in a bowl.
2.   Heat 1 tablespoon of olive oil in a frying pan, add the shrimp and cook until opaque and pink, stirring occasionally.
3.   In a separate bowl, combine the cooked shrimp, olives, red onion, capers, lemon zest and juice. Toss gently then add the cauliflower and cucumber noodles. Mix well and ensure a good coating of the mixture on the cauliflower and cucumber.
4.   Drizzle the remaining olive oil in the bowl and season with the black pepper. Toss a little more and enjoy!

Oregano Chicken Salad

Ingredients:

- 3 pound chicken breast (grilled, diced)
- 2 large green bell peppers (diced)
- 2 tablespoons Greek yogurt
- 2 teaspoons fresh oregano
- 3 ounces Parmesan cheese (grated)
- Salt to taste
- Pepper to taste

Directions:

1. Add all the ingredients except the parmesan cheese to a mixing bowl and carefully mix them together.
2. Transfer to a serving bowl or divide between two serving plates. Top with grated parmesan cheese and serve immediately.

Almond Crusted Chicken

Ingredients:

- Cooking oil spray
- 3 ounces almond flour
- 2 pound chicken breasts (boneless, skinless, cut into slices)
- ¼ cup whole milk
- 3 ounces mozzarella cheese (grated)
- ¼ teaspoon ground paprika
- ½ teaspoon dried parsley
- Salt to taste
- Pepper to taste

Directions:
1. Preheat the oven to 400°F and grease a baking tray with cooking oil spray. Set out three plates, which will be used for preparing the chicken with three different mixtures.
2. Combine almond flour, salt and pepper. Mix well and pour on the first plate.

3.   Pour whole milk on the second plate.

4.   Put the grated mozzarella, paprika and dried parsley on the third plate. Mix well.

5.   Dip the chicken slices into the almond flour first, then the milk, and then roll in the cheese mixture.

6.   Once all of the slices are coated with all the mixtures, lay them on the greased baking tray and roast in the oven for about 15 minutes, until golden brown and totally cooked.

Celery Chicken Soup

Ingredients:

- 1 tablespoon olive oil
- 1 onion (chopped)
- 2 celery stalks (sliced)
- 3 cloves garlic (minced)
- 5 cups all-natural chicken broth
- 3 1/2 pound chicken breast (boneless, skinless, cut into thin slices)
- 1 teaspoon garlic powder
- Salt to taste
- Pepper to taste

Directions:

1.   Heat the olive oil in a saucepan over a medium heat. Sauté the onion and celery for about 5 minutes or until they are soft. Add the garlic, stir and sauté for about 2 minutes, careful not to burn it.

2.   Pour in the broth and bring to a boil. Reduce the heat to low, add the chicken strips, and let simmer for about 10 minutes, until the chicken is cooked through.

3.   Add the garlic powder and stir to combine. Season the soup with a pinch of salt and ground black pepper. Let it simmer until everything is heated through.

4.   Divide between two serving bowls. Serve immediately!

Thyme Grilled Orange Chicken

Ingredients:

- 1 pound chicken filets
- 1 tablespoon olive oil
- 2 teaspoons heavy cream
- 2 tablespoons Dijon mustard
- 1 tablespoon orange zest
- 1 tablespoon orange juice
- 1 teaspoon dried thyme
- Black pepper to taste
- Salt to taste

Directions:

1.   Place the heavy cream, mustard, thyme, orange zest, orange juice, pepper and salt in a bowl. Mix well to combine.
2.   Place chicken filets in a Ziploc bag and pour the mustard mixture over them. Shake the bag to coat the chicken with the marinade.
3.   Let it marinate for about 20 minutes in the fridge.
4.   Heat a frying pan with olive oil. Grill the chicken over medium heat until cooked through.

Indian Style Chicken Cubes

Ingredients:

- 1 bunch of fresh kale (shredded)
- 1 pound chicken breast (boneless, skinless, cut into cubes)
- 4 tablespoons olive oil
- 5 whole black peppercorns
- 4 whole cloves
- 3 green cardamom pods
- 1 onion (chopped)

- 2 red chilies (chopped, without seeds)
- 4 garlic cloves (chopped)
- 1 ounce fresh ginger (grated)
- 1/4 tablespoon cumin
- 1 teaspoon ground coriander
- 1 teaspoon ground turmeric
- 1 ounce Greek yogurt
- Salt to taste

Directions:

1. Add the olive oil to a large frying pan over medium heat. Sauté the peppercorns, cloves and cardamom for 2 minutes.
2. Add the chopped onion, red chilies, ginger and garlic. Sauté for a few minutes until the onions are soft.
3. Add the chicken, cumin, coriander, turmeric and salt. Stir continuously for a few minutes.
4. Once the chicken is slightly browned, add the shredded kale and season with more salt to taste.
5. Once the kale is wilted and the chicken is tender, turn off heat and add the Greek yogurt.
6. Divide between two serving plates and serve right away.

Citrus Shrimp Salad

Ingredients:
- 1 yellow bell pepper (sliced)
- 1 green bell pepper (sliced)
- 3 large tomatoes (chopped)
- 1 bunch of fresh parsley (chopped)
- 1 pound fresh shrimp (peeled and deveined)
- 1 lemon (juice)
- 1 tablespoon olive oil
- Salt to taste
- Pepper to taste

Directions:

1.   Heat the olive oil in a frying pan, add the shrimp and cook until opaque and pink, stirring occasionally. Set aside.
2.   Put the bell peppers in a large bowl. Add the chopped tomatoes and parsley, then squeeze the lemon juice over the top.
3.   Add the cooked shrimp and stir or toss gently to mix the salad together. Season with salt and pepper to taste.
4.   Divide between two plates or bowls. Garnish with parsley.

Refreshing Cucumber Salad

Ingredients
2 small cucumbers, thinly sliced
1/2 small red onion, thinly sliced
1 large tomato, halved and sliced
3 tablespoons mayonnaise
1 tablespoon white vinegar
1/4 teaspoon salt
1/2 teaspoon ground black pepper

Directions
In a medium bowl, toss together the cucumbers, red onion and tomato. Gently stir in the mayonnaise, vinegar, salt and pepper until coated. Cover and refrigerate for at least 1 hour before serving.

Ginger Vinegar Cod Zucchini Noodles

Ingredients:

- 3 large zucchini, spiralized (alternatively, use a julienne peeler or slice into thin strips)
- 1 1/2; pounds fresh cod fillets
- 2 inches fresh ginger (finely chopped)
- 3 tablespoons soy sauce
- 2 tablespoons rice vinegar
- 1 green onion (chopped)
- 1 garlic clove (minced)
- 1 cup vegetable broth
- 1 bunch fresh parsley (finely chopped)

Directions:

6. Use a spiralizer, mandolin, julienne or vegetable peeler to turn the zucchini into noodles.
7. Combine the chopped ginger, garlic, soy sauce, vegetable broth, green onions and vinegar in a medium bowl.
8. Chop the cod fillets into strips and put them in the bowl with the mixture. Turn the strips over to ensure they are fully coated in the mixture and let them marinate for 40 minutes.
9. Heat a large nonstick frying pan over a medium heat, add some olive oil and cook the cod for about 4 minutes on each side. Add the marinade to the pan, bring to a boil and then immediately remove from the heat.
10. Divide the noodles into four portions, add the cod on top and pour the sauce over the fish. Sprinkle chopped parsley on top and serve right away.

Walnut Salmon Salad

Ingredients:

Salad
- 5 ounces baby spinach leaves
- 2 ripe avocados (chopped)
- 8 ripe strawberries (chopped)
- 5 ounces cherry tomatoes (halved)
- 2 ounces walnuts (chopped)

- 1 pound fresh salmon fillets
- 1 teaspoon olive oil

Vinaigrette
- 2 tablespoons fresh lemon juice
- 6 tablespoons olive oil
- 1 teaspoon Dijon mustard
- 1 pinch cayenne pepper

Directions:
1. Preheat the oven to 400°F.
2. Heat a cast iron or oven-proof pan over a medium-high heat and add the olive oil once the pan is hot.
3. Place the salmon in the pan skin-side down and cook the fillets for about 4 minutes.
4. Transfer the pan to the middle shelf in the oven and continue cooking for about 4 minutes (depending on the thickness) until cooked through.
5. Add the spinach, chopped avocado, strawberries, cherry tomatoes and walnuts to a large bowl.
6. Mix the freshly squeezed lemon juice with the Dijon mustard in another small bowl and whisk. Continue to whisk while gradually adding the olive oil. Once the vinaigrette is well combined, season it with cayenne pepper.
7. Divide the salad between two plates or bowls, add the salmon on top of each serving and then drizzle the vinaigrette over the top. Serve right away!

Cherry Tomatoes Tuna

Ingredients:
- 10 ounces cherry tomatoes
- 2 tablespoons olive oil
- Salt to taste
- Ground black pepper to taste
- 1 1/2 pounds fresh tuna fillets (cut into cubes)
- 2 teaspoons ground turmeric
- 1 bunch fresh parsley (chopped)

Directions:

1.   Preheat the oven to 400°F.

2.   Add the tomatoes, olive oil, salt, and black pepper to a bowl and mix well. Pour this mixture into a baking tray and spread it out evenly.

3.   Place the tuna on top of the tomato mixture. Coat the tuna with the oil from the baking tray using a pastry brush or the back of a spoon. Then, sprinkle turmeric, more salt and ground black pepper over the top of the tuna.

4.   Roast the fish in the oven for about 15 minutes or until the tuna flakes easily when tested with a fork.

5.   Garnish with chopped parsley.

Bacon Spinach Salad

Ingredients :

4 eggs
8 slices bacon
1 (10 ounce) package fresh spinach
1 small onion, chopped
6 tablespoons vegetable oil
3 tablespoons lemon juice
2 cloves garlic, minced
Salt and pepper to taste

Directions :

Place eggs in a saucepan and cover with cold water. Bring water to a boil; cover, remove from heat, and let eggs stand in hot water for 10 to 12 minutes. Remove from hot water, cool, peel and chop.

Place bacon in a large, deep skillet. Cook over medium high heat until evenly brown. Drain, crumble and set aside.

In a large bowl, combine the eggs, bacon, spinach and onion.

In a small bowl, whisk together the oil, lemon juice, garlic and salt and pepper. Pour over salad and toss well to coat.

Curry Crusted Chicken

Ingredients:

- 2 medium chicken thighs
- 1 egg
- 1/4 cup almond flour
- ¼ teaspoon salt
- 1 1/2 teaspoon curry powder
- Pepper to taste
- 4 tablespoons fresh parsley (chopped)

Directions:
1. Preheat the oven to 425°F. Grease a baking sheet or line with parchment paper. Set aside.
2. In a mixing bowl, mix the almond flour, curry, salt, parsley and pepper.
3. In another bowl beat the egg.
4. Dip the chicken thighs into the egg, and then toss in the almond mixture to coat evenly.
5. Arrange the chicken on the prepared baking sheet and bake in the oven about 30 minutes, until cooked through.
6. Turn 2 times during the cooking to brown on both sides.

Oven-Baked Rib-eye Steak

Ingredients:

3 medium rib-eye steaks
3 tablespoons butter
1 tablespoon paprika
1 tablespoon garlic powder
Pinch of salt and ground black pepper

Directions:

Rub the rib-eye steaks with salt, pepper, paprika and garlic powder. Place it in a lightly-greased baking dish. Bake the steaks in a 250°F oven for 45 minutes.

Use a cooking thermometer to check for the steak's doneness. If it reaches 120°F then the steak is ready. Remove the steak from the oven and let it stand for 5 minutes.

Heat the butter in a pan over medium flame. Once the oil is hot, place the steaks on the pan and sear each side of the meat for 30-40 seconds. Serve immediately.

Honey Chicken Breast with Citrus Sauce

Ingredients:

3 chicken breast halves, skin intact
2 cups kale leaves, washed and stems discarded
½ teaspoon butter
2 tablespoons heavy cream
3 tablespoons olive oil
2 tablespoons organic honey
½ teaspoon dried rosemary
1 cup fresh orange juice
Pinch of salt and ground black pepper

Directions:

Season the chicken breast with salt and pepper. Place it in a pan over medium-high flame and cook each side for 8-10 minutes. Set aside.

While the chicken breasts are cooking, heat the olive oil in a pan over medium flame. Add in the rosemary, orange juice and honey and simmer for 5-7 minutes. Pour in the heavy cream and cook for 3 minutes. Turn off the heat and set aside.

Place the butter and kale leaves on the same pan where the chicken breast was cooked. Cook the greens for 3-5 minutes or until the leaves wilt.

Transfer the wilted greens on a plate and arrange the chicken breasts on top of it. Pour the orange sauce on top of the dish. Serve immediately.

Pork Ribs With Bell Pepper

Ingredients:

- 2 pound pork ribs
- 4 tablespoons fresh sage (chopped)
- 3 tablespoons butter
- 2 bell peppers (seeded, chopped)
- Salt to taste
- Pepper to taste

Directions:
1. Preheat oven to 400°F. Grease a baking pan with butter.
2. Season pork ribs with salt and pepper to taste.
3. Heat the butter in a large frying pan over medium heat. Add the pork ribs and quickly brown them.
4. Transfer the pork ribs to the greased baking pan. Sprinkle with sage and chopped bell peppers.
5. Cover the baking pan with aluminum foil. Bake for about 25 minutes. Remove the foil and bake for 5 additional minutes or until the bell peppers are browned.
6. Serve right away!

Mushroom Beef

Ingredients:
- 3 pound ground beef
- 1 ½ pound fresh white mushrooms (sliced)
- 4 ripe tomatoes (seeded and chopped)

- 2 tablespoons fresh basil (chopped)
- 1/4 cup vegetable broth
- 3 tablespoons olive oil
- Salt to taste
- Pepper to taste

Directions:

1. Heat olive oil in a large pan over medium heat. Add the ground beef and cook for about 8 minutes or until browned, stirring frequently.
2. Add the tomatoes and cook for about 5 minutes, stirring.
3. Add vegetable broth. Reduce the heat to low and cook for about 20 minutes. Add more liquid if needed.
4. Add in sliced mushrooms and cook until they change texture. Turn off the heat, season with salt and pepper to taste.
5. Garnish with chopped basil, serve and enjoy!

Creamy Chives Pork Tenderloin

Ingredients:
- 4 ½ pound pork tenderloin (cut into strips)
- 1 onion (chopped)
- 1 garlic clove (minced)
- 1 1/4 cup vegetable broth
- 1/2 cup heavy cream
- 4 tablespoons fresh chives (chopped)
- 1 pinch ground cumin
- 1 pinch ground turmeric
- 2 tablespoons butter
- Salt to taste
- Pepper to taste

Directions:

1. Add butter to a large frying pan and place over medium heat.

2.   Once the butter is hot, add the pork and cook for about 3 minutes, until browned.
3.   Stir in garlic and onion. Sauté for about 5 minutes.
4.   Stir in vegetable broth, turmeric, cumin, salt and pepper. Cook over low heat for about 15 minutes or until the broth is evaporated.
5.   Finally, add heavy cream and chopped chives. Then cook for additional 2 minutes.
6.   Serve right away!

Coconut Crusted Chilli Shrimp

Ingredients:

450 grams shrimps, peeled and deveined
2 tablespoons coconut flour
1 cup dried coconut flakes
2 egg whites
1 red chili, minced
½ cup crushed pineapple
1 tablespoon lemon juice
1½ tablespoons white vinegar
Pinch of red pepper flakes

Directions:
Preheat the oven to 225°F [400°] and line a baking sheet with parchment paper.
Beat the egg whites until soft white peaks form. Set this aside. Place the coconut flour and coconut flakes in separate bowls.
Dip each shrimp in this order: coconut flour, egg whites then coconut flakes. Arrange the shrimps on the baking sheet until all seafood has been coated. Place the shrimps in the oven and bake for 5 minutes. Turn off the oven and arrange the shrimp on a serving platter.
To make the dip, mix together the crushed pineapple, lemon juice, vinegar and pepper flakes. Place the mixture in a sauce bowl and serve alongside the coconut shrimp.

Sesame Beef Noodles

- 5 to 6-ounce Cellophane noodles
- 1/3 cup Soy sauce
- 5 tablespoons Sesame oil
- 1 clove minced garlic
- 1/3 cup brown sugar
- 1 1/2 tablespoons apple vinegar
- 12 ounces skirt steak (1/4 inch thick slices)
- 1/4-inch wedges onion
- Kosher salt to taste
- 10 ounces Shiitake mushrooms (remove stems)
- 1 cup shredded carrots
- 6 cups baby spinach

Directions:

1. In the first step, you have to soak noodles in water (warm water) for almost 5 – 10 minutes. Drain water and snip noodle into pieces with kitchen scissors.
2. It is time to take a bowl and mix sesame oil (3 tablespoons), soy sauce, garlic, vinegar and brown sugar. Keep it aside. It is time to put beef to another and add two tablespoons soy sauce mixture. Keep it aside.
3. Take a large cooking pan and heat two teaspoons oil. Add salt and onion in this pan and cook for two minutes. Now, add beef and let it cook for a few minutes. Transfer beef in a bowl and keep it aside.
4. Rinse your cooking pan and heat two teaspoons oil again. Add carrots and mushroom and cook for three minutes. It is time to add noodles and two tablespoons soy sauce blend. Cook for one minute and add only 1/3 cup water and cook to make noodles tender. It will take almost three minutes. Transfer noodles in a bowl with beef.
5. Clean skillet again and keep it on the heat again and add remaining sesame oil. Add remaining mixture of soy sauce and spinach and cook them for one minute. It is time to add beef and mix them well.

Italian Style Turkey Meatballs

Ingredients:

- 1 lb. turkey meat, ground
- ½ cup mozzarella cheese, cut into bite sized cubes
- ½ cup grated Romano cheese
- 1 egg
- 5 garlic clove, minced
- 2 teaspoons fresh parsley, chopped
- 1 cup whole wheat panko bread
- ½ cup warm water
- 6 tablespoons olive oil
- 3 teaspoons Italian seasoning
- ½ teaspoon sugar
- 1 teaspoon salt
- ½ teaspoon red pepper flakes, crushed
- 1 can tomatoes, crushed
- 2 pinch of salt
- 1 pinch of pepper
- Salt and black pepper to taste

Directions:

1. Mix the turkey meat, egg, cheese, seasoning, parsley, half of the minced garlic, panko bread, salt and pepper. Mix well until you can shape it into meatballs
2. Preheat oven at 200 degrees Celsius.
3. Prepare a skillet over medium heat and add olive oil.
4. Use a tablespoon to scoop a piece of meat onto a baking sheet, place the cheese on top and cover it with another piece of meat. Roll the meat into meatballs.

5.	Add the meatballs into your skillet to fry them. Fry the meatballs on all sides for about 1-2 minutes.

6.	Take the meatballs out and place them back on the baking sheet to be baked in the oven for 10-12 minutes.

7.	Add oil to your skillet pan over medium heat.

8.	Add remaining garlic to be sautéed till golden.

9.	Add the remaining ingredients (seasoning, pepper flakes, sugar, tomatoes, salt and pepper) to create your sauce. Simmer the mix for about 8 minutes. Add salt and pepper to taste.

10.	By this time, your meatballs are ready to be added into the sauce mix.

Mushroom Steak and Scramble Eggs

Ingredients:

- ½ cup lean sirloin steaks, cut into bite sized cubes
- 2 free range eggs
- 4 egg whites
- 2 teaspoons olive oil
- 1 medium potato, cut into bite sized cubes
- 1 teaspoon skim milk
- ¼ cup mushrooms
- 2 teaspoons Worcestershire sauce
- 2 tablespoons low-fat cheese, shredded
- 30 ml onions, chopped
- Paprika to taste
- Salt and black pepper to taste

Directions:

1.	Heat a skillet pan over a medium-high heat.

2.	Add oil, potatoes, onions, paprika and cook for 5 minutes. You may add salt and pepper to taste.

3.	In a separate bowl, beat the eggs. Add milk as you continue to beat the egg.

4. Now, coming back to your pan, add Worcestershire sauce, mushrooms and the main dish, steak. Cook for about 4-6 minutes.
5. There will be excess fat from the pan mix. Drain the excess fat.
6. Add the eggs mix to the pan and scramble them together for about 4 minutes.
7. Once again, the dish is ready to serve. Sprinkle cheese to the dish and watch it melt just right.

Oregano Almond Steak Salad

Ingredients:

- ½ pound sirloin steak (thinly sliced)
- 2 cups lettuce (shredded)
- 1 cup arugula leaves
- 1 pinch paprika
- 2 ounces almonds (chopped)
- 3 tablespoons fresh oregano (chopped)
- 1 tablespoon soy sauce
- 4 tablespoons olive oil
- Salt to taste
- Pepper to taste

Directions:

1. Heat 2 tablespoons of olive oil in a large frying pan and cook sirloin slices until golden brown. Season with paprika, salt and pepper. Set aside.
2. In a large bowl, mix lettuce, almonds and arugula. Set aside.
3. In a small bowl, whisk soy sauce, oregano and remaining olive oil until smooth.
4. Add the cooked sirloin slices and the soy sauce mixture to the large bowl. Toss well to combine with the leaves.
5. Serve immediately!

Pork Curry

Ingredients:

- 2 pound pork loin (thinly sliced)
- 3 cups cauliflower (florets)
- 1 cup heavy cream
- 2 garlic cloves (minced)
- 1 teaspoon curry powder
- 2 tablespoons butter
- Salt to taste
- Pepper to taste

Directions:

1. Season pork loin with curry, salt and pepper.
2. Add 1 tablespoon of butter to a frying pan and melt over medium heat. Place pork in frying pan and sauté for about 5 minutes. Remove from frying pan and set aside.
3. Heat remaining butter in the same frying pan and sauté garlic until slightly brown.
4. Add in the cauliflower, sauté until tender, add a little water if needed.
5. Stir in the heavy cream, salt and pepper. Cook over medium heat for about 5 minutes. Transfer this mixture to a food processor and blend until creamy.
6. Place the pork loin slices in serving plates and top with the cauliflower sauce.
7. Serve warm!

Spicy Beef Ribs

Ingredients:

- 3 pound beef ribs
- 1 onion (sliced)
- 4 ripe tomatoes (chopped)
- 2 red bell peppers (seeded, chopped)
- 1 cup vegetable broth
- 1 bunch fresh parsley (chopped)
- 1 teaspoon paprika
- 1/2 teaspoon chili powder
- 2 tablespoons olive oil
- Salt to taste
- Pepper to taste

Directions:
1.   Season beef ribs with salt and pepper to taste.
2.   Heat olive oil in a pan, add beef ribs and cook until golden brown. Then stir in onions and sauté until soft.
3.   Add in tomatoes, bell peppers, paprika and chili. Sauté for about 3 minutes. Then pour in vegetable broth. Cover and cook over low heat for about 40 minutes, add more broth if needed.
4.   Taste the sauce and add more salt or spices to taste.
5.   Garnish with fresh parsley. Serve warm!

Rosemary Walnut Pork Lion

Iingredients:

*   1 pound pork loin
*   5 tablespoons fresh rosemary (chopped)
*   8 tablespoons sour cream
*   2 ounces walnuts (chopped)
*   ¼ cup olive oil
*   Salt to taste
*   Pepper to taste

Directions:

1.   Preheat oven to 375°F.
2.   Mix olive oil, rosemary, salt and pepper in a bowl. Evenly coat the pork loin with this mixture.
3.   Place the pork on a baking pan. Cover the pan with aluminum foil. Bake for about 30 minutes. Then remove foil and bake until golden brown.
4.   Remove from oven and wait about 5 minutes to slice. Place the slices on a serving plate, top them with sour cream and sprinkle with chopped walnuts.

Chilli Pork and Veggie Sandwich

Ingredients:

900 grams lean ground pork
½ cup tomato sauce
1 large white onion, minced
2 eggs
Slices of tomato and cucumber
1½ tablespoons melted butter
½ teaspoon paprika
½ teaspoon chili powder
Pinch of salt and black pepper

Directions:

Place the chopped onions in a pan over medium-high heat then pour in the melted butter. Cook the onions for 3 minutes then let it cool.

In a large bowl, mix together the pork, tomato sauce, eggs and cooked onions. Season it with salt, pepper, chili powder and paprika then mix thoroughly. Divide the pork mixture into 6 patties and place them on a parchment-lined baking sheet. Bake the patties in a 350°F oven for 45 minutes.

Once the patties are cooked, remove it from the oven and allow them to cool. Slice each patty horizontally in the middle to make 2 loaves. Place a patty slice on a plate, top with cucumbers and tomatoes then cover it with the other patty. Serve immediately.

Easy Healthy Soup

Ingredients:
- 4 large zucchini
- 1 pound sea bass fillets, cut into strips
- 1 red onion (thinly sliced)
- Zest and juice from one lemon
- 6 tablespoons coriander leaves (chopped)

- 1 ½ cups soy milk
- 1 tablespoon extra-virgin olive oil
- 10 ounces tomato paste
- 2 teaspoons curry powder

Directions:

1. Spiralize the zucchini and set aside.
2. Heat the olive oil in a large stockpot. Sauté the onion for 4–5 minutes until translucent.
3. Add the zucchini noodles and cook for 4–6 minutes until the edges become brown.
4. Pour the soy milk then add the sea bass, lemon juice, and half of the coriander.
5. Add the tomato paste and curry powder.
6. Bring the soup to a boil, lower the heat and simmer for 10 minutes.
7. Garnish with coriander and lemon zest.

Zucchini Sesame Sardine Noodles

Ingredients:

- 4 zucchini
- 10 ounces canned sardines (drained)
- 2 small red onions (chopped)
- 2 celery stalks (chopped)
- 1/4 cup parsley (chopped)
- 1 tablespoon dried oregano
- 3 tablespoons black sesame seeds
- 4 tablespoons apple cider vinegar
- 2 tablespoons Tamari
- 1 inch fresh ginger root (minced or grated)
- 2 tablespoons extra virgin olive oil
- 1 teaspoon chili powder or hot pepper sauce
- salt and black pepper, to taste

Directions:
1.   Spiralize the zucchini to create the noodles.
2.   Prepare the dressing by combining the soy sauce, oregano, apple cider vinegar and chili powder in a mixing bowl. Whisk in the olive oil little by little until you get a thick sauce.
3.   In a large serving bowl, combine the zucchini noodles, sardines, onions, ginger, chopped celery and parsley. Coat with the dressing and top with sesame seeds to serve.

Spicy Vegies Chicken Soup

Iingredients:

- 2 carrots (sliced)
- 1/4 cup bamboo shoots
- 1 red Poblano pepper (finely chopped)
- 2 celery stalks (chopped)
- 4 pound of boneless, skinless chicken breasts (cut into bite-sized pieces)
- 5 cups vegetable stock
- Zest and juice from 1 lime
- 1 cup Champignon mushrooms (chopped)
- 2 green onions (sliced)
- 1 teaspoon curry powder (or 3 curry leaves)
- 1 tablespoon white wine vinegar
- 2 tablespoons ginger powder
- 2 tablespoons Tamari
- 1 teaspoon turmeric powder
- 2 tablespoons dry white wine
- 2 tablespoons olive oil
- Salt and pepper, to taste

Directions:
1.   Heat the olive oil in a large skillet over medium heat.
2.   Add the spices, salt and pepper, and cook for about 1 minute.
3.   Add the meat to the pan and cook for 5 minutes per side, until golden.

4.   Stir in the onions, mushrooms, carrots, celery and bamboo shoots. Cook for 5 more minutes.

5.   Finally, add the soy sauce, lime juice and zest, white wine vinegar, dry white wine and vegetable stock. Cover and simmer for about 25 minutes, until the veggies are soft. Serve hot.

Pork Stuffed

FOR THE STUFFING
2 tablespoons olive oil, divided
1 teaspoon minced garlic
3 tablespoons finely chopped onion
⅓ cup spinach
2 ounces Muenster cheese, shredded
1 egg, beaten
FOR THE PORK CHOPS
2 (6- to 8-ounce) bone-in pork chops
½ teaspoon salt
¼ teaspoon finely ground black pepper
To make the stuffing

1.
In a large oven-safe skillet over medium-high heat, heat 1 tablespoon of olive oil for 1 minute. Add the garlic and sauté until fragrant, about 1 minute. Add the onion and spinach. Lower the heat to medium and cook for 2 to 3 minutes. Transfer the mixture to a small bowl to cool.

2.
Once cooled, add the Muenster cheese and the egg. Mix well to combine.
To make the pork chops

1.
Preheat the oven to 375°F.

2.
On a flat surface, cut the pork chops through the middle horizontally to the bone. Open the meat up like a butterfly. Stuff half of the spinach mixture into each pork chop. Fold the chop together over the stuffing and secure the edges with toothpicks, if necessary. Season with the salt and pepper.

3.
In the large oven-safe skillet, heat the remaining tablespoon of olive oil over medium-high heat. Place the chops into the skillet and sear each side for 2 minutes. Once seared, remove the skillet from the heat and place it into the preheated oven. Bake for 15 minutes, or until the internal temperature reaches 150°F.

4.
Serve with your preferred side dishes.

Balsamic Pork Medallion

Ingredients:

1 (1-pound) pork tenderloin, sliced into 1½-inch-thick medallions

¼ teaspoon salt

¼ teaspoon freshly ground black pepper

2 tablespoons olive oil

4 tablespoons butter, divided

1 garlic clove, minced

1 shallot, minced

3 tablespoons balsamic vinegar

1 teaspoon soy sauce

4 fresh rosemary sprigs

4 fresh thyme sprigs

1.

Preheat the oven to 475°F.

2.

Season each medallion with the salt and pepper.

3.

In a large oven-safe skillet over medium-high heat, heat the olive oil and 1 tablespoon of butter for 1 minute. Add the garlic and shallot and sauté until fragrant, about 1 minute. Add the pork medallions to the skillet. Sear on each side for about 2 minutes.

4.

Add the balsamic vinegar, soy sauce, rosemary, thyme, and the remaining 3 tablespoons of butter to the skillet. Stir to combine. Spoon the balsamic mixture over the pork. Bring to a simmer and cook for about 2 minutes.

5.

Remove the skillet from the heat and place it into the preheated oven. Bake for 5 minutes. Flip the medallions and spoon the balsamic mixture over each piece. Continue baking for an additional 5 minutes, or until the internal temperature reaches 150°F.

6.

Remove from the oven and allow the pork to rest for 2 to 3 minutes before serving.

7.

Serve with your preferred sides and any remaining balsamic sauce from the pan.

Cauliflower Beef

Ingredients

FOR THE CAULIFLOWER SALAD
3½ cups cauliflower florets
4 hardboiled eggs, roughly chopped
1 cup mayonnaise
2 tablespoons mustard
1 teaspoon minced garlic
½ teaspoon salt
¼ teaspoon freshly ground black pepper
¼ teaspoon paprika
1 cup chopped onion
3 tablespoons minced dill pickles
1 teaspoon chopped fresh parsley
FOR THE RUB
2 tablespoons powdered stevia, or other sugar substitute
2 tablespoons paprika
1 tablespoon garlic powder
1 tablespoon onion powder
1 teaspoon cayenne pepper
1 tablespoon ground cumin
1 teaspoon salt
1 tablespoon freshly ground black pepper
1 tablespoon chili powder
FOR THE BRISKET
1 (7- to 8-pound) beef brisket
2 tablespoons olive oil
1½ cups beef stock, divided
1 cup chopped onion
1 tablespoon liquid smoke
To make the cauliflower salad
1.
Bring a large pot of water to a boil. Add the cauliflower and cook for 10 minutes, or until tender. Drain the cauliflower. Set aside in a large bowl to cool.

2.

Once cooled, roughly chop the cauliflower. Add the eggs and stir to combine.

3.

In another large bowl, whisk together the mayonnaise, mustard, garlic, salt, pepper, and paprika. Add the cauliflower and egg mixture, onions, pickles, and parsley. Mix thoroughly to combine. Refrigerate, covered, for at least 2 hours, or until ready to serve.

To make the rub

In a medium bowl, mix together the stevia, paprika, garlic powder, onion powder, cayenne pepper, cumin, salt, black pepper, and chili powder.

To make the brisket

1.

Cover the beef brisket with the rub, massaging it into the meat thoroughly.

2.

In a large skillet over medium-high heat, heat the olive oil for 1 minute. Add the brisket to the skillet. Brown on all sides for about 3 minutes per side. Once browned, remove the beef brisket from the skillet. Set aside.

3.

Add ½ cup of beef stock to the skillet and scrape the bottom of the pan to loosen any browned bits. Remove the skillet from the heat and pour the drippings into a large slow cooker.

4.

To the slow cooker, add the remaining 1 cup of beef stock, onions, and liquid smoke. Whisk to combine with the drippings.

5.

Add the brisket to the slow cooker. Spoon some liquid over it to coat. Cover and cook on low for 6 hours, 30 minutes, or until tender.

6.

Serve the brisket sliced and with a spoonful of the cauliflower salad.

Bacon-Double Cheese Burger

Ingredients:

1 pound 80 percent lean ground beef
1 shallot, minced
1 teaspoon minced garlic
1 tablespoon Worcestershire sauce
½ teaspoon salt
¼ teaspoon freshly ground black pepper

4 (1-ounce) slices thick-cut bacon, cooked, grease reserved and cooled
1 tablespoon butter
4 (1-ounce) slices American cheese
4 low-carb buns or lettuce wraps (optional)

1.
In a large bowl, mix together the ground beef, shallot, garlic, Worcestershire sauce, salt, pepper, and reserved bacon grease. Divide the mixture into 4 equal portions and form into patties.

2.
In a large cast iron (or other heavy-bottomed) skillet over medium-high heat, heat the butter for 1 minute.

3.
Add the patties to the skillet and cook for 3 to 4 minutes. Flip and cook 2 to 3 minutes more for medium-rare.

4.
Lower the heat to medium-low. Place 1 slice of cheese on each patty. Cover the skillet and melt the cheese for 1 to 2 minutes.

5.
Remove the patties from the skillet. Top each with 1 slice of bacon.

6.
Serve with your favorite condiments, on a low-carb bun, or with a lettuce wrap

---

Beff Fajitas

Ingredients:

FOR THE RUB
1 teaspoon cumin
½ teaspoon chili powder
½ teaspoon garlic powder
½ teaspoon onion powder
¼ teaspoon paprika
¼ teaspoon salt
¼ teaspoon freshly ground black pepper
FOR THE STEAK
1 (1-pound) skirt steak
3 tablespoons olive oil, divided
1 red bell pepper, sliced

1 green bell pepper, sliced

1 jalapeño pepper, sliced

1 serrano pepper, minced

1 onion, sliced

2 garlic cloves, minced

2 tablespoons fresh cilantro, chopped

1 lime, quartered

3 low-carb tortillas (optional)

To make the rub

In a large bowl, mix together the cumin, chili powder, garlic powder, onion powder, paprika, salt, and pepper.

To make the steak

1.

Coat the steak with the rub, massaging it thoroughly into the meat. Set aside.

2.

In a large skillet over medium-high heat, heat 1 tablespoon of olive oil for 1 minute. Add the red peppers, green peppers, jalapeño peppers, serrano peppers, onions, and garlic. Sauté for 6 to 7 minutes, until browned and tender. Transfer the pepper and onion mixture to a bowl. Set aside.

3.

Add 1 more tablespoon of olive oil to the skillet. Heat on medium-high for 1 minute. Place the seasoned steak into the pan and sear it for 3 to 4 minutes per side for medium-rare. Remove the steak from the skillet. Set aside to rest for at least 3 minutes.

4.

Add the remaining tablespoon of olive oil to the skillet. Heat on medium-high heat for 1 minute.

5.

Add the peppers and onions back into the skillet. Sauté for 2 minutes.

6.

Slice the steak into ¼-inch-thick strips. Add the steak strips to the skillet with the peppers. Cook for 2 to 3 minutes until browned. Add the chopped cilantro. Remove from the heat.

7.

Serve garnished with a lime wedge and with the low-carb tortillas

Spinach Orange Duck Breast

Ingredients:
1/2 tsp. orange extract
1 tbsp. swerve sweetener
1/4 tsp. sage
1 tbsp. heavy cream
2 tbsp. butter
1 cup spinach
6 oz. duck breast

Directions:

1. Season the entire duck breast with salt and pepper, and score the top.
2. Heat a pan over medium-low, and add the butter and swerve. Cook until the butter begins to brown.
3. Add the orange extract and sage. Cook until the butter turns deep amber in color.
4. While this is cooking, set another pan on the stove and heat over medium-high. Add the duck breast to this pan.
5. Cook for a few minutes, or until the skin turns crisp. Then flip.
6. Now add the heavy cream to the butter mixture, and mix well.
7. When hot, pour the mixture over the duck breast, and cook for a further few minutes.
8. Toss the spinach into the pan and cook until wilted.
Enjoy!

Delicious Thyme Ribeye

Ingredients:

1 ribeye steak (~16 oz.)
1 tbsp. butter
1 tbsp. duck fat
1/2 tsp. thyme
Salt and pepper to taste\

Directions:

1. Preheat your oven to 400☐F.
2. Place a cast iron skillet in the oven as it is warming.
3. Once the oven is up to temperature, remove the pan and place on the stove over medium heat.
4. Add the oil and steak to the pan. Sear the steak for about 2 minute
5. Turn over the steak, and bake in the oven for about 5 minutes.
6. Again remove the pan, and place over low heat on the stove.
7. Add your butter and thyme to the pan and mix with the oil.
8. Baste the steak for 4 minutes.
9. Let the steak rest for 5 minutes. Serve and Enjoy

Yummy Chili Turkey Legs

Ingredients:

1/2 tsp. onion powder
1 tsp. liquid smoke
1/2 tsp. thyme (dried)
1/2 tsp. pepper
2 tsp. salt
1/4 tsp. cayenne pepper
1/2 tsp. garlic powder
1 tsp. Worcestershire sauce
1/2 tsp. ancho chili powder
2 turkey legs (about 1 lbs. each without bone)
2 tbsp. duck fat

Directions:

1. Combine all dry spices in a bowl, then toss in the wet ingredients and mix thoroughly.
2. Dry the turkey legs with paper towel, and then rub in the seasoning.
3. Preheat oven to 350☐F.
4. Heat a pan over medium-high, and add the duck fat.
5. When the oil begins to smoke, add the turkey legs and sear for 1 to 2 minutes per side.
6. Bake in the oven for 55 to 60 minutes or until completely cooked. Enjoy

Slow Roasted Pork Shoulder

Ingredients:

1 tsp. black pepper
2 tsp. oregano
1 tsp. onion powder
1 tsp. garlic powder
3 1/2 tsp. salt
8 lbs. pork shoulder

Directions:
1. Preheat oven to 250°F.
2. Dry the pork, then rub with the salt and spices.
3. Place the shoulder on a wire rack (a foiled baking sheet works too), and bake for 8 to 10 hours.
Or until your meat thermometer reads 190°F.
4. Remove from the oven, and raise oven temperature to 500°F.
5. Cover the shoulder with foil and let rest for about 15 minutes.
6. Remove the foil from the shoulder, and roast in the oven for another 20 minutes, while
rotating every 5 minutes.
7. Remove from oven and let rest for 20 minutes. Enjoy

Asian Style Spiced Chicken

Ingredients:

1 tsp. ginger (minced)
1 tsp. garlic (minced)
1/4 tsp. xanthan gum
1 tsp. red pepper flakes
1 tbsp. ketchup (sugar free)
1 tbsp. olive oil
1 tbsp. rice wine vinegar
2 tsp. sriracha
4 cups spinach
6 chicken thighs (bone in and skin on)

Salt and pepper to taste

Directions:
1. Preheat your oven to 425 F.
2. Dry your chicken and season the skin with salt and pepper.
3. Mix all of the sauce ingredients until a paste begins to form
4. Rub this sauce all over the chicken.
5. Lay the chicken on a wire rack
6. Bake for 45 to 50 minutes, or until the skin is crisp and slight charring appears.
7. Mix the spinach, some salt and pepper, red pepper flakes, and leftover chicken fat together, and serve alongside the baked chicken.
Enjoy!

Coconut Honey Grilled Fillet

Ingredients:

3 Tilapia fillets
2 tablespoons lime zest
1 teaspoon sea salt
1 tablespoon lemon pepper seasoning
1 teaspoon garlic powder
1 tablespoon melted coconut oil
2 cups arugula, washed and drained
1 tablespoon lemon juice
1 tablespoon olive oil
1 teaspoon honey

Directions:

To make the arugula salad, mix together the arugula leaves, lemon juice, olive oil and honey until the leaves are well-coated. Set this aside.
In another bowl, combine the lime zest, sea salt, lemon pepper seasoning and garlic powder.
Place the tilapia fillets into the spice mixture and coat evenly.
Grease the grill pan with the coconut oil and place it over medium-high flame. Place the tilapia on the grill pan and cook each side for 3-5 minutes.

Once the fillets are cooked, arrange them on a serving plate. Serve the tilapia with the prepared arugula salad.

Mozzarella Garlic Meaty Pizza

Ingredients:

1 pound of beef (minced)
1 free range egg
1 1/2 cups of keto-friendly Marinara Sauce
1/2 teaspoon of powdered onion
1/2 teaspoon of powdered garlic
Salt and pepper to taste
1 teaspoon of oregano (dried)
1/4 cup of parmesan (grated)
15 slices of pepperoni
11/2 cups of mozzarella (shredded)

Directions:

Set your oven to 400°F. Mix together the egg and meat. Add in the parmesan and garlic and seasoning.
Cover the base of a pie plate, so that you have a crust. Bake for about twenty minutes or until the meat loses its pink tinge and is cooked through.
Take out of the oven and top with marinara sauce.
Top this with the mozzarella and the pepperoni.
Bake for another few minutes until the cheese has melted.

Coconut Onion Stir-Fried Pork

Ingredients:

1 medium-sized sweet onion
2 tablespoons of melted coconut oil
3 cloves of crushed garlic
1 pound of pork (finely ground)
1 big zucchini
10 ounces of spinach
1 cup of broccoli (cooked and chopped)
1 teaspoon of dried sage
1 teaspoon of garlic flakes
1 teaspoon of onion flakes
Salt and pepper to taste
1/2 teaspoon of flaked red pepper (omit if you don't like spicy food)
1 big avocado (cubed)

Directions:

Set your stove to medium-high.
Fry the garlic and onion in the coconut oil until softened and transparent. Add in the zucchini and fry until softened.
Fry the pork until all traces of pink are gone. Once the meat is done, add in the spinach and allow it to wilt.
Add in all the remaining ingredients except the avocado and heat through.
Divide into four equal portions, top with the avocado, and serve.

Mushroom Cabbage Beef

Ingredients:

1 (1-pound) beef roast
¼ teaspoon salt
¼ teaspoon freshly ground black pepper
1 tablespoon olive oil
½ cup diced onion
1 cup chopped mushrooms
1 teaspoon minced garlic

4 cups sliced cabbage

1½ cups beef broth

½ cup heavy (whipping) cream

½ cream cheese, at room temperature

1 teaspoon tomato paste

1.

Season the roast with the salt and pepper. Set aside.

2.

In a large skillet over medium-high heat, heat the olive oil for about 1 minute. Add the roast to the skillet Brown on all sides, about 2 minutes per side. Remove the roast from the skillet, reserving any juices, and set aside.

3.

Add the onion, mushrooms, and garlic to the skillet. Cook for 2 minutes, or until tender.

4.

In a large slow cooker, layer the cabbage on the bottom. Top with the roast. Transfer the onion mixture to the cooker.

5.

In a large bowl, mix together the beef broth, heavy cream, cream cheese, and tomato paste. Add to the slower cooker and cover.

6.

Cook the roast on low for about 7 hours.

7.

With a fork or tongs, shred the roast. Serve with the cabbage.

Cumin Chili Beef

Ingredients:

FOR THE CHILI

3 tablespoons olive oil

2 cups diced onion

5 garlic cloves, minced

2 green bell peppers, diced

2 poblano peppers, diced

3 serrano peppers, minced

3 jalapeño peppers, diced

2 to 3 habanero peppers, minced (adjust for heat level; optional)

3 pounds 80 percent lean ground beef

1 cup tomato paste

2¼ cups crushed tomatoes

1½ cups diced tomatoes

2 cups dark beer

1½ tablespoons dark chili powder

½ teaspoon paprika

1 teaspoon salt

1 teaspoon freshly ground black pepper

½ teaspoon cumin

FOR THE TOPPINGS

2 cups shredded Cheddar cheese

1 cup sour cream

Chopped fresh cilantro, for garnish (optional)

To make the chili

1.

In a large stockpot over medium heat, heat the olive oil for 1 minute. Add the onion and garlic. Cook for 3 minutes until tender.

2.

Add the bell peppers, poblano peppers, serrano peppers, jalapeño peppers, and habanero peppers (if using) to the pot. Mix well. Cook for 3 to 4 minutes.

3.

Add the ground beef to the peppers and onions. Crumble with the back of a spoon while browning for 4 minutes.

4.

Add the tomato paste, crushed tomatoes, and diced tomatoes to the pot. Mix well.

5.

Add the beer. Increase the heat to high and bring the mixture to a boil.

6.

Once the chili boils, cover and lower the heat to medium-low. Cook for 1½ hours.

7.

Add the chili powder, paprika, salt, pepper, and cumin. Stir to incorporate. Cook for 5 more minutes, stirring occasionally.

8.

Serve the chili with the shredded cheese and sour cream. Garnish with cilantro (if using).

Delicious Beef Tacos Salad

Ingredients:

FOR THE TACO MEAT
2 tablespoons olive oil
½ cup diced onion
2 garlic cloves, minced
1 green bell pepper, diced
1 jalapeño pepper, diced
6 ounces diced tomatoes, divided
1 pound 80-percent lean ground beef
½ teaspoon cumin
½ teaspoon paprika
¼ teaspoon salt
¼ teaspoon freshly ground black pepper
1 avocado, diced
FOR THE TOPPINGS
½ cup shredded Cheddar cheese
¼ cup sour cream
Fresh cilantro, chopped
To make the taco meat
1.
In a large skillet over medium-high heat, heat the olive oil for about 1 minute. Add the onion and garlic. Cook for 2 minutes, until tender.
2.
Add the bell pepper, jalapeño pepper, and 3 ounces of diced tomatoes to the skillet. Cook for 3 to 4 more minutes.
3.
Transfer the mixture to a large bowl. Set aside. Reserve any liquid left in the skillet and place back over the heat.
4.
Add the ground beef to the skillet. Cook for 8 to 10 minutes, crumbling the meat, until browned.
5.
Add the cumin, paprika, salt, and pepper. Stir to combine.
6.
Transfer the beef to the large bowl with the onion and pepper mixture. Toss to combine.

7.

Mix in the remaining 3 ounces of tomatoes.

8.

Gently stir in the avocado. Do not overmix.

9.

Plate each serving of taco salad with a portion of the Cheddar cheese, sour cream, and cilantro toppings.

Bacon Crusted Stuffing

Ingredients:

4 medium-sized bell peppers (green peppers have the lowest carb count)
1/2 cup of mild onion (chopped)
1 tablespoon of good quality olive oil
1 pound of beef (finely ground)
4 rashers of bacon (cubed)
2 cloves of crushed garlic
1 big tomato (cubed)
2 teaspoons of dried Italian seasoning
1/2 cup of cheddar (shredded)
1/2 cup of mozzarella (shredded)
1/4 cup of keto-friendly Marinara sauce

Directions:

Set your oven to 375°F. Take the top third off the pepper and deseed them. Put to one side. Set your stove to medium.

Fry the garlic and onion in the heated olive oil until they become transparent. Brown the ground beef. Add the tomato, bacon, and seasoning and mix well. Add the marinara sauce.

Divide the mixture evenly and stuff the peppers. Stand them in an oven-proof dish upright, and bake for about fifty minutes. The meat should reach a temperature of 165°F.

Turn on the broiler and sprinkle the peppers with cheese.

Allow to broil for a few minutes until the cheese starts to bubble and the peppers start charring. Serve immediately.

Garlic Rosemary Thyme Cottage Pie

Ingredients:

2 celery stalks (finely diced)
1 1/2 pounds of lamb (finely ground)
3 cloves of crushed garlic
1 medium-sized onion (finely diced)
1 medium-sized zucchini (finely diced)
2 tablespoons of coconut oil
1 teaspoon of rosemary (dried)
1 teaspoon of thyme (dried)
Salt and pepper to taste
1/2 teaspoon of powdered garlic
3 tablespoons of farm butter
4 cups of cooked cauliflower
1/4 cup of double cream
1/2 teaspoon of garlic salt
3/4 cup of cheddar (shredded)

Directions:

Set the oven to 350°F. Fry the garlic and onions in the oil until translucent. Fry the zucchini and celery until softened.
Add the ground lamb and seasoning, and cook until browned. Put the meat into an oven-proof dish and set aside. Process the cauliflower, butter, and cream until smooth. Layer on top of the ground lamb and sprinkle the cheese over that. Bake for around half an hour until heated through, and allow to stand for a few minutes before you serve it.

Yummy Heavy Cream Garlic Fried Hake Fillet

Ingredients
- 10 oz. hake filets
- 1+ 1 tbsp. coconut oil
- ¼ onion, minced
- 2 cloves garlic
- 16 oz. spinach
- ⅓ cup heavy cream
- salt and pepper

Directions:

1.   Heat 1 tbsp. coconut oil in a large frying pan. Add the hake, skin side down, and cook for 5-6 minutes. Flip and cook for another 3-4 minutes until the flesh is opaque throughout.
2.   Meanwhile, heat 1 tbsp. coconut oil in a medium frying pan. Add the onions and garlic and cook for 2-3 minutes. Add the spinach and cook just until wilted.
3.   Add the cream to the spinach and season with salt and pepper. Simmer for 2 minutes more until the cream thickens. Serve the hake with the spinach on the side.

Coconut Caramelized Onions Baked Hake Fillet

Ingredients

- 2 onions, thinly sliced
- 2 + 2 tbsp. coconut oil, melted
- 10 oz. hake filets

- 1 cup cherry tomatoes
- salt and pepper

Directions:

1.   In a large pan, heat 2 tbsp. coconut oil and add the onions. Cook over medium heat, stirring frequently, until they are golden brown and reduced greatly, about 30 minutes.
2.   Meanwhile, lay the hake filets in a baking pan lined with parchment paper. Toss the cherry tomatoes with 2 tbsp. coconut oil and add them to the pan. Use a spoon to spread any excess oil onto the fish.
3.   Bake the fish and tomatoes for 15-20 minutes at 350°F until the hake is opaque and flakes easily.
4.   Serve with the caramelized onions.

Coconut Almond Crusted Tilapia

Ingredients
- 10 oz. tilapia filets
- ¼ cup ground almonds
- ¼ cup shredded coconut
- 2 tbsp. coconut oil, melted
- 1 clove garlic, minced
- 1 tsp. lime zest
- salt and pepper
- 1½ cups green beans
- 2 tbsp. slivered almonds
- 1 tbsp. butter

Directions:

1.   Lay the tilapia on a baking sheet.
2.   Mix the ground almonds, coconut, coconut oil, garlic, lime zest, salt, and pepper together and spread evenly over the fish.
3.   Bake for 15-20 minutes at 350°F until the tilapia is opaque and the crust is crunchy.

4.   Meanwhile, steam the green beans in the microwave or on the stove top until bright green. Toss with the butter and slivered almonds and serve with the tilapia.

Delight Curry soup with chicken

Ingredients:
* 1 tablespoon curry paste
* 1 teaspoon salt
* 1 tablespoon turmeric
* ½ teaspoon ground black pepper
* 1 tablespoon minced garlic
* 10 oz chicken
* 5 cups water
* ½ tablespoon mustard
* 1 teaspoon dill
* 1 cup collard greens

Directions:
1.   Chop the chicken roughly and put it in the saucepan.
2.   Pour water and cook the mixture on the medium heat for 15 minutes.
3.   Meanwhile, combine the curry paste, salt, turmeric, ground black pepper, and minced garlic together. You should get homogenous mass.
4.   After this, add mustard and dill. Stir it carefully again.
5.   Chop the collard greens.
6.   Transfer the spice mixture in the soup and stir it carefully till the curry paste is dissolved.
7.   Cook it for 5 minutes more.
8.   Then add chopped collard green and cook the soup on the low heat for 10 minutes.
9.   When the soup is cooked – let it rest for 10 minutes more.
10.   Then ladle the soup into the serving bowl and serve it immediately.
11.   Enjoy!

Delicious Spicy bacon soup

Ingredients:
- 10 oz bacon
- 1 tablespoon olive oil
- 4.2 oz green pepper
- 4 cups chicken stock
- 1 teaspoon chili pepper
- 1 teaspoon ground black pepper
- 1 jalapeno pepper
- 5.3 oz cauliflower
- 2 tablespoon full-fat cream
- 1 teaspoon salt

Directions:

1. Chop the bacon and sprinkle it with salt. Mix up the bacon with the help of hands.
2. Then preheat the pan and toss the bacon in the pan.
3. Cook it for 5 minutes on the medium heat. Stir it frequently.
4. After this, remove the bacon from the pan and leave it.
5. Remove the seeds from the green pepper and chop it.
6. Wash the cauliflower carefully and make the small florets.
7. Pour olive oil into the preheated pan and toss the cauliflower and green pepper.
8. Stir it and cook on the high heat for 1 minute. Stir it frequently.
9. After this, pour the chicken stock in the saucepan and add vegetables and bacon.
10. Close the lid and cook the soup for 20 minutes.
11. Then add full-fat cream, chili pepper, ground black pepper, and salt. Cook the soup for 5 minutes more.
12. When the soup is cooked – ladle it into the bowl and serve immediately.

Nutritional value: calories: 297, fat: 22.8g, total carbs: 4.0g, sugars: 1.8g, protein: 18.7g

Tasty Tender onion soup

Ingredients:

- 4.2 oz white onion
- 1 garlic clove
- 2 fl oz coconut milk
- 1 teaspoon salt
- 8 oz beef brisket
- 1 teaspoon paprika
- 3 large eggs
- 4 cups water
- 1 tablespoon butter

Directions:

1. Chop the beef brisket roughly and transfer it to the saucepan.
2. Add water and sprinkle it with the salt.
3. Cook the beef for 30 minutes with the closed lid.
4. Meanwhile, peel the onion and garlic clove.
5. Chop the vegetables and sprinkle them with the paprika.
6. Beat the eggs in the separate bowl and whisk them.
7. Add almond milk and mix up the liquid.
8. Then remove the meat from the liquid and chill it.
9. Add the egg mixture to the soup and stir it constantly during adding.
10. Add butter and onion mixture.
11. Stir the soup carefully and cook it for 15 minutes more.
12. Then take the hand blender and blend the soup until smooth.
13. Remove the soup from the heat and leave it for 5 minutes more.
14. Ladle it into the bowl and sprinkle with the cooked beef brisket.
15. Serve and Enjoy

Almond Chicken soup

Ingredients:
- 13 oz chicken breast, skinned, boneless
- 1.4 oz white onion
- 2.5 oz green beans
- ¼ cup almond milk
- 5 cups water
- ¼ cup cream cheese
- 5.3 oz zucchini
- 1 garlic clove
- 1 teaspoon salt
- ½ tablespoon dill

Directions:
1. Chop the chicken breast roughly and sprinkle it with salt.
2. Add dill and mix up the mixture with the help of the hands.
3. After this, pour water into the saucepan and toss chicken mixture.
4. Close the lid and cook it for 15 minutes.
5. Meanwhile, peel the onion and chop it.
6. Combine the chopped onion and green beans together. Mix it up.
7. After this, chop the zucchini and add it to the chicken mixture.
8. Cook it for 5 minutes more.
9. Then add chopped onion mixture, cream cheese, and almond milk.
10. Add garlic clove and cook the soup for 10 minutes on the medium heat.
11. When the soup is cooked – stir it carefully with the help of the spoon and serve it immediately.
12. Enjoy!

Rosemary Mushroom soup

Ingredients:
- 10.5 oz white mushrooms
- 2.8 oz white onion
- 1 teaspoon salt
- ¼ cup almond milk
- 1 teaspoon olive oil

- 1 tablespoon butter
- 4 cups chicken stock
- 1.3 oz almond flour
- ½ tablespoon tahini
- 10 oz chicken thighs
- ½ teaspoon rosemary

Directions:
1. Put the chicken thighs in the saucepan and pour chicken stock.
2. Sprinkle the mixture with salt and almond milk.
3. Cook the mixture over the medium heat with the closed lid for 15 minutes.
4. Meanwhile, slice the mushrooms and chop the onion.
5. Combine the vegetables together and sprinkle the mixture with the tahini, almond flour, rosemary, and olive oil. Stir the mixture carefully.
6. Preheat the pan and toss the butter in it.
7. Transfer the mushroom mixture to the pan and cook it on the medium heat for 5 minutes.
8. Stir it frequently.
9. After this, transfer the mushrooms in the soup and mix up it carefully with the help of the spoon till you get homogenous mass.
10. Cook the soup for 15 minutes more.
11. When all the ingredients in the soup are soft – remove it from the heat and ladle the in the serving bowls.

Kale soup

Ingredients:
- 10.6 oz kale (Italian dark-leaf)
- 5 cups beef broth
- 14 oz chicken fillet
- 1 teaspoon paprika
- 1 teaspoon turmeric
- ½ teaspoon thyme
- 1 teaspoon basil
- 5.3 oz zucchini
- 5.3 oz eggplant
- 1 oz walnuts
- 1 teaspoon salt

Directions:

1. Chop the kale and sprinkle it with salt. Stir the mixture and leave it until the kale gives the juice.
2. Cut the chicken into the strips and sprinkle with the paprika and turmeric. Stir it carefully with the help of the hands.
3. After this, wash the zucchini and chop it into the medium pieces.
4. Peel the eggplant and chop it into the same pieces as the zucchini.
5. Combine the chopped vegetables together in the mixing bowl and sprinkle them with the basil and thyme.
6. Pour the beef broth into the saucepan and add chicken strips.
7. Start to cook the soup on the medium heat for 20 minutes.
8. Then add chopped vegetable mixture and cook it for 6 minutes more.
9. After this, add chopped kale. Cook it for 5 minutes on the medium heat.
10. Crush the walnuts.
11. When the soup is cooked – all the ingredients should be soft.
12. Ladle the soup into the serving bowls and sprinkle with the crushed walnuts.
13. Serve the dish immediately.

Oregano Beef soup with the green peppers

Ingredients:
- ½ cup spinach
- 13 oz beef brisket
- 1 teaspoon salt
- 1 teaspoon ground black pepper
- 2 green peppers
- 1 garlic clove
- 1 tablespoon butter
- 2 fl oz almond milk
- 1 teaspoon oregano
- ½ teaspoon paprika
- ¼ cup flax meal
- ½ cup bok choy
- 4 cups water

Directions:

1.   Chop the spinach and bok choy.
2.   Combine the chopped vegetables together in the mixing bowl and add salt and flax meal.
3.   Mix up the mixture.
4.   After this, chop the beef brisket roughly and toss it in the saucepan.
5.   Pour water and cook the meat on the medium heat with the closed lid for 20 minutes.
6.   Peel the garlic clove and mince it.
7.   Combine the minced garlic with paprika, oregano, almond milk, and butter.
8.   Mix up the mixture carefully.
9.   Then sprinkle the meat with the ground black pepper and salt.
10.   Add the minced garlic mixture and cook the soup for 5 minutes more.
11.   Then add spinach mixture and cook the soup for 10 minutes on the medium heat with the closed lid.
12.   When the soup is cooked – remove it from the heat and leave it for at least 5 minutes to rest.
13.   Ladle the soup into the serving bowls and enjoy!

Zested Butter Rainbow Trout

Ingredients

*   10 oz. rainbow trout filets
*   1 recipe Avocado Dressing
*   1 tsp. lemon zest
*   2 tbsp. butter, melted

Directions:
1.   Pat the filets dry with paper towel and brush both sides with melted butter. Broil for 4-6 minutes until fish is opaque and flakes easily.
2.   Meanwhile, make the avocado dressing, adding 1 tsp. lemon zest.
3.   Serve the fish warm with the avocado sauce on the side.

Ginger Broccoli Beef Stir-Fry

Ingredients:

2 tablespoons soy sauce
2 garlic cloves, minced
2 tablespoons sake –vodka
1 tablespoon grated fresh ginger
½ teaspoon Chinese five-spice powder
1 (1-pound) skirt steak, sliced into 1-inch strips, then halved crosswise
3 tablespoons coconut oil
1 cup diced onion
4 cups broccoli florets
½ cup sliced scallions

1.
In a large bowl, mix together the soy sauce, garlic, sake, ginger, and five-spice powder. Add the steak strips. Cover. Refrigerate to marinate for at least 15 minutes.

2.
In a large deep skillet or wok over medium-high heat, heat the coconut oil for about 1 minute. Add the onion. Sauté for 2 minutes, or until tender.

3.
Add the beef and marinade to the skillet. Cook for 4 to 5 minutes, stirring occasionally.

4.
Add the broccoli and scallions to the skillet. Sauté for 2 minutes. Cover and reduce the heat to medium-low. Cook, covered, for another 2 to 3 minutes, or until the broccoli is tender.

5.
Stir the ingredients to mix well, and serve.

Butter Rainbow Trout

Ingredients

- 10 oz. rainbow trout filets
- 1 recipe Avocado Dressing
- 1 tsp. lemon zest
- 2 tbsp. butter, melted

Directions:

1. Pat the filets dry with paper towel and brush both sides with melted butter. Broil for 4-6 minutes until fish is opaque and flakes easily.
2. Meanwhile, make the avocado dressing, adding 1 tsp. lemon zest.
3. Serve the fish warm with the avocado sauce on the side.

Mayo Baked Fish Fillet

Ingredients
- 10 oz. Arctic char filet
- 2 tbsp. mayonnaise
- ½ cup sour cream
- 3 tbsp. thinly sliced chives
- 2 cups steamed broccoli (serve on the side)

Directions:

1. Lay the Arctic char skin side down on a baking sheet. Use the back of a spoon to spread the mayonnaise over the top; this helps keep the fish moist while baking.
2. Bake at 400°F for 10-13 minutes, until the fish is opaque and flakes easily.
3. Serve fish topped with sour cream and chives and steamed broccoli on the side.

Delicious Coconut Fish Curry

Ingredients

- 1 tbsp. coconut oil
- ½ onion, chopped
- 1 red pepper, chopped
- 3 cloves garlic, minced
- ½ inch ginger, minced
- 1 15 oz. can coconut milk
- 2 tbsp. lime juice
- 1 tbsp. curry paste
- 8 oz. hake, in 4-5 pieces.
- handful fresh cilantro, roughly chopped

Directions:

1.   Heat the coconut oil in a large pan and add the onions and red pepper. Cook for 3 minutes or so, then add the garlic and ginger and cook for 2-3 minutes.
2.   Stir the coconut milk, lime juice, and curry paste together and pour into the pan. Bring to a simmer and add the hake. Cover and cook gently for 6-9 minutes, until the fish is opaque and flakes easily.
3.   Ladle the curry into bowls and serve with fresh cilantro.

Stuffed onion rings

Ingredients:

- 2 big onions
- 1 teaspoon salt
- 7 oz ground chicken
- 6 oz ground beef
- 1 teaspoon paprika
- 1 tablespoon coconut oil
- 2 tablespoon almond flour
- 1 large egg
- 3 tablespoon chicken stock
- 3 tablespoon butter

Directions:

1. Peel onions and slice them into the thick circles.
2. Take the mixing bowl and combine salt, ground chicken, and paprika together.
3. Add egg.
4. Stir the mixture carefully with the help of the hands.
5. Take the tray and cover it with the baking paper.
6. Transfer the onion circles in the tray.
7. Then stuff the onion circles with the meat mixture.
8. Add butter and pour the dish with the chicken stock.
9. After this, sprinkle the onions with the almond flour and coconut oil.
10. Preheat the oven to 370 F and transfer the tray with onions.
11. Cook the dish for 20 minutes.
12. When it is cooked – remove the circles from the oven and chill them little.
13. Serve the dish immediately.

Thai Pad Gra Pow

Ingredients:

- 14 oz ground chicken
- 2 tablespoon basil
- 1 jalapeno pepper
- 1 teaspoon chili pepper
- ½ cup chicken stock
- 3 celery stalks
- 1 teaspoon salt
- 1 white onion
- 1/3 teaspoon thyme

Directions:
1. Remove the seeds from the jalapeno pepper and slice it.
2. Take the form and transfer ground chicken. Sprinkle the meat with thyme, salt, and chili pepper.
3. Stir the mass and sprinkle it with sliced jalapeno.
4. Then peel the onion and dice it.
5. Chop the celery stalk.
6. Sprinkle the meat with the diced onion and then add chopped celery stalk.
7. Pour the raw dish with the chicken stock and cover with the foil.
8. Preheat the oven to 380 F.
9. Transfer the dish to the oven and cook it for 25 minutes.
10. Then remove the foil from the dish and cook it for 10 minutes more.
11. Remove the cooked dish from the oven and chill it little.
12. Serve it.

Parmagiana Dish

Ingredients:
- 10 oz chicken breast

- 1 tablespoon coconut oil
- 1 teaspoon ground black pepper
- 1 teaspoon salt
- ½ teaspoon turmeric
- 1 tablespoon tomato puree
- 1 tablespoon apple cider vinegar
- 1 teaspoon basil
- ¼ cup chicken stock
- 2 eggs
- 1 tablespoon butter
- 3 oz Cheddar cheese

Directions:

1. Beat the chicken breast little and rub it with the ground black pepper.
2. Then sprinkle the meat with the salt, turmeric, and basil.
3. Sprinkle the meat with the apple cider vinegar and leave for at least 5 minutes.
4. Beat the eggs in the mixing bowl and whisk them.
5. Preheat the skillet and pour coconut oil.
6. Toss the chicken breast in the preheated skillet and cook it for 5 minutes from the both sides.
7. Grate Cheddar cheese.
8. Take the form and pour chicken stock.
9. Add the fried chicken breasts and sprinkle them with the whisked egg.
10. Add butter and sprinkle with the grated Cheddar cheese.
11. Preheat the oven to 370 F.
12. Transfer the chicken breasts to the oven and cook the meat for 25 minutes.
13. When the meat is cooked – remove it from the oven, chill it little.
14. Serve the dish immediately.

Nutritional value: calories: 255, fat: 12.5g, total carbs: 0.6g, sugars: 0g, protein: 32.7g

Easy Keto Thai Moussaka

Ingredients:
- 6 oz bacon

- 10 oz ground beef
- 3 tablespoon butter
- 1 teaspoon salt
- 7 oz cauliflower
- 4 oz Parmesan cheese
- 1 teaspoon ground black pepper
- 3 eggs
- ½ cup chicken stock
- 1 teaspoon tomato puree
- 1 tablespoon coconut oil

Directions:

1. Take the mixing bowl and combine ground beef, butter, salt, ground black pepper, and eggs together.
2. Stir the mixture carefully with the help of the hands.
3. After this, wash the cauliflower and chop it.
4. Preheat the pan well and pour coconut oil.
5. Toss the chopped cauliflower in the pan and roast the vegetables for 5 minutes. Stir it frequently.
6. Grate Parmesan cheese.
7. Take the big form and transfer the meat mixture.
8. Add roasted cauliflower and tomato puree.
9. After this, sprinkle the dish with the grated cheese and pour the chicken stock.
10. Cover the form with the foil and transfer it to the oven.
11. Cook the dish for 25 minutes.
12. When the dish is cooked – remove it from the oven and chill little.
13. Then remove the foil from the dish and serve it on the serving plates.

Rosemary Beef stew

Ingredients:
- 1-pound beef brisket

- 1 teaspoon rosemary
- 2 cups beef broth
- 1 oz walnuts
- 1 tablespoon mustard
- 1/3 oz flax meal
- 1 teaspoon salt
- 1 teaspoon paprika
- ½ teaspoon ground black pepper
- ¼ cup cream cheese
- 10 oz asparagus
- 7 oz avocado, pitted

Directions:

1.   Chop the beef brisket and put the meat in the mixing bowl.
2.   Sprinkle the chopped beef with the rosemary, mustard, salt, paprika, and ground black pepper.
3.   Stir the mixture carefully with the help of the hands. Leave the mixture.
4.   Meanwhile, chop the avocado and cut the asparagus into 4 parts.
5.   Crush the walnuts.
6.   Pour the beef broth into the saucepan and start to preheat it.
7.   When the liquid becomes to boil – add chopped beef brisket and simmer it for 15 minutes on the medium heat.
8.   After this, add asparagus and cream cheese.
9.   Continue to cook the stew for 15 minutes more.
10.   Then combine the chopped avocado and cream cheese together. Stir the mixture.
11.   Sprinkle the mass with the flax meal and stir it gently again.
12.   Transfer the cream cheese mixture in the stew and stir it carefully till you get homogenous mass.
13.   Close the lid and cook the stew for 10 minutes more.
14.   Remove the stew from the heat and sprinkle it with the walnuts.
15.   Serve the dish immediately.

Turmeric Bacon and cabbage stew

Ingredients:
- 7 oz bacon strips
- 1 teaspoon salt
- ½ teaspoon nutmeg
- 1 teaspoon turmeric
- 1 teaspoon ground black pepper
- 7 oz white cabbage
- 2 cups bone broth
- 1 tablespoon almond milk
- 1 teaspoon butter
- 2 green peppers

Directions:
1. Remove the seeds from the green peppers and chop them roughly.
2. Preheat the skillet on the medium heat and toss butter.
3. Add chopped green peppers and cook it for 2 minutes on the high heat.
4. Stir it constantly.
5. Chop the cabbage.
6. Chop the bacon strips roughly.
7. Take the mixing bowl and transfer the chopped cabbage. Sprinkle it with salt and nutmeg. Stir the mixture.
8. Sprinkle the chopped bacon with the turmeric, ground black pepper, and almond milk. Stir it.
9. Take the big saucepan and put the spiced bacon.
10. Add bone broth and cook the dish for 5 minutes.
11. Then add chopped cabbage and green peppers.
12. Stir the mixture.
13. Close the lid and simmer the dish for 15 minutes more.
14. Then mix up the stew and serve it immediately.

Seared Scallops with Lemon Juice

Ingredients:

2 tsp canola oil
3 oz sea scallops
2 tsp lemon juice
1/2 tsp ground sage
1 1/2 cups cubed roasted acorn squash
2 cups kale sautéed in 2 tsp olive oil

Directions:
Warm canola oil in a huge nonstick skillet over high warmth
Include scallops and cook without mixing until all around seared, around two minutes. Flip scallops and cook until the sides are firm and focuses misty, 30 to 90 seconds. Shower with lemon squeeze, and sprinkle sage on top. Present with squash and kale.

Herb Lamb Chops

Ingredients:

1 pound lamb chops
2 tablespoons Dijon mustard
4 fresh rosemary sprigs, chopped
4 fresh thyme sprigs, chopped
3 tablespoons almond flour
4 garlic cloves, minced
1 teaspoon onion powder
¼ teaspoon salt
¼ teaspoon freshly ground black pepper
4 tablespoons olive oil, divided
1.
Preheat the oven to 350°F.
2.
Coat the lamb chops with the mustard. Set aside.

3.

To a blender or food processor, add the rosemary, thyme, almond flour, garlic, onion powder, salt, and pepper. Pulse until finely chopped. Slowly add about 2 tablespoons of olive oil to form a thick paste.

4.

Press the herb paste firmly around the edges of the mustard-coated chops, creating a crust.

5.

In a large oven-safe skillet over medium heat, heat the remaining 2 tablespoons of olive oil for 2 minutes. Add the chops to the skillet on their sides to brown. Cook, undisturbed, for 2 to 3 minutes so the crust adheres properly to the meat. Turn and cook on the opposite edge for 2 to 3 minutes more. Transfer the chops to a baking sheet.

6.

Place the sheet in the preheated oven. Cook for 7 to 8 minutes, for medium.

7.

Remove the sheet from the oven. Serve immediately

Hot Sauce Bacon Cheese Burgers

Ingredients:

1 pound of beef (finely ground)
3 tablespoons of onion (finely chopped)
1/3 cup of double cream
1 clove of crushed garlic
1/8 teaspoon of hot sauce (can be left out)
Salt and pepper to taste
4 slices of cheddar
4 rashers of bacon
1 sliced avocado
2 tablespoons of Keto-friendly Mayo

Directions:

Put on the broiler. Mix well together the beef, cream, seasoning, onion, and garlic. Divide into four evenly sized patties and broil for around four minutes per side or till cooked to your liking.

Turn oven on to broil. Put a piece of cheese on each burger and broil for a little while longer until the cheese melts.

Add the bacon and avocado, put on mayo to taste, and serve.

Delicious Pulled Pork Cabbage Slaw

Ingredients:

FOR THE SLAW
¾ cup shredded cabbage

¼ cup shredded carrot

⅛ cup sliced scallions

3 tablespoons mayonnaise

1 teaspoon mustard

¼ teaspoon salt

¼ teaspoon freshly ground black pepper

FOR THE RUB
4 tablespoons stevia, or other sugar substitute

1 tablespoon paprika

2 teaspoons garlic powder

2 teaspoons onion powder

2 teaspoons mustard powder

1 teaspoon ground cumin

1 teaspoon salt

1 teaspoon freshly ground black pepper

½ teaspoon chili powder

FOR THE PORK
1 (4- to 5-pound) boneless pork shoulder roast

2½ tablespoons olive oil

¾ cup light beer

3 tablespoons apple cider vinegar

3 tablespoons tomato paste

8 low-carb buns or lettuce wraps (optional)

To make the slaw

In a large bowl, combine the cabbage, carrots, scallions, mayonnaise, mustard, salt, and pepper. Mix thoroughly. Refrigerate until ready to serve.

To make the rub

In a medium bowl, mix together the stevia, paprika, garlic powder, onion powder, mustard powder, cumin, salt, pepper, and chili powder.

To make the pork

1.

Cover the pork shoulder with the rub, massaging it thoroughly into the meat.

2.

In a large skillet over medium-high heat, heat the olive oil for 1 minute. Add the pork to the skillet, browning on all sides for about 3 minutes per side. Once browned, remove the pork from the skillet and set aside.

3.

Pour the beer into the skillet and scrape the bottom of the pan to loosen any browned bits. Remove the skillet from the heat and pour the drippings into a large slow cooker.

4.

To the slow cooker, add the apple cider vinegar and tomato paste. Whisk to combine with the pork drippings.

5.

Place the pork in the slow cooker and spoon some of the liquid over it. Cover. Cook on low for 8 hours. Insert a meat thermometer into the center of the pork to check the internal temperature. It should be between 180°F and 200°F.

6.

Remove the pork from the slow cooker and place it in a large bowl to cool.

7.

In a large skillet over high heat, add the remaining liquid from the slow cooker and bring to a boil. Lower the heat to medium-low and reduce the liquid by at least half over the next 10 minutes.

8.

Using two forks, shred the cooled pork until you have bite-size chunks.

9.

Pour the reduced liquid over the meat. Mix until it is coated evenly.

10.

Serve the shredded pork with the slaw on its own, or on a low-carb bun or a lettuce wrap (if using).

Kale Zucchini Noodles Spicy Beef Soup

Ingredients:

3 large zucchini (spiralized or peeled into strips)
1 pound grass-fed ground beef
2 carrots (sliced)
4 cups chicken broth
2 heads kale (chopped)
4 green onions (thinly sliced)
1 tablespoon fresh ginger (grated)
2 teaspoons chili paste
1 tablespoon sesame oil

Directions:

1.   Heat a large saucepan over medium heat.
2.   Brown the beef for 5–6 minutes. Remove from heat and set aside.
3.   Heat the oil in the same saucepan, over medium-high heat, and add the veggies, chicken broth, kale, chili paste, ginger and onions.
4.   Bring to a boil, reduce heat to low and simmer for 20 minutes, until the vegetables are soft.
5.   Stir in the ground beef and continue cooking together for another 10 minutes. Serve hot.

Sweet Juicy lamb ribs

Ingredients:

*   17 oz lamb ribs
*   1 tablespoon Stevia
*   1 tablespoon lemon juice
*   2 tablespoon olive oil
*   ½ cup chicken stock
*   1 teaspoon ground black pepper
*   1 teaspoon oregano

- 1 teaspoon salt

Directions:
1. Chop the lamb ribs roughly.
2. Transfer the lamb ribs in the mixing bowl and sprinkle it with the ground black pepper, oregano, and salt.
3. Mix up the mixture carefully.
4. After this, combine stevia and lemon juice together. Stir it.
5. Sprinkle the meat with the stevia mixture and stir it carefully again.
6. Preheat the skillet and pour olive oil.
7. Toss the lamb ribs in the preheated skillet and fry them for 2 minutes on the high heat from the both sides.
8. After this, transfer the meat in the pan and pour chicken stock.
9. Close the lid and simmer the ribs for 30 minutes on the medium heat.
10. When the ribs are cooked – remove them from the oven and chill them little.
11. Serve the dish.

Nutritional value: calories: 344, fat: 23.2g, total carbs: 0.8g, sugars: 0g, protein: 31.7g

Rosemary Chicken liver pate

Ingredients:
- 2 cups water
- 12 oz chicken liver
- 1 teaspoon salt
- ½ teaspoon rosemary
- 1 teaspoon basil
- 1 teaspoon oregano
- 1 teaspoon paprika
- 1 teaspoon ground black pepper
- 1 oz bay leaf
- 3 medium celery stalks
- 3 tablespoon butter

Directions:

1.   Take the saucepan and pour water.
2.   Sprinkle the liquid with the salt, rosemary, and basil.
3.   Add bay leaf.
4.   Transfer the chicken liver and celery stalk in the water and close the lid.
5.   Cook the liver for 20 minutes or until cooked.
6.   Then remove the chicken liver from the liquid and transfer to the mixing bowl.
7.   Take the hand blender and blend it until you get soft and fluffy mass.
8.   After, this, add a celery stalk and continue to blend it for 5 minutes more.
9.   Then add oregano, paprika, and ground black pepper.
10. Stir it gently and add butter.
11. Mix up the mass until you get smooth and homogeneous consistency.
12. Serve the liver pate immediately.

Mustard Spicy beef steak

Ingredients:
- 15 oz beef steak
- 1 tablespoon lemon juice
- 1 tablespoon coconut oil
- 1 tablespoon almond milk
- 1 teaspoon turmeric
- 1 teaspoon basil
- 1 teaspoon oregano
- 1 teaspoon ground black pepper
- 1 teaspoon cilantro
- 1 tablespoon rosemary
- 2 tablespoon butter
- 1teaspoon mustard
- 1 teaspoon apple cider vinegar

Directions:
1.   Beat the steaks gently.
2.   Take the shallow bowl and combine turmeric, basil, oregano, ground black pepper, cilantro, and rosemary together. Stir the mixture gently.

3.   Then sprinkle the meat with the spice mixture and stir it carefully.
4.   After this, rub the steaks with the mustard and sprinkle them with the apple cider vinegar.
5.   Leave the meat for 5 minutes.
6.   Meanwhile, combine the butter, almond milk, and coconut oil together. Stir it.
7.   Preheat the skillet well and pour the almond milk mixture.
8.   Then transfer the meat to the skillet and cook it for 15 minutes from the both sides on the medium heat.
9.   When the meat is soft – remove it from the skillet and serve it hot.
10. Enjoy!

Easy Meatloaf

Ingredients:
- 8 oz ground beef
- 8 oz ground chicken
- 1 tablespoon chicken stock
- 2 large eggs
- ½ tablespoon salt
- 1 teaspoon oregano
- 2 teaspoon cilantro
- 2 tablespoon butter
- 3 oz Parmesan cheese
- 1 teaspoon mustard
- 1 tablespoon almond flour

Directions:
1.   Take the mixing bowl and combine ground beef and ground chicken together.
2.   Beat the eggs in the ground meat mixture.
3.   Then sprinkle the mixture with the salt, oregano, and cilantro.
4.   Take the spoon and stir the mass very carefully.
5.   After this, grate Parmesan cheese.
6.   Combine the grated cheese and mustard together. Stir the mixture.
7.   Add chicken stock and stir it again.
8.   After this, preheat the oven to 365 F.
9.   Take the loaf form and transfer the meat mixture.

10. Sprinkle the meat loaf with the grated cheese mixture.
11. After this, sprinkle it with the almond flour.
12. Cover the meatloaf with the foil and transfer it to the preheated oven.
13. Cook the dish for 30 minutes.
14. Then remove the foil from the dish and cook it for 5 minutes more.
15. When the dish is cooked – remove it from the oven and chill it.
16. Slice it and serve immediately.

Delicious oysters

Ingredients:
- 10 oz oysters
- 4 garlic cloves
- 1 teaspoon paprika
- 1 tablespoon lemon juice
- 1 teaspoon basil
- 1 teaspoon oregano
- 1 teaspoon cilantro
- 1 teaspoon coconut oil

Directions:
1. Take the mixing bowl and combine paprika, basil, oregano, and cilantro together.
2. Then open the oysters and sprinkle them with the spice mixture.
3. Preheat the grill.
4. Peel the garlic cloves and mince them.
5. Combine the oysters with the garlic cloves and stir the mixture again.
6. After this, transfer the oysters in the grill and cook it for 8 minutes.
7. Sprinkle the dish with coconut oil during cooking.
8. Remove the oysters from the grill and sprinkle with the lemon juice.
9. Serve it immediately.

Nutritional value: calories: 108, fat: 5.0g, total carbs: 7.1g, sugars: 1.2g, protein: 8.8g

Chili Prawns with asparagus

Ingredients:

- 8 oz asparagus
- 2 tablespoon butter
- 1 teaspoon salt
- 1 teaspoon chili flakes
- 14 oz prawns
- 1 teaspoon ground black pepper
- 1 tablespoon coconut oil
- 1 teaspoon rosemary

Directions:
1. Wash the asparagus carefully.
2. Take the tray and cover it with foil.
3. Transfer the asparagus to the tray.
4. Preheat the oven to 365 F and transfer the asparagus to the tray.
5. Sprinkle the asparagus with the coconut oil.
6. Cook the vegetables for 5 minutes.
7. Meanwhile, peel the prawns and transfer them to the mixing bowl.
8. Sprinkle the seafood with the chili flakes, salt, ground black pepper, and rosemary.
9. Mix up the mass carefully.
10. After this, remove the tray with the asparagus from the oven and add shrimps.
11. Sprinkle the mixture with the butter and transfer in the oven again.
12. Cook the dish for 7 minutes more.
13. Then remove the dish from the oven and serve it immediately.

Oregano Basil Chili lobster

Ingredients:
- 2-pound lobsters
- 1 tablespoon lemon juice
- 1teaspoon ground black pepper
- 1 teaspoon oregano
- 1.2 tablespoon basil
- ½ teaspoon cilantro
- 1 teaspoon chili flakes
- 1 cup water
- 2 tablespoon butter
- 4 garlic cloves
- 1 teaspoon salt
- 4 cups water

Directions:
1. Wash the lobsters carefully and sprinkle the seafood with the salt.
2. Take the pan and pour water.
3. Transfer the lobsters to the water and cook the dish for 10 minutes with the closed lid.
4. Then remove the lobsters from the water.
5. Take the shallow bowl and combine ground black pepper, oregano, basil, cilantro, and chili flakes. Stir the mixture.
6. Peel the garlic cloves and slice them.
7. Combine the sliced garlic and butter together. Stir the mixture.
8. Add lemon juice and stir it again.
9. Sprinkle the lobsters with the spices.
10. Then preheat the oven to 365 F and transfer the lobsters.
11. Cook the seafood for 10 minutes.
12. Then rub the lobsters with the butter mixture and serve it immediately.
13. Enjoy!

Fish Lover rolls

Ingredients:
- 10 oz smoked salmon, sliced
- ½ cup cream cheese
- 1 tablespoon butter
- 1 tablespoon dill
- 1 teaspoon cilantro
- ½ teaspoon minced garlic
- 1 oz walnuts
- 1 teaspoon salt
- 1 tablespoon oregano
- 1 teaspoon nutmeg

Directions:
1. Take the mixing bowl and combine the cream cheese and butter together.
2. Take the hand mixer and mix the mixture carefully till you get smooth and fluffy mass.
3. Then sprinkle the mixture with the dill, cilantro, minced garlic, salt, oregano, and walnuts.
4. Stir the cream mixture very carefully with the help of the spoon.
5. After this, crush the walnuts and sprinkle the cream mixture.
6. Stir it again until homogenous.
7. Then take the sliced salmon and cover every slice with the cream mixture.
8. Roll the salmon slices.
9. Transfer the salmon rolls in the fridge and keep them for 10 minutes there.
10. Remove the dish from the fridge and serve it immediately.

Mustard Spinach Chicken

Ingredients:

- 3 pound chicken breast (cut into strips)
- 2 cups spinach leaves
- 1 teaspoon smoked paprika
- 1 tablespoon Dijon mustard

- 4 tablespoons butter (divided)
- 2 tablespoons heavy cream
- Fresh oregano (for garnish)
- ½ teaspoon Himalayan pink salt
- Pepper to taste

Directions:

1. Pound the chicken breast strips with a meat mallet until they are about ¾-inch thick.
2. Combine the paprika, salt and pepper in a shallow dish.
3. Coat the chickefn evenly with the mixture.
4. Meanwhile, melt 2 tablespoons of butter in a frying pan over medium heat.
5. Cook the chicken breast strips in the butter for 5 minutes per side until golden brown. Transfer the chicken to a serving plate.
6. In the same frying pan, melt remaining butter and add the spinach. Sauté for about 3 minutes.
7. In a small bowl, mix the mustard and the heavy cream.
8. To serve, place the chicken on the top of the spinach followed by the mustard.
9. Garnish with fresh oregano and enjoy.

Keto Salmon

Ingredients:

Salmon:
1 tbsp. duck fat
1 tsp. tarragon (dried)
1 tsp. dill weed (dried)
1 1/2 lbs. salmon fillet
Salt and pepper to taste.
Dill Sauce:
1/2 tsp. dill weed (dried)
1/4 cup heavy cream
1/2 tarragon (dried)
2 tbsp. butter

salt and pepper to taste

Directions:
1. Slice your salmon so you have two fillets.
2. Season the meaty side with all of your salmon spices, and season the skin side with salt and pepper.
3. Heat a skillet over medium, and add the duck fat. When hot, add the salmon with the skin down.
4. Cook for about 5 minutes as the skin crisps. Once the skin is crispy, flip the salmon and reduce heat to low.
5. Cook for about 10 minutes, or until it is cooked to your liking.
6. When the salmon is removed from the pan, toss in all your spices for the dill sauce, and stir until they begin to turn brown.
7. Add the cream, and stir until hot. Serve

Spicy Lemon grilled shrimps

Ingredients:
* 15 oz shrimps
* 1 tablespoon lemon juice
* 3 tablespoon butter
* 1 tablespoon minced garlic
* 1 teaspoon basil
* 1 teaspoon oregano
* 1 teaspoon cilantro
* 1 teaspoon rosemary
* ¼ tablespoon turmeric
* 1 teaspoon salt
* 2 tablespoon coconut oil
* 1 tablespoon hot chili pepper

Directions:
1.   Peel the shrimps and sprinkle them with salt.
2.   Take the shallow bowl and combine basil, oregano, cilantro, rosemary, and turmeric together. Stir the mixture.

3.   After this, combine the butter and minced garlic together in the separate bowl. Stir the mixture carefully.

4.   Combine the peeled shrimps and spice mixture, Add hot chili pepper and stir the mass carefully with the help of the spoon.

5.   Leave the shrimps for 10 minutes.

6.   Meanwhile, preheat the grill.

7.   Transfer the shrimps in the grill and sprinkle them with the coconut oil.

8.   Cook the seafood for 3 minutes on the medium heat.

9.   Then add ½ of the butter mixture. Cook the dish for 2 minutes more.

10.   When the shrimps are cooked – transfer them to the serving plate.

11.   Sprinkle the hot shrimps with the butter mixture again and serve them immediately.

Nutritional value: calories: 361, fat: 23.2g, total carbs: 4.7g, sugars: 0.5g, protein: 32.8g

Fish nuggets

Ingredients:
*   8 oz tilapia fillet
*   2 eggs
*   1 teaspoon salt
*   1 teaspoon turmeric
*   1 teaspoon onion powder
*   1 teaspoon cilantro
*   1 tablespoon cream
*   5 oz Parmesan cheese
*   1 tablespoon butter

Directions:
1.   Cut the tilapia fillet into the nuggets pieces.

2.   Take the bowl and combine salt, turmeric, onion powder, and cilantro. Stir the mixture gently.

3.   Combine the tilapia and spice mixture. Stir it carefully with the help of the hands.

4.   After this, beat the eggs in the separate bowl and whisk it until homogenous.

5.   Grate Parmesan cheese.

6.   Combine the whisked egg and cream together. Stir it.

7.   Preheat the skillet and pour butter.
8.   Deep the tilapia fillets in the egg mixture and then combine them with the grated cheese.
9.   Transfer the nuggets to the skillet and cook the dish for 4 minutes from the both sides on the medium heat.
10.   Then remove the nuggets from the skillet carefully – chill them for 3 minutes.
11.   Serve the dish immediately.

Juicy Pork Cutlets

Ingredients:
*   10 oz ground pork
*   2 tablespoon butter
*   1 teaspoon rosemary
*   1 teaspoon paprika
*   1 teaspoon salt
*   ½ teaspoon turmeric
*   1 tablespoon oregano
*   2 teaspoon coconut oil
*   2 eggs
*   1 tablespoon almond flour

Directions:
1.   Combine the ground pork and butter together in the mixing bowl.
2.   Add rosemary and paprika.
3.   Then sprinkle the mixture with the salt, turmeric, and oregano.
4.   After this, mix up the mixture carefully with the help of the hands.
5.   Make the medium cutlets.
6.   Whisk the eggs in the separate bowl until homogenous.
7.   Preheat the skillet and pour coconut oil.
8.   Preheat the coconut oil well.
9.   After this, deep the pork cutlets in the whisked egg mixture.
10.   Then sprinkle them with the almond flour.
11.   Transfer the cutlets to the skillet and cook them on the medium heat for 7 minutes from the both sides.

12. Then remove the cutlets from the skillet and discard the excess fat.
13. Serve the dish immediately.

Delicious Beef Goulash

Ingredients:
- 13 oz beef brisket
- 1 teaspoon marjoram
- 1 teaspoon salt
- ½ teaspoon ground black pepper
- 1 tablespoon paprika
- 2 cups water
- 1 green pepper
- 1 white onion

Directions:

1. Chop the beef into the medium cubes and transfer the meat to the mixing bowl.
2. Sprinkle it with the salt, ground black pepper, and paprika. Stir the mixture carefully and leave it for 5 minutes to rest.
3. Meanwhile, peel the onion and remove the seeds from the green pepper.
4. Chop the green pepper and dice the onion.
5. After this, take the big saucepan and pour water.
6. Add chopped beef brisket and close the lid.
7. Cook the meat for 20 minutes on the medium heat.
8. Then add chopped green pepper and diced onion.
9. Stir the mixture and close the lid.
10. Cook the dish for 15 minutes more.
11. Then sprinkle the goulash with the marjoram and simmer the dish for 5 minutes more.
12. Stir the final dish very carefully and serve it immediately.

Carbonade

Ingredients:
- 2 lbs. beef chuck
- 1 tablespoon salt
- 4 garlic cloves
- 1 white onion
- 1 tablespoon coconut oil
- 1 cup water
- 1 teaspoon ground black pepper
- 1 tablespoon mustard
- 1 teaspoon chili pepper
- 1 teaspoon thyme
- 1 teaspoon coconut flour

Directions:

1. Take the big plastic bag and put the coconut oil, ground black pepper, mustard, chili pepper, and thyme inside.
2. Chop the beef chunk roughly and transfer it into the plastic bag.
3. Peel the onion and garlic cloves. Slice the vegetables.
4. Then transfer the sliced vegetables in the plastic bag and seal it.
5. Stir it gently until homogenous.
6. Take the big pan and pour water.
7. Preheat the water until boiled and toss the meat mixture in the water.
8. Sprinkle the meat with the coconut flour and stir it carefully until homogenous.
9. Reduce the heat and close the lid.
10. Simmer the carbonade for 35 minutes on the low heat.
11. When the meat is cooked – remove it from the heat.
12. Let it rest little and serve immediately.
13. Enjoy!

Roasted meat mixture

Ingredients:
- 8 oz lamb
- 5 oz chicken
- 7 oz beef brisket
- 3 oz pork
- 1 white onion
- 6 oz asparagus
- 4 tablespoon butter
- 1 teaspoon salt
- 1 teaspoon cayenne pepper
- 1 tablespoon oregano
- 1 teaspoon basil
- 2 cups water

Directions:

1. Take the lamb, chicken, and beef brisket and cut them into the strips.
2. Transfer the meat strips in the mixing bowl and sprinkle with the salt, cayenne pepper, oregano, and basil.
3. Mix up the mixture and leave it.
4. Chop the asparagus and peel the onion.
5. Dice the onion roughly.
6. Preheat the skillet and toss the butter. Melt the butter.
7. After this, transfer the meat strips in the skillet and fry them on the high heat for 4 minutes. Stir it frequently.
8. After this, transfer the fried meat in the pan and pour water.
9. Add chopped asparagus and diced onion.
10. Stir the mixture carefully with the help of the spoon and close the lid.
11. Simmer the dish on the medium heat for 40 minutes.
12. When the dish is cooked – serve it in the bowls.
13. Enjoy!

Prawn Avocado with eggs

Ingredients:

- 12 oz avocado, pitted
- 4 oz prawns
- 3 boiled eggs
- 1 tablespoon coconut oil
- ½ white onion
- 1 teaspoon cilantro
- 1 teaspoon oregano
- 1 teaspoon salt
- ¼ teaspoon nutmeg
- 1 tablespoon butter
- 1 teaspoon garlic powder

Directions:

1. Remove the meat from the avocado and mash it with the help of the spoon.
2. Peel the prawns and combine the seafood with the cilantro, oregano, salt, and nutmeg. Stir the mixture.
3. Take the skillet and pour coconut oil.
4. Preheat the coconut oil and toss the prawns in the skillet.
5. Chop the onion and dice it.
6. Add the chopped onion in the skillet.
7. Cook the prawn mixture for 5 minutes on the medium heat. Stir them frequently.
8. After this, peel the boiled eggs and chop them.
9. Combine the shrimps and chopped eggs and stir the mixture.
10. Add butter and leave it.
11. Then add the chopped eggs in the avocado mixture and add prawn mixture.
12. Stir it carefully until homogenous.
13. Fill the avocado with the seafood mixture.
14. Serve it immediately.

Coconut Bok Choy muffins

Ingredients:

- 2 cup bok choy
- ½ cup almond flour
- ½ cup coconut milk
- 1 tablespoon minced garlic
- 1 teaspoon salt
- 3 eggs
- ½ teaspoon baking soda
- 1 teaspoon apple cider vinegar
- 3 tablespoon butter
- 1 tablespoon coconut oil
- ½ white onion

Directions:
1. Chop the bok choy into the tiny pieces.
2. Dice the onion and combine it with the chopped bok choy.
3. Preheat the pan and pour coconut oil.
4. Toss the bok choy mixture and cook it on the medium heat for 5 minutes.
5. Stir it frequently.
6. After this, beat the eggs in the mixing bowl and pour coconut milk. Mix up the mixture with the help of the hand mixer.
7. Then add baking soda, apple cider vinegar, salt, minced garlic, and coconut flour.
8. Stir the mixture carefully till you get smooth mass.
9. Then add the bok choy mixture and mix up the dough till you get homogenous mass.
10. Preheat the oven to 365 F.
11. Take the muffin from and toss the small amount of butter in every form.
12. Then fill the ½ of every form with dough.
13. Transfer the muffins to the preheated oven and cook for 20 minutes.
14. When the muffins are cooked – remove them from the oven and chill little.
15. Then discard muffins from the forms and serve.
16. Enjoy!

Vegetable lasagna

Ingredients:
- 15 oz eggplants
- 7 eggs
- 1 teaspoon salt
- 1 teaspoon paprika
- 3 tablespoon butter
- 1 teaspoon ground black pepper
- 1 teaspoon rosemary
- 1 tablespoon coconut oil
- 1 teaspoon minced garlic
- 8 oz Parmesan cheese
- 8 oz Cheddar cheese
- 1/3 cup cream
- 1 teaspoon chili pepper
- 1 cup spinach

Directions:
1. Wash the eggplants carefully and slice.
2. Sprinkle the sliced eggplants with the paprika and salt.
3. After this, sprinkle the vegetables with the coconut oil.
4. Preheat the oven to 365 F.
5. Put the sliced eggplants in the tray and transfer the tray to the oven.
6. Cook the vegetables for 10 minutes.
7. Meanwhile, chop the spinach roughly and steam it for 5 minutes.
8. Then grate Cheddar and Parmesan cheese.
9. Combine the grated cheeses together.
10. Sprinkle the mixture with the ground black pepper, rosemary, and chili pepper. Stir it.
11. After this, remove the eggplants from the oven.
12. Take the big form and toss the butter.
13. Whisk the eggs. Make the crepes from the whisked egg mixture.
14. Make the layer from the sliced eggplants in the form.
15. Then add chopped spinach. Sprinkle the mixture with the grated cheese.
16. After this, add the egg crepe. Repeat the same steps 3 times.
17. Then combine the cream and minced garlic together. Stir the mixture until homogenous.
18. After this, pour the liquid in the lasagna. Transfer the dish to the oven and cook it at 365 F for 15 minutes.
19. When the lasagna is cooked – remove it from the oven and chill little.
20. Serve it immediately.

Low carb risotto

Ingredients:

- 12 oz cauliflower rice
- 1 tablespoon tomato puree
- 1/3 cup tomatoes
- 2 cups chicken stock
- 1 teaspoon salt
- 1 teaspoon paprika
- 1 white onion
- 7 oz Parmesan cheese
- 4 garlic cloves
- ¼ cup cream
- 3 tablespoon butter
- 1 tablespoon parsley

Directions:
1. Peel the onion and dice it.
2. Combine the diced onion with the tomato puree and paprika. Stir the mixture.
3. After this, add parsley and stir it carefully.
4. Preheat the saucepan and pour chicken stock. Add cauliflower rice and cook it for 10 minutes.
5. Then add diced onion mixture and butter.
6. Grate the cheese and chop the tomatoes.
7. When the cauliflower mixture soaks the ½ of the liquid – add chopped tomatoes.
8. Peel the garlic cloves and slice them.
9. Sprinkle the cauliflower mixture with the sliced garlic.
10. After this, add butter and tomato puree. Mix up the mixture carefully with the help of the spoon.
11. Sprinkle the dish with grated Parmesan and stir it thoroughly.
12. Simmer the risotto for 10 minutes more.

13. When the risotto is cooked – remove it from the heat.
14. Serve the dish immediately.

Rosemary juicy pork cutlets

Ingredients:
- 10 oz ground pork
- 2 tablespoon butter
- 1 teaspoon rosemary
- 1 teaspoon paprika
- 1 teaspoon salt
- ½ teaspoon turmeric
- 1 tablespoon oregano
- 2 teaspoon coconut oil
- 2 eggs
- 1 tablespoon almond flour

Directions:
1. Combine the ground pork and butter together in the mixing bowl.
2. Add rosemary and paprika.
3. Then sprinkle the mixture with the salt, turmeric, and oregano.
4. After this, mix up the mixture carefully with the help of the hands.
5. Make the medium cutlets.
6. Whisk the eggs in the separate bowl until homogenous.
7. Preheat the skillet and pour coconut oil.
8. Preheat the coconut oil well.
9. After this, deep the pork cutlets in the whisked egg mixture.
10. Then sprinkle them with the almond flour.
11. Transfer the cutlets to the skillet and cook them on the medium heat for 7 minutes from the both sides.
12. Then remove the cutlets from the skillet and discard the excess fat.
13. Serve the dish immediately.

Sardine fritters

Ingredients:
- 2-pound sardines
- ¼ cup spinach
- 2 tablespoon butter
- 4 tablespoon coconut milk
- 1 teaspoon salt
- ½ tablespoon ground ginger
- 1 teaspoon cilantro
- 3 tablespoon fish stock

Directions:
1. Mince the sardines and sprinkle the mixture with salt, ground ginger, and cilantro.
2. Stir it carefully.
3. After this, chop the spinach roughly and then blend it in the blender for 1 minute.
4. Combine the blended spinach and sardines mixture together.
5. Make the balls from the mixture and then flatten the balls with the help of the hands.
6. Toss butter in the skillet and preheat it.
7. Transfer the fritters to the skillet and cook them for 2 minutes from the one side on the medium heat.
8. Then turn the fritters into another side and pour coconut milk and fish stock.
9. Close the lid and simmer the dish for 10 minutes on the medium heat.
10. When the time is over – remove the fritters from the skillet and serve the dish immediately.
11. Enjoy!

Delicious Stuffed zucchini

Ingredients:
- 2 zucchini

- 10 oz ground chicken
- 1 white onion
- 1 tablespoon tomato puree
- 1 teaspoon ground black pepper
- 1 teaspoon salt
- 1 tablespoon almond milk
- 1 cup chicken stock
- 6 oz Cheddar cheese
- 1 tablespoon butter

Directions:
1. Wash the zucchini carefully and cut it into 6 parts.
2. Then remove the meat from the zucchini and chop the zucchini meat.
3. Take the mixing bowl and transfer the zucchini meat. Add ground chicken, ground black pepper, and tomato puree.
4. Stir the mixture carefully.
5. After this, peel the onion and dice it.
6. Combine the diced onion and ground meat mixture together.
7. Preheat the pan and toss the butter.
8. Add the ground meat mixture and start to cook it on the medium heat for 4 minutes.
9. Stir it frequently.
10. Sprinkle the mixture with salt, stir it, and remove from the heat.
11. Grate Cheddar cheese.
12. Fill the zucchini with the ground meat mixture.
13. Then sprinkle with the grated cheese.
14. Take the big tray and transfer the zucchini.
15. Pour almond milk.
16. Preheat the oven to 370 F and transfer the tray with zucchini.
17. Cook the dish for 15 minutes.
18. When the dish is cooked – chill it little and serve immediately.
19. Enjoy!

Fish meatballs

Ingredients:
- 15 oz salmon
- 1 tablespoon dill
- 1 teaspoon parsley
- 1 teaspoon salt
- ¼ cup almond flour
- ½ teaspoon chili flakes
- 4 tablespoon butter
- ¼ cup fish stock
- 2 eggs
- 1 teaspoon minced garlic

Directions:
1. Chop the salmon roughly and transfer to the blender. Blend it for 2 minutes or till you get smooth mass.
2. After this, take the shallow bowl and combine dill, parsley, salt, and chili flakes together.
3. Stir the mixture.
4. Combine the smooth salmon mixture and spices together.
5. Add eggs and minced garlic. Stir the mixture carefully till you get homogeneous consistency.
6. Make the medium meatballs from the fish mixture.
7. Take the pan and toss the butter.
8. Melt the butter.
9. Sprinkle the salmon meatballs with the almond flour and transfer them to the preheated pan.
10. Fry the meatballs on the high heat for 1 minute from the both sides.
11. After this, pour the fish stock in the pan and close the lid.
12. Simmer the dish for 10 minutes on the medium heat.
13. Serve the salmon meatballs immediately.

Coconut Stuffed cod

Ingredients:
- 1-pound cod
- 4 garlic cloves
- 1 white onion

- 6 oz white mushrooms
- 1 tablespoon butter
- 1 teaspoon salt
- ½ teaspoon ground black pepper
- 2 tablespoon coconut oil
- 1 teaspoon lemon juice

Directions:
1. Wash the cod carefully and dry it with the help of the paper towel.
2. After this, peel the onion and chop it roughly.
3. Peel the garlic and slice it.
4. Slice the mushrooms.
5. Combine the mushrooms with the garlic and chopped onion. Stir the mixture.
6. After this, sprinkle the mushroom mixture with the ground black pepper.
7. Stuff the cod with the mushroom mixture.
8. Then sprinkle the fish with the coconut oil and wrap it in the foil.
9. Preheat the oven to 370 F and transfer the fish.
10. Cook the cod for 25 minutes.
11. When the fish is cooked – all the ingredients should be soft.
12. Remove the foil and sprinkle with the lemon juice.
13. Serve the dish immediately.

Garlic Grilled salmon

Ingredients:
- 2-pound salmon fillet
- 1 tablespoon minced garlic
- ¼ cup almond milk
- 1 teaspoon ground black pepper
- 1 teaspoon ginger
- 1 tablespoon coconut oil
- 1 teaspoon onion powder

Directions:

1. Take the shallow bowl and combine minced garlic, ground black pepper, ginger, and onion powder together. Stir the mixture gently.
2. After this, rub the salmon fillets with the spice mixture carefully.
3. Leave the fish for 10 minutes to rest.
4. After this, pour the almond milk in the salmon.
5. Preheat the grill and transfer the fish to the grill.
6. Cook it for 7 minutes from the both sides. Sprinkle the fish with the coconut oil during the cooking.
7. When the fish is cooked – serve it hot.

Onion Vegetable Beef Soup

Ingredients
2 pounds lean ground beef
4 (15 ounce) cans mixed vegetables
4 (16 ounce) cans diced tomatoes
1 onion, chopped
Ground black pepper to taste
Salt to taste

Directions

In a large soup pot, cook ground meat over medium heat until browned. Drain grease from the pot.
Add chopped onion, mixed vegetables, and tomatoes. Give it a stir. Reduce heat, and simmer for about 3 to 4 hours. Season to taste with salt and pepper.

Delightful Seafood salad

Ingredients:
- 8 oz scallops
- 2 tablespoon butter
- 1 teaspoon onion powder
- ½ teaspoon salt
- 1 cucumber
- 1 tomato
- ½ cup spinach
- 1 teaspoon paprika
- 1 tablespoon coconut oil

Directions:

1. Combine the scallops with the onion powder and paprika. Stir the mixture and add salt.
2. Preheat the skillet on the medium heat and toss butter. Melt the butter.
3. After this, transfer the scallops in the preheated skillet and cook the seafood for 4 minutes on the medium heat.
4. Chop the spinach slice the cucumber.
5. Chop the tomato.
6. Take the mixing bowl and combine the cooked scallops, chopped spinach, sliced cucumbers, and chopped tomatoes.
7. Sprinkle salad with salt and coconut oil.
8. Stir the salad carefully and transfer the salad to the serving bowl.
9. Serve the dish immediately.

Shrimp and avocado Macadamia salad

Ingredients:
- 1-pound shrimps
- 1 tablespoon onion powder

- 1 teaspoon garlic powder
- 7 oz avocado, pitted
- 1 oz macadamia nuts
- 1 green pepper
- 1 teaspoon paprika
- 2 tablespoon coconut oil
- 1 teaspoon basil
- 1 teaspoon oregano
- 1 teaspoon turmeric
- 1 teaspoon cilantro
- 1 teaspoon dill
- 4 oz red cabbage
- 2 cups water

Directions:
1. Slice the avocado and transfer in the salad bowl.
2. Pour water into the saucepan and add shrimps.
3. Cook the shrimps for 15 minutes.
4. Then remove the shrimps from the water and peel the seafood.
5. Add the peeled shrimps in the sliced avocado.
6. Sprinkle the mixture with the basil, paprika, oregano, turmeric, cilantro, and dill.
7. Chop the red cabbage and add to the salad.
8. Then combine the coconut oil, garlic powder, and onion powder. Stir the mixture.
9. Remove the seeds from the green pepper and chop it.
10. Crush the macadamia nuts.
11. Combine the crushed macadamia nuts and chopped green pepper together and transfer the mixture in the salad mass.
12. Sprinkle the salad with the coconut oil liquid and stir it carefully with the help of the spoon.
13. Serve the salad immediately.

Healthy Salad

Ingredients:
- 2 tomatoes
- 1 tablespoon coconut oil
- 1 teaspoon minced garlic
- 7 oz avocado, pitted
- 5 oz mozzarella
- 1 teaspoon basil
- 1 teaspoon oregano
- 1 teaspoon lemon juice
- 8 olives

Directions:
1. Cut the mozzarella balls into 2 parts.
2. Slice the tomatoes and avocado.
3. Take the shallow bowl and combine basil, oregano, lemon juice, and coconut oil. Stir the mixture,
4. Slice olives.
5. Take the serving plate and transfer the sliced tomato.
6. Then add sliced avocado and olives.
7. After this, put the mozzarella pieces.
8. Sprinkle the salad with the coconut sauce and serve it immediately. Enjoy

Greek salad

Ingredients:
- 6 oz Parmesan cheese
- 1 teaspoon basil
- 1 teaspoon oregano
- 1 tablespoon coconut oil
- 1 white onion
- 3 oz black olives
- 2 tomatoes
- 1 cucumber
- 1 teaspoon salt
- ½ teaspoon ground black pepper

Directions:
1. Wash the cucumber and tomatoes carefully and chop the vegetables.
2. Put the chopped vegetables in the mixing bowl.
3. Cut Parmesan cheese into the cubes and add to the mixing bowl too.
4. Peel the onion and slice it.
5. Add the sliced onion to the salad mixture.
6. After this, cut the black olives into 2 parts and add in the salad too.
7. Sprinkle the salad with the basil, oregano, coconut oil, salt, and ground black pepper.
8. Stir the salad carefully with the help of the spoon.
9. Serve the dish immediately.
10. Enjoy!

Delicious Sauerkraut Salad

Ingredients:
- 3 tablespoon salt
- 2-pound white cabbage
- 1 tablespoon black pepper
- 1 teaspoon basil
- 1 cup water
- 1 garlic clove

Directions:
1. Wash the cabbage carefully and chop it.
2. Take the big mixing bowl and combine chopped cabbage, black pepper, basil, and salt.
3. Stir the mixture carefully with the help of the hands.
4. Then peel the garlic clove and chop it.
5. Add the chopped garlic in the cabbage mixture and stir it carefully again.
6. Then take the glass jar and transfer the cabbage mixture in the jar.
7. Add the cup of water and cover the jar with the lid.
8. Leave it for at least 20 minutes.
9. Keep the salad in warm dark place.

Nutritious Bacon Salad

Ingredients:
- 1-pound bacon strips
- 1 teaspoon salt
- 1 teaspoon ground ginger
- 1 teaspoon cilantro
- 3 boiled eggs
- 4 oz Cheddar cheese
- 1 teaspoon almond milk
- 2 tablespoon butter
- 7 oz eggplant
- 2 tomatoes
- 1 oz spinach

Directions:
1. Chop the bacon strips and transfer it to the mixing bowl.
2. Add salt, ground ginger, and cilantro. Stir the mixture.
3. Preheat the skillet and put the 1 tablespoon of butter. Melt the butter.
4. Then put the chopped bacon in the preheated skillet and fry the bacon for 5 minutes on the medium heat.
5. Chop the spinach and grated Cheddar cheese.
6. Peel the eggs and chop them too.
7. Wash the tomatoes and dice them.
8. Combine the diced tomatoes, chopped eggs, and spinach together. Stir the mixture and sprinkle it with the grated cheese.
9. Add almond milk.
10. Peel the eggplants and dice them.
11. Take the pan and put the 1 tablespoon of the butter. Add diced eggplants and roast the vegetables for 8 minutes on the medium heat.
12. Add the roasted eggplants and cooked bacon in the salad and stir it carefully.
13. Serve the salad immediately.

Yummy Chinese Egg Soup

Ingredients
4 cups seasoned chicken broth
1/2 cup frozen green peas

1 egg, beaten

Directions
Bring chicken broth and peas to a boil in a large saucepan.
Slowly add egg to the boiling broth, stirring constantly. Serve hot, garnished with chopped green onions.

Cauliflower Soup

Ingredients :

2 stalks celery, chopped
1 onion, chopped
3/4 cup shredded carrots
2 tablespoons olive oil
1 head cauliflower, coarsely chopped
6 cups chicken broth
Ground black pepper to taste

Directions
In a large saucepan over medium heat, saute the celery, onion and carrot in olive oil for 5 minutes, or until onion is translucent. Remove from heat and set aside.
Steam cauliflower in a colander over boiling water or in a steamer until tender. Mash.
Add the mashed cauliflower to the vegetable mixture, return to stovetop over medium heat and add the chicken broth. Pepper to taste and simmer for 15 minutes or until soup is heated thoroughly.

Delicious Teriyaki Veggies Beef

Ingredients:

- ☐ 3 oz grass-fed beef tenderloin, cubed
- ☐ 2 Tbsp reduced-sodium teriyaki sauce
- ☐ 1 Tbsp light honey-mustard dressing
- ☐ 2 tsp olive oil
- ☐ 1/4 cup sliced carrots
- ☐ 1/2 cup chopped broccoli
- ☐ 1/4 cup sliced water chestnuts
- ☐ 1/4 cup sliced peppers
- ☐ 1/2 cup cooked brown rice

Directions:

Marinate hamburger in teriyaki and dressing for 30 minutes.
Warm olive oil in a skillet, and cook meat one to two minutes. Include veggies, and cook for another five to seven minutes until hamburger is seared. Serve over rice.

Tasty Coconut Cheesy Chili Beef

Ingredients

- 2 + 2 tbsp. coconut oil
- 1 large onion, chopped
- 2 green peppers, seeded and chopped
- 3 cloves garlic, minced
- 12 oz. 80% lean ground beef
- 2 cups water
- 1 15 oz. can diced tomatoes
- 1 tbsp. cocoa powder
- 2 tsp. Worcestershire sauce
- 1 tsp. oregano
- 1-2 tsp. chili powder
- salt and pepper
- ½ cup sour cream
- ½ cup shredded cheddar cheese

- green onions, thinly sliced

Directions:

1. Heat 2 tbsp. coconut oil in a large skillet. Add the onions, peppers, and garlic and cook until softened.
2. Meanwhile, heat 2 tbsp. coconut oil in a soup pot. Add the ground beef and cook until browned.
3. Add the peppers, onions, tomatoes, water, cocoa powder, Worcestershire sauce oregano, chili powder, salt, and pepper to the pot with the beef. Simmer, covered, for about 2 hours. Add more water if needed.
4. Serve with cheese, sour cream, and green onions.

Creamy Avocado and Bacon Soup

Ingredients :

1/2 pound bacon
1 medium onion, chopped
2 stalks celery, chopped
1 quart chicken stock
2 avocados - peeled, pitted, and chopped
1/2 cup white wine
1 lime, juiced
1 cup heavy cream
Salt and pepper to taste

Directions :

In a skillet over medium heat, cook the bacon until evenly brown. Drain, reserving 1 tablespoon grease in the skillet, chop, and set aside. Place onion and celery in the skillet, and cook until tender.

Transfer the onion and celery to a blender or food processor. Pour in 1/2 the chicken stock, add avocados, and blend until smooth.

Transfer blender mixture to a large pot over medium heat. Whisk in remaining stock, wine, lime juice, and heavy cream. Season with salt and pepper. Cook, stirring often, until heated through, but do not boil. Garnish with chopped bacon to serve.

Mustard Nutty Salmon

Ingredients:

1/4 tsp. dill
1 tbsp. olive oil
1 tbsp. dijon mustard
2 salmon fillets (3 oz. each)
1/2 cup walnuts
2 tbsp. maple syrup (sugar free)
Salt and pepper to taste

Directions:
1. Preheat your oven to 350□F.
2. Dump your syrup, mustard, and walnuts into a blender or food processor.
3. Pulse until you have a paste.
4. Heat a stovetop pan on high. Once hot, place your salmon skin side down in the pan.
5. Sear the salmon for about 3 minutes until the skin is crisp.
6. While searing the skin side, add the walnut paste to the side facing up.
7. Once done searing, transfer to the oven and bake for 7 to 8 minutes.
All done, enjoy!

Keto Celery Chili Beef

Ingredients:
340 grams ground beef
1 cup broccoli, segregated
½ cup broth of your choice
¾ can spicy tomatoes
¼ can green chili
2 stalks celery, sliced
½ small onion, sliced
1/2 tablespoon butter

1 teaspoon chili powder

1 teaspoon cumin

¾ teaspoon garlic powder

½ teaspoon dried, crushed oregano

½ teaspoon paprika

½ teaspoon onion powder

Directions:

1. Bring a pot large enough to hold broccoli to a boil.
2. Place pan with butter over high heat. Once butter has melted, add ground beef, salt, and pepper.
3. Allow ground beef to brown.
4. Once pot for broccoli comes to a boil, add broccoli. Boil until partially tender and drain.
5. Add onion to ground beef once it starts to sizzle.
6. Mix half of the onion in with ground beef.
7. Once beef has cooked, remove it from heat.
8. Toss spicy tomatoes, green chili, celery, remainder of onion into the crock pot.
9. Over top, sprinkle chili powder, cumin, garlic powder, oregano, paprika, and onion powder.
10. Over top, add ground beef and onions from pan.
11. Finally, dump the drained broccoli into the slow cooker.
12. Fold ingredients into each other until everything is well incorporated and has a nice coating of the spices.
13. Put slow cooker on highest heat setting and let sit for 20 minutes.
14. Once 20 minutes has passed, pour broth overtop.
15. Cover and still on high heat, let cook for 3 hours.
16. Remove lid and let cook until most liquid has evaporated.
17. Separate into two bowls and enjoy!

Crispy Bacon Burgers

Ingredients

- ½ lb. 80% lean ground beef
- 1 tsp. Worcestershire sauce
- 2 slices cheddar cheese
- 4 strips crispy bacon
- 2 slices red onion
- ½ head butter or Bibb lettuce
- 1 avocado, sliced
- 1 tomato, sliced
- 1 large dill pickle, sliced
- mustard to taste

Directions:

1. Mix the ground beef with the Worcestershire sauce and form into two patties. Grill or pan fry over medium until no pink remains in the center, 5-7 minutes per side.
2. When the burgers are almost done, lay a slice of cheese on top and allow to melt.
3. Divide the lettuce between two plates and set the burgers on top. Top with red onion, avocado, tomato, bacon, pickle, and mustard.

Garlic Applewood Pork Chops

Ingredients:
1/2 tsp. garlic powder
1 tsp. grill mates Applewood rub
1/2 tsp. black pepper
1/2 tsp. Mrs. Dash (table blend)
1 tsp. salt
2 tbsp. olive oil
2 2tsp. hidden valley powdered ranch
4 pork chops (bone in)

Directions:
1. Combine all of the spices and rub into the pork chops.
2. Heat a pan on medium, and add the olive oil.
3. When hot, add the pork chops and cover.

4. Cook for about 10 minutes and then flip the chops.

5. Cook for a further 5 minutes (covered).

6. Turn the heat up to high, and flip chops again. Keep the pan uncovered now.

7. Cook for 2 minutes, and then let rest for 4 minutes

Serve and enjoy!

Hot Wing Sauce Chicken Stew

Ingredients:

2 tsp. garlic (minced)

3 tbsp. butter

2 tsp. paprika

2 tsp. ranch seasoning

1 tsp. red pepper flakes

1 tsp. oregano

1/2 cup sliced tomatoes

1 1/2 tomato sauce

3 lbs. chicken thigh

1 green pepper

1/3 cup hot wing sauce

3 cups mushrooms

Directions:

1. Finely slice your mushrooms and pepper.

2. Set your crock pot on high and add the thighs, tomato slices, garlic, spices, tomato sauce, and hot sauce.

3. Also toss in peppers and mix.

4. Let the mixture cook for 2 hours.

5. Now turn the pot to low, give the mix a stir, and cook for 4 to 5 hours.

6. Dump in 3 tbsp. of butter and give another stir.

7. Remove the lid, and cook for an hour. Serve and enjoy

Chili Asian Pork Chops

Ingredients:
1/2 tbsp. sambal chili paste
1/2 tsp. five spice
1/2 tbsp. ketchup (sugar free)
1 stalk lemon grass
4 garlic cloves (halved)
1 tbsp. almond flour
1 tbsp. fish sauce
1/2 tsp. peppercorns
1 1/2 tsp. soy sauce
1 tsp. sesame oil
1 medium star anise
4 boneless pork chops

Directions:

1. Pound the pork chops to 1/2 inch thickness
2. Grind the peppercorns and star anise to a fine powder.
3. Combine the pepper, anise, lemongrass, and garlic. Grind until a paste forms.
4. Marinade the chops with the paste
5. Let the chops marinate for about 2 hours at room temperature.
6. Heat a pan on high. Coat your pork chops with the almond flour.
7. Sear the chops in the pan. This should take about 1 to 2 minutes per side.
8. Once the pork is cooked, cut them into slices.
9. Mix the sambal and ketchup to create your sauce.
Serve and enjoy.

Healthy Keto Burger

Ingredients:
Bun:
1 tsp. oregano
1 clove garlic
1/2 tbsp. coconut oil
2 Portobello mushroom caps
1 pinch each of salt and pepper
Burger:
1 tsp. each of salt and pepper
6 oz. beef
1 tbsp. dijon mustard
1/4 cup cheddar cheese

Directions:
1. Preheat a griddle on high
2. In a container, combine the oil and spices for the bun
3. Scrape out the insides of the mushrooms, and marinate in the oil and spices
4. In a separate bowl, combine the meat, salt, pepper, cheese, and mustard.
5. Use your hands to form your burger patties.
6. Now add your mushrooms to the griddle and cook about 8 minutes.
7. Remove the mushrooms and toss the patties on. Cook about 5 minutes per side.
8. Assemble your burger with whatever toppings you like.

Cheddar Bacon Soup

Ingredients:

1 tsp. garlic powder
1/2 tsp. celery seed
1 tsp. thyme (dried)
1 tsp. onion powder
3/4 cup heavy cream
1/2 tsp. cumin
3 cups chicken broth
4 tbsp. butter
1/2 lbs. bacon
8 oz. cheddar cheese

Salt and pepper to taste
4 jalapeno peppers (diced)

Directions:
1. Chop up the bacon to 1 inch slices. Cook until crisp and save the fat.
2. Now dice your jalapenos and cook in the saved bacon fat.
3. Now toss the bacon fat (we're still using it!) into a pot, along with the butter, spices, and broth. Bring the pot to a boil.
4. Once boiling, reduce heat and simmer for 15 minutes.
5. Use a food processor or immersion blender to puree the mixture. Then add the cream and shredded cheese.
6. Stir everything together and keep simmering. Salt and pepper to taste.
7. Add jalapenos and bacon to the pot and simmer for a final 5 minutes.
Enjoy!

Delicious BBQ Chicken Pizza

Ingredients:

Crust:
1 1/2 tsp. Italian seasoning
6 tbsp. parmesan cheese
3 tbsp. psyllium husk powder
6 large eggs
salt and pepper to taste
Toppings:
1 tbsp. mayonnaise
4 tbsp. tomato sauce
6 oz. rotisserie chicken (shredded)
4 tbsp. BBQ sauce
4 oz. cheddar cheese

Directions:
1. Pre heat your oven to 425□F.
2. Combine all ingredients for the crust in a blender and pulse until thick. An immersion blender will serve this purpose as well.
3. Now spread the dough into a circle on a baking sheet or oven stone. Be sure you grease the surface first.
4. Bake for 10 minutes.

5. Flip the crust over, and pile up your toppings.
6. Broil for a further 10 minutes.
Serve and enjoy

Best Beef and Mushroom Ragu

Ingredients:
- ½ pound ground beef
- ½ pound fresh white mushrooms (sliced)
- 4 ripe tomatoes (seeded and chopped)
- 2 tablespoons fresh basil (chopped)
- ¼ cup vegetable broth
- 3 tablespoons olive oil
- Salt to taste
- Pepper to taste

Directions:

1.   Heat olive oil in a large pan over medium heat. Add the ground beef and cook for about 8 minutes or until browned, stirring frequently.
2.   Add the tomatoes and cook for about 5 minutes, stirring.
3.   Add vegetable broth. Reduce the heat to low and cook for about 20 minutes. Add more liquid if needed.
4.   Add in sliced mushrooms and cook until they change texture. Turn off the heat, season with salt and pepper to taste.
5.   Garnish with chopped basil, serve and enjoy!

Pork Tenderloin with Chives

Ingredients:
- ½ pound pork tenderloin (cut into strips)
- 1 onion (chopped)
- 1 garlic clove (minced)
- ¼ cup vegetable broth
- ½ cup heavy cream
- 4 tablespoons fresh chives (chopped)
- 1 pinch ground cumin
- 1 pinch ground turmeric
- 2 tablespoons butter
- Salt to taste
- Pepper to taste

Directions:
1. Add butter to a large frying pan and place over medium heat.
2. Once the butter is hot, add the pork and cook for about 3 minutes, until browned.
3. Stir in garlic and onion. Sauté for about 5 minutes.
4. Stir in vegetable broth, turmeric, cumin, salt and pepper. Cook over low heat for about 15 minutes or until the broth is evaporated.
5. Finally, add heavy cream and chopped chives. Then cook for additional 2 minutes.
6. Serve right away!

Pecan Nuts Smoked salmon salad

Ingredients:
- 1/3 cup cream cheese
- 8 oz smoked salmon
- 2 oz pecan nuts
- 1 tablespoon lemon juice
- 1/3 cup coconut milk
- 3 tomatoes

- ½ cup lettuce
- 1 teaspoon salt
- ½ teaspoon basil
- ½ teaspoon oregano
- 1 cucumber

Directions:

1. Slice the smoked salmon into the thin pieces and transfer the fish to the mixing bowl.
2. Crush the pecan nuts and add them to the mixing bowl too.
3. After this, chop the lettuce and tomatoes.
4. Dice the cucumbers.
5. Transfer all the vegetables to the fish mixture.
6. Mix up the mass till it is homogenous.
7. Then combine the cream cheese. Lemon juice, coconut milk, salt, basil, and oregano together. Stir the mixture till you get homogenous mass.
8. Transfer the salad to the serving plates and sprinkle with the cream cheese sauce.
9. Serve the salad immediately.

Nutritional value: calories: 206, fat: 16.3g, total carbs: 6.9g, sugars: 3.4g, protein: 10.1g

Ginger Sauté Chicken

Ingredients:

- ½ pound chicken breast (cut into slices)
- 3 teaspoons olive oil
- 1 tablespoon soy sauce
- 1 red bell pepper (thinly sliced)
- 1 teaspoon garlic (minced)
- 2 ounces fresh ginger (grated)
- 1 tablespoon lemon juice
- 2 tablespoons fresh dill (chopped)

- Lemon wedges
- Salt to taste

Directions:

1. Place the chicken in a bowl, spoon the soy sauce over and toss to coat.
2. Add 2 tablespoons of olive oil to a large frying pan over medium heat.
3. Place the chicken in the frying pan and cook for 5 minutes or until cooked through.
4. Remove from the frying pan and set aside.
5. Add the remaining oil to the same pan and keep over medium heat.
6. Add the garlic, bell pepper, and ginger and cook, until lightly golden and fragrant, about 2 minutes.
7. Return the chicken to the pan and sauté for another 2 minutes.
8. Add the lemon juice. Mix well and continue cooking, stirring it frequently, until the mixture is heated through.
9. Place the chicken in a serving dish, sprinkle with chopped fresh dill, season with salt and serve with lemon wedges.

Spicy Squid Salad

Servings: 4
Preparation time: 15 minutes
Cooking time: 7 minutes
Ingredients:
- 10 oz squid
- 1 white onion
- 3 tomatoes
- 1 tablespoon apple cider vinegar
- 1 teaspoon coconut oil
- 1 tablespoon lemon juice
- 1 teaspoon chili flakes
- ½ teaspoon cayenne pepper
- 2 garlic cloves
- 3 cups water

Directions:
1. Take the large saucepan and pour water.
2. Preheat the liquid until it is boiled.
3. Wash the squid carefully and transfer it to the boiled water.
4. Cook the squid for 7 minutes on the medium heat.
5. Meanwhile, peel the onion and slice it.
6. Wash the tomatoes carefully and chop them roughly.
7. Chill the cooked squid little and slice it.
8. Take the mixing bowl and transfer the sliced squid.
9. Sprinkle it with the apple cider vinegar, lemon juice, cayenne pepper, and chili flakes. Stir the mixture carefully and leave it for 5 minutes.
10. Meanwhile, peel the garlic clove and slice it.
11. Add the sliced garlic cloves in the squid mixture.
12. Then add chopped tomatoes and sliced onion.
13. Sprinkle the salad with the coconut oil and stir it carefully till you get homogenous mass.
14. Serve the salad immediately.

Stuffed Meatballs with Mustard Sauce

Ingredients:
For the meatballs
- ½ pound ground beef
- 3 ounces mozzarella cheese (cubed)
- 1 teaspoon paprika
- ¼ teaspoon ground cumin
- 1 tablespoon olive oil
- Salt to taste
- Pepper to taste

For the mustard sauce
- ½ cup heavy cream
- 4 tablespoons Dijon mustard
- 4 tablespoons fresh parsley (chopped)
- Salt to taste
- Pepper to taste

Directions:
1.   Preheat oven to 375°F.
2.   To make the meatballs, add the ground beef, paprika, cumin, salt and pepper to a bowl and mix well to combine. Shape the mixture into small balls, stuffing cheese into meatballs. Set aside.
3.   Grease a baking pan with olive oil, place meatballs on it.
4.   Bake in the preheated oven for about 20 minutes or until golden brown.
5.   To prepare the mustard sauce, heat heavy cream over low heat for about 3 minutes. Turn off heat, then stir in Dijon mustard, parsley, salt and pepper.
6.   Serve the meatballs covered with the sauce. Enjoy!

Almonds and Oregano Steak Salad

Ingredients:
*   ½ pound sirloin steak (thinly sliced)
*   2 cups lettuce (shredded)
*   1 cup arugula leaves
*   1 pinch paprika
*   2 ounces almonds (chopped)
*   3 tablespoons fresh oregano (chopped)
*   1 tablespoon soy sauce
*   4 tablespoons olive oil
*   Salt to taste
*   Pepper to taste

Directions:
1.   Heat 2 tablespoons of olive oil in a large frying pan and cook sirloin slices until golden brown. Season with paprika, salt and pepper. Set aside.
2.   In a large bowl, mix lettuce, almonds and arugula. Set aside.
3.   In a small bowl, whisk soy sauce, oregano and remaining olive oil until smooth.
4.   Add the cooked sirloin slices and the soy sauce mixture to the large bowl. Toss well to combine with the leaves.
5.   Serve immediately!

Pork Curry With Cauliflower Sauce

Ingredients:
- ½ pound pork loin (thinly sliced)
- 3 cups cauliflower (florets)
- ½ cup heavy cream
- 2 garlic cloves (minced)
- ½ teaspoon curry powder
- 2 tablespoons butter
- Salt to taste
- Pepper to taste

Directions:
1. Season pork loin with curry, salt and pepper.
2. Add 1 tablespoon of butter to a frying pan and melt over medium heat. Place pork in frying pan and sauté for about 5 minutes. Remove from frying pan and set aside.
3. Heat remaining butter in the same frying pan and sauté garlic until slightly brown.
4. Add in the cauliflower, sauté until tender, add a little water if needed.
5. Stir in the heavy cream, salt and pepper. Cook over medium heat for about 5 minutes. Transfer this mixture to a food processor and blend until creamy.
6. Place the pork loin slices in serving plates and top with the cauliflower sauce.
7. Serve warm!

Tasty Roast Beef   Wrap

Ingredients:

- ☐ 2 Tbsp 2% plain Greek yogurt
- ☐ 1 Tbsp horseradish sauce
- ☐ 2 leaves Bibb lettuce
- ☐ 4 slices lean deli-style roast beef
- ☐ 4 slices tomato
- ☐ 1 cup fresh raspberries

Directions:

Join yogurt and horseradish, and spread on lettuce.
Best with dish meat and tomato, and move into a wrap.
Top with raspberries.

Walnuts Rosemary Pork Loin

Ingredients:
- 1 pound pork loin
- 5 tablespoons fresh rosemary (chopped)
- 8 tablespoons sour cream
- 2 ounces walnuts (chopped)
- ¼ cup olive oil
- Salt to taste
- Pepper to taste

Directions:
1.   Preheat oven to 375°F.
2.   Mix olive oil, rosemary, salt and pepper in a bowl. Evenly coat the pork loin with this mixture.
3.   Place the pork on a baking pan. Cover the pan with aluminum foil. Bake for about 30 minutes. Then remove foil and bake until golden brown.
4.   Remove from oven and wait about 5 minutes to slice. Place the slices on a serving plate, top them with sour cream and sprinkle with chopped walnuts.

Low Carb Chili Vegies Beef

Ingredients:

- 1 ¼ pound grass-fed ground beef
- 3 Roma tomatoes (chopped)
- 2 green onions (chopped)
- 8 ounces canned tomatoes (chopped with juice)
- 1 medium green bell pepper (chopped)
- 1 carrot (sliced)
- 2 celery stalks (chopped)
- 1½ teaspoons ground cumin seeds
- 2 chili peppers (chopped)
- Salt and pepper to taste
- ¾ cup vegetable stock, or as needed

Directions:

1. Brown the ground beef in a large skillet for 5–6 minutes.
2. Remove the fat and season with salt and pepper.
3. Add the onions and bell pepper to the ground beef and cook for 2 minutes more.
4. Stir in the Roma tomatoes, carrot, celery, and canned tomatoes. Mix well. Add the water and bring to a boil.
5. Reduce the heat to low, add the cumin seeds and chili peppers and allow to simmer for about 90–120 minutes until slightly thickened, stirring occasionally.
6. Serve hot.

Yummy Tuna Steaks

Ingredients:
- 1 ½ pounds fresh tuna steaks
- 2 tablespoons truffle oil
- 3 tablespoons olive oil
- 2 tablespoons chopped fresh oregano

Directions:

1.   Sprinkle the truffle oil over both sides of the tuna steaks, distributing it evenly.
2.   Add the olive oil to a large frying pan over high heat.
3.   Once the oil is hot, add the tuna steaks and cook for about 4 minutes on each side. Serve right away!

Onion Tuna-Avocado Sandwich

Ingredients:

- ☐ 1/3 avocado, mashed
- ☐ 1/2 Tbsp lemon juice
- ☐ 4 oz white albacore tuna, drained
- ☐ 1 thick slice tomato
- ☐ 1 piece butter lettuce
- ☐ 1 slice red onion
- ☐ 1 slice whole-grain bread

Directions:
Join avocado with lemon squeeze, and overlay in fish. Stack tomato, lettuce, onion, and avocado and fish blend on bread for an open-confront sandwich.

Delicious Thai Chicken & Rice

Ingredients

- 1 pc. of cauliflower head
- 3 to 4 pcs. of cooked chicken breasts or meat from 1 whole chicken, shredded
- 3 medium-sized eggs
- 3 pcs. of chilies (any preferred variety will do)
- 1 Tbsp. of ginger, freshly grated
- 3 cloves of regular-sized garlic, crushed
- Coconut oil for cooking
- Salt to taste
- 1 Tbsp. of tamari soy sauce or coconut aminos (optional)
- ½ cup of cilantro, chopped (for garnishing)

Directions:

10.   Separate the cauliflower into florets, then process in a food processor until a rice-like texture is achieved. It may be done in several batches, if necessary.

11.   Get a large pan and cook the processed cauliflower in coconut oil. If necessary, do it in batches or in 2 separate pans. Set the heat to medium and continue to stir.

12.   In a new pan, heat some coconut oil, then scramble the eggs.

13.   Combine the scrambled eggs with the rice-like cauliflower.

14.   Add the chopped chilies, garlic, and ginger.

15.   Once the cauliflower rice softens, gently mix the shredded chicken meat in.

16.   Add the tamari soy sauce or coconut aminos to the mix. Sprinkle some salt to taste. Mix everything well.

17.   Transfer the dish to a large bowl and garnish with cilantro.

18.   Serve immediately; best consumed when hot.

Slow Cooker Roast Beef with Honey Citrus Sauce

Ingredients:

900 grams beef chuck roast
2 tablespoons fresh lime juice
2 tablespoons fresh orange juice
1 tablespoon honey
½ cup olive oil
3 garlic cloves, minced
½ cup chopped cilantro
1 large shallot, minced
1 teaspoon chili powder
2 teaspoons oregano powder
2 teaspoons sea salt
¼ teaspoon cumin
¼ teaspoon coriander
¼ cup water

Directions:

Place the beef chuck inside the slow cooker. Let it stand for 20-30 minutes.
In a food processor, mix together the lime juice, orange juice, honey, olive oil, cilantro, shallot, chili powder, oregano, salt, cumin and coriander. Pour the mixture into the pot, making sure to coat the beef evenly. Pour in the water then cover the pot.
Set the temperature to high and cook the beef for 4 hours, turning the meat every hour. After 4 hours, turn off the slow cooker and tilt the cover of the pot to let the heat dissipate. Leave it for 20 minutes.
Remove the beef from the pot and place it on a serving plate. Slice the meat according to preferred thickness and pour the citrus sauce over it. Serve immediately.

Spicy sauce Beef Ribs

Ingredients:
- ½ pound beef ribs
- 1 onion (sliced)
- 4 ripe tomatoes (chopped)

- 2 red bell peppers (seeded, chopped)
- 1 cup vegetable broth
- ¼ bunch fresh parsley (chopped)
- 1 teaspoon paprika
- ¼ teaspoon chili powder
- 2 tablespoons olive oil
- Salt to taste
- Pepper to taste

Directions:

1. Season beef ribs with salt and pepper to taste.
2. Heat olive oil in a pan, add beef ribs and cook until golden brown. Then stir in onions and sauté until soft.
3. Add in tomatoes, bell peppers, paprika and chili. Sauté for about 3 minutes. Then pour in vegetable broth. Cover and cook over low heat for about 40 minutes, add more broth if needed.
4. Taste the sauce and add more salt or spices to taste.
5. Garnish with fresh parsley. Serve warm!

Coconut Stir-Fried Spinach Almond

Ingredients
- 1 lb. of spinach leaves
- 3 Tbsp. of almond slices
- 1 Tbsp. of coconut oil to cook with
- Salt to taste

Directions:

1. Heat the 1 Tbsp. of coconut oil in a large-sized pot on medium heat setting.

2. Put in the spinach and allow it to cook down a bit.
3. When the spinach has cooked down, sprinkle some salt to taste. Stir
4. Stir the almond slices in.
5. Transfer the contents into a cup.
6. Serve and enjoy.

Garlic Sauce Grilled Chicken

Ingredients:

For the Skewers
- 1 lb. of chicken breast, cut into 1"-sized cubes
- 2 pcs. of bell peppers, chopped
- 1 pc. of zucchini
- 1 pc. of onion, chopped

For the Garlic Sauce
- 1 pc. of garlic head, peeled
- ¼ cup of lemon juice
- 1 tsp. of salt
- 1 cup of olive oil

For the Marinade
- 1 tsp. of salt
- ½ cup of olive oil

Directions:

1. Start up the grill and set it to high. When using wooden skewers, make sure to soak them first in water.
2. To prepare the garlic sauce, mix the garlic cloves with salt, and process in a blender. Add about ½ cup of the olive oil and 1/8 cup of the lemon juice.

3.   Blend everything for around 10 seconds before slowing the blender down. Alternately drizzle some olive oil and lemon juice. Stop only once you hear a subtle sound shift in the blender. By then, you should notice the sauce achieving a mayo-like consistency. In case this does not happen, do not worry. Although your sauce may not look great, it will still have the desired taste.**

4.   Set aside ½ of the garlic sauce which will be used when serving the finished dish. Take the rest of the sauce and mix with a tsp. of salt and half a cup of olive oil. Make sure to mix well. This will be your marinade.

5.   Mix the chopped chicken, bell peppers, onion, and zucchini in a mixing bowl with the prepared marinade.

6.   Put the cubed ingredients on skewers. Put the grill on high heat setting and grill the skewers until the chicken is done. To achieve a charred look grill on the bottom first for a couple of minutes before moving the skewers to a higher rack while the lid is closed to make sure that the chicken is cooked well.

7.   Remove from heat and serve with the garlic sauce you previously set aside.

8.   Enjoy hot.

Delux Keto Beef Stew

Ingredients

- 3 tbsp. coconut oil
- 1 lb. high-fat beef stew meat, such as chuck, cut into 1″ pieces
- 1 onion, chopped
- ¼ lb. carrots, chopped
- ¼ lb. parsnips, chopped
- 4 cloves garlic, chopped
- handful fresh parsley
- salt and pepper
- ½ tsp. thyme
- 2 bay leaves
- 2 tsp. Worcestershire sauce
- 1 cup Guinness stout
- 1 qt. beef broth

Directions:

1.   Heat the coconut oil in a soup pot and add the beef. Brown, then add the rest of the ingredients.
2.   Simmer for 1½ - 2 hours until the beef is tender and the broth is thickened, adding more water as needed.

Zucchini Noodle Stir-Fry Chicken

Ingredients:

*   4 medium zucchini
*   1 cup of chicken breast (cut into bite-sized pieces)
*   1 carrot (diced)
*   1 medium head kale (chopped)
*   2 chives (thinly sliced)
*   1 red hot chili pepper (thinly sliced)
*   ¼ cup almonds (chopped)
*   ¼ cup fresh parsley (chopped)
*   ½ tablespoon grated fresh ginger root
*   3 tablespoon of Tamari
*   1 tablespoon of coconut oil for cooking (deodorized)
*   ½ tsp of curry powder
*   Salt and freshly ground black pepper, to taste

Directions:

1.   Create zucchini noodles with a spiralizer.
2.   Heat the coconut oil in a skillet.
3.   Brown the chicken pieces on all sides.

4.   Reduce the heat to medium. Add the zucchini, chili pepper, carrot, kale, chives, cilantro, ginger, and curry powder. Season with salt and pepper to taste and cook for 5–10 minutes, or until the zucchini becomes tender and the kale wilts.

5.   Add the soy sauce and stir in the almonds. Cook for another 5 minutes.

6.   Remove the saucepan from heat. Let rest for 10 minutes before serving.

Yummy Shrimp Macaroni Pasta Salad

Ingredients:
- 4 oz cooked shrimp
- 1/2 cup cooked whole-wheat elbow macaroni
- 1/2 steamed broccoli
- 4 sun-dried tomatoes, halved
- 1 tsp capers
- 2 Tbsp red wine vinegar
- 1/4 tsp onion powder
- 1/2 tsp oregano

Directions:
Toss all ingredients together, and serve cold.

Mayo Baked Avocado Crab Dynamite

Ingredients
- 1 medium-sized avocado, skin on, halved & pitted
- 1 ½ oz. of real crabmeat, no juices (drained)
- 1 tsp. of coconut aminos, tamari, or soy sauce
- 2 tsp. of mayonnaise
- ¼ tsp. of black pepper, freshly ground

Directions:

1. Pre-heat oven to 3500 F.
2. Place the avocado halves in a small-sized shallow baking dish, hole-side up.
3. Combine the crabmeat with mayonnaise, pepper, and coconut aminos in a small-sized bowl. Mix well.
4. Scoop the mixture into the avocado cavities.
5. Bake for about 20 minutes.
6. Dish is best served hot. Enjoy!

Spicy-Creamy Sesame Beef

Ingredients:

- ½ lb. of 90% lean meat, ground
- Mexican spices or taco seasoning
- 2 oz. of hot pepper cheese, shredded
- 1 oz. of sour cream
- ½ Tbsp. of sesame seeds
- Water

Directions:

1. Cook the ground beef in a small-sized skillet until brown. Add a Tbsp. of water, or more, if necessary.
2. Sprinkle with a dash of taco seasoning or Mexican spices to taste.
3. Thoroughly mix. Allow to simmer for around 10 – 15 minutes.
4. Transfer the dish into a plate. Top the beef with shredded hot pepper cheese.

5.   Combine the sour cream and sesame seeds for use as siding.

6.   Immediately serve with sour cream mixture siding. If preferred, you can mix desired amount of the mixture with the dish to make the texture creamy.

Coconut Thai Curry Fish

Ingredients :

- 2 lbs. of white fish or salmon
- 5 Tbsp. of butter or ghee
- 1 can of coconut cream
- 2 Tbsp. of green or red curry paste
- 2/3 cup of cilantro, fresh & chopped
- Butter or olive oil to use for greasing the baking dish

Directions:

1.   Set and pre-heat oven at 4000 F.

2.   Grease a medium-sized, deep enough baking dish that can accommodate the fish. Put the fish in the dish.

3.   Sprinkle some salt & pepper on the fish. Put a Tbsp. of butter on each pc. of fish.

4.   Combine the curry paste, coconut cream, and cilantro in a small-sized bowl. Mix well and then spread over the fish.

5.   Bake until well-done or around 20 minutes.

6.   Serve and enjoy while hot. Best served with cooked rice or boiled veggies such as cauliflower and broccoli.

Chapter 4 KETOGENIC DESSERTS

Sunday Almond Butter Fudge

Ingredients
- 1 cup of unsweetened almond butter
- 1 cup of coconut oil
- ¼ cup of coconut milk
- 1 tsp. of vanilla extract
- Stevia (to sweeten/to taste)

Directions:

1. Combine the almond butter with coconut oil and melt until soft.
2. Put all the ingredients in a blender.
3. Process until everything is well-blended.
4. Pour the blended mixture into a baking pan.
5. Refrigerate for around 2 to 3 hours or until it sets.
6. Remove from the refrigerator and cut into around 12 pcs.
7. Serve and enjoy immediately.

Gluten-Free Bourbon Chocolate Truffles

Ingredients
- 2 pcs. of avocado, ripe, skinned, & pitted
- ½ cup of premium cocoa powder
- 1 Tbsp. of heavy whipping cream
- 1 Tbsp. of granulated sugar substitute
- 2 Tbsp. of SF choco-flavored syrup
- 2 Tbsp. of bourbon (if desired)

- 2 Tbsp. coconut oil
- ½ cup of pecans, chopped

Directions:
1.   Process all ingredients in in a food processor or blender, except the pecans, until a smooth consistency is achieved.
2.   Chill the mixture until firm enough or around 1 hour.
3.   Form 1″ balls from the mixture and roll each ball in the pecans. Refrigerate until the balls are firm.
4.   Serve and enjoy!

Low Carb Chocolate Mousse

Ingredients:

- 2 pcs avocados
- ½ cup of premium cocoa powder
- 2 Tbsp. of coconut oil
- 3 Tbsp. of sugar free chocolate flavored syrup
- 1 Tbsp. of heavy cream

Directions:

For the Pudding
1.   Put all ingredients in the blender
2.   Puree until consistency is smooth. Adjust the sweetness, as needed. If the mixture is too thick, add a bit of heavy cream until the desired consistency for the pudding is achieved.
For the Mousse
1.   Whip a cup of heavy cream with a tsp. of stevia sweetener until it becomes stiff.
2.   If available, use a rubber spatula to fold 1/3 of the whipped cream gently into the pudding.
3.   Fold the pudding mixture slowly into the remaining whipped cream until smooth and well-blended.
Notes: If you do not know what folding is, it is simply what it means literally. Just scoop from under the mixture and slowly "fold" or flip it together until blended. This is done to keep the fluffiness. If you just recklessly whip it, you will release air into the cream. Your work will wind up in a mess. Thus, it is important to fold gently.

Delicious Coconut Bars

Ingredients:

1 tsp. cinnamon
1/4 cup butter (melted)
1/2 cup cashews
1/4 cup maple syrup (sugar free)
1 cup almond flour
1/4 cup shredded coconut
1 pinch salt

Directions:
1. Add the almond flour and melted flour to a large bowl. Mix well.
2. Now (with dramatic flourish) toss in the salt, syrup, coconut, and cinnamon.
3. Roughly chop the cashews and toss into the mixture. Make sure everything is well combined.
4. Place parchment paper in a baking dish and evenly spread the coconut mixture.
Chill for at least 2 hours.
Slice and enjoy

Coconut Pumpkin Ice Cream

Ingredients:

2 cups coconut milk
1/2 tsp. xanthan gum
20 drops liquid stevia
1/2 cup pumpkin puree
1/2 cup cottage cheese

1/3 cup erythritol

3 large egg yolks

1 tsp. maple extract

1/2 cup pecans (toasted and chopped)

2 tbsp. butter (Salted)

1 tsp. pumpkin spice

Directions:

1. Heat a pan on the stove and toss in the butter and pecans.

2. Now blend the remaining ingredients in either a blender, food processor, or immersion blender.

3. Now add the blended mixture to your ice cream machine, along with the pecans and butter.

4. Follow the churning instructions on your ice cream maker.

Simple as that, go eat!

Delight Rosemary Panna Cotta and Sour Cream

Ingredients

- 1 ½ cups of sour cream
- 1 ½ cups of heavy whipping cream
- 2 medium-sized sprigs of rosemary, fresh & w/ extra leaves (for garnishing)
- 2 tsp. of unflavoured powdered gelatine
- 1 tsp. of sea salt

Directions:

1.   Put the sour cream, heavy cream, and rosemary sprigs in a small-sized saucepan and cook at medium heat setting. Stir until everything melts and blends together.

2.   Whisk the salt and gelatine in while continuously stirring

3.   Reduce heat to low setting and allow to simmer for 4 minutes. Keep on stirring.

4.   Take the rosemary sprigs out.

5.   Pour the mixture into 6 small ramekins or glasses

6.   Refrigerate for 6 hours or overnight until the mixture sets.

7.   Remove from the refrigerator and garnish the glasses with rosemary leaves.

8.   Serve and enjoy!

Butter Creamy Lemon Bars

Ingredients
- 4 oz. of melted butter
- 1 cup of pecans
- 3 oz. of unflavoured powdered gelatine
- 8 oz. of softened cream cheese
- ¼ cup of coconut flour
- 1 Tbsp. of lemon zest
- 2 Tbsp. of fresh lemon juice
- 1 cup of boiling water
- ¼ cup of granular Swerve

Directions:

1.   Mix the pecans, melted butter, and coconut flour in a small-sized bowl.
2.   Spread the mixture into an 8x8″ baking dish or silicone glass. Set aside.
3.   Put the gelatine in a medium-sized bowl with boiling water. Stir for around two minutes.
4.   Add the rest of the ingredients into the bowl.
5.   Thoroughly mix until all the lumps are gone.
6.   Pour the mixture over the pecan crust.
7.   Refrigerate to set.
8.   Divide into 8 individual bars.
9.   Best served chilled.

Chocolate Orange Truffles

Ingredients:

For the Ganache
- 3 oz. of baking chocolate, unsweetened
- 2 Tbsp. of heavy cream
- 2 Tbsp. of confectioners Swerve
- ½ tsp. of liquid orange flavor
- 2 drops of stevia glycerite
- 1 Tbsp. of butter

For the Coating
- 2 tsp. of unsweetened cocoa powder
- 1 tsp. of confectioners Swerve
- 1 tsp. of orange zest, fresh

Directions:

1. Melt the chocolate over medium heat setting in a small-sized double boiler, while stirring slowly.
2. Add the butter, Swerve, cream, orange flavor, and stevia to the chocolate. Stir until everything is well-blended.
3. Take out of the heat. Continue to stir for around 10 seconds more.
4. Refrigerate the saucepan for around 1 hour or until the ganache congeals.
5. Use a spoon to scoop the ganache and make 9 balls from the mixture. Do this while wearing plastic gloves to keep the chocolate from sticking to your hands.
6. Create a coating powder by mixing the confectioners Swerve, orange zest and cocoa powder on a plate.
7. Thinly coat the ganache balls by rolling each ball through the coating powder.
8. To achieve the best consistency, refrigerate if the room temperature is over 70° F.

Cream Gorgonzola Panna Cotta

Ingredients
- 12 oz. of crumbled Gorgonzola or blue cheese
- 12 pcs. of pecan halves
- 2 tsp. of powdered gelatine, unflavoured
- 1 ½ cups of heavy whipping cream

Directions:

1.   Melt Gorgonzola and heavy cream in a small-sized saucepan for 2 minutes over medium heat setting. Remove the clots using a whisk.
2.   Whisk the gelatine in until it is blended completely.
3.   Pour the mixture into 6 small-sized ramekins or glasses evenly.
4.   Refrigerate to set for 6 hours or overnight.
5.   Garnish every glass w/ 2 pecan halves.
6.   Serve and enjoy!

Cinnamon Pumpkin Pie Mousse

Ingredients :

*   4 oz. cream cheese, softened
*   4 oz. of canned pumpkin purée
*   ½ cup of heavy cream
*   ½ tsp. of pumpkin pie spice
*   ½ tsp. of cinnamon (for topping)
*   8 drops of liquid stevia
*   ½ tsp. of vanilla extract

Directions:

1.   Using a hand-held blender set on high, mix heavy cream in a small-sized mixing bowl until stiff peaks are formed.
2.   Get a separate bowl and combine the pumpkin and cream cheese. Mix using a hand-held blender until consistency becomes smooth.
3.   Fold the whipped cream until fully incorporated into the cheese mixture.
4.   Put mousse in 3 separate serving dishes topped with cinnamon.
5.   Serve and enjoy immediately. If desired, cover and refrigerate first before serving.

Tasty Herbs & Goat Cheese Panna Cotta

Ingredients:

- ¾ cup of sour cream
- 1 ½ cups of heavy whipping cream
- 6 oz. goat cheese, soft
- 2 tsp. of unflavoured powdered gelatine
- 1 tsp. sea salt
- 1 tsp. of Herbes de Provence

Directions:

1.   Combine the goat cheese, Herbes de Provence, heavy cream, and sour cream in a small-sized saucepan. Cook on medium heat setting. Stir constantly until the cheese melts.
2.   Add salt and gelatine and whisk until everything is mixed completely.
3.   Set heat to low and simmer for around 5 minutes while constantly stirring.
4.   Pour the mixture into 6 small-sized glasses or ramekin evenly.
5.   Refrigerate overnight or not less than 6 hours to set.
6.   Serve in glasses. If preferred, dip glass in warm water first to loosen the panna cotta, and then invert the glass to transfer the contents to a small plate before serving.
7.   Enjoy!

Blueberry Coconut Cream Bars

Ingredients :

- 1 cup of fresh blueberries
- 8 oz. of butter
- ¾ cup of coconut oil
- 4 oz. of softened cream cheese, softened
- ¼ cup of coconut cream
- ¼ cup of granular Swerve

Directions:

1. Crush the blueberries gently in a small-sized bowl. Pour contents into an 8x8″ glass or silicone baking dish.
2. Melt coconut oil and butter in a medium-sized saucepan over medium heat setting.
3. Take the dish away from heat. Allow to cook for around 5 minutes.
4. Put the remaining ingredients in the saucepan. Mix thoroughly using a wooden spoon.
5. Top the blueberries with the mixture. Put them in the freezer to set.
6. Take the saucepan out of the freezer and let it warm up a bit for around 15 minutes.
7. Cut the dish into 20 bars of equal size.
8. Serve and enjoy!

Turmeric Panna Cotta

Ingredients
- 1 ½ cups of beef stock, homemade
- 1 ½ cups of coconut milk, refrigerated and water separated from cream
- 1 Tbsp. of turmeric
- ½ tbsp. of sea salt
- 1 ½ Tbsp. of unflavored powdered gelatin

Directions:

1.   Heat the beef stock and coconut cream in a small-sized saucepan over medium heat setting.
2.   Gradually whisk the gelatine in until it is completely incorporated.
3.   Add some salt and turmeric, then allow to simmer for about 5 minutes.
4.   Divide the mixture equally among 6 small-sized glasses or ramekins.
5.   Refrigerate to set for 6 hours or overnight.
6.   The dessert is best served and enjoyed cold.

Sugar-Free Peach Cobblers

Ingredients:

*   ¼ cup of Heart Smart Bisquick
*   1 large-sized egg
*   ½ cup of skim milk
*   1 tsp. of Splenda
*   8 oz. of Del Monte Lite Peaches (diced and drained)

Directions:

1.   Drain diced peaches and separate into 4 oven-safe, individual dessert cups.
2.   Place Bisquick, egg, Splenda, and skim milk in a small-sized bowl, then mix well.
3.   Pour ¼ of the mixture on top of each peach cup.
4.   Bake for around 15 minutes at 400 degrees or until the topping turns brown.
5.   Can be served hot or cold.

Stevia Vanilla Gelatin Cake

Ingredients:

- 1 teaspoon vanilla extract
- 3 tablespoon gelatin powder
- 2 tablespoon stevia extract
- 1 cup cream
- 1 cup almond milk
- 1 teaspoon cinnamon
- 5 tablespoon water

Directions:
1. Combine the cream and almond milk together, stir the mixture and preheat it until warm.
2. Then boil the water and transfer it to the bowl.
3. Add gelatin powder and stir it carefully until gelatin powder is dissolved.
4. After this, add stevia extract and vanilla extract. Stir the mixture thoroughly till you get homogenous mass.
5. After this, pour the gelatin mixture in the warm cream liquid whisk it thoroughly.
6. When you get smooth mass – add cinnamon.
7. Preheat the cream liquid until boiled and remove the liquid from the heat.
8. Chill it little and pour the cream mixture into the silicone mold.
9. Put the silicon form with the cake in the freezer and freeze it for 2 hours.
10. Serve it.

Coconut Sweet bombs

Ingredients:
- 4 oz coconut
- 2 eggs
- 2 tablespoon Erythritol
- 1 cup almond flour
- 1 tablespoon butter
- 1 teaspoon vanilla extract

Directions:

1. Take the mixing bowl and beat the eggs.
2. Whisk the eggs with the help of the hand whisker.
3. After this, add Erythritol and vanilla extract. Stir the mixture.
4. Then add almond flour and coconut.
5. Knead the dough. Then add butter and mix up the mixture carefully till you get smooth and homogenous mass.
6. Preheat the oven to 360 F.
7. Make the small bombs from the dough and transfer them to the tray.
8. Put the tray with the sweet bombs in the preheated oven and cook the dessert for 15 minutes.
9. Then remove the bombs from the oven and chill them well.
10. Serve the dish immediately.
11. Enjoy!

Chocolate blackberry muffins

Ingredients:

- 1 cup almond flour
- 1 teaspoon baking soda
- 1 tablespoon apple cider vinegar
- ½ cup blackberries
- 1 tablespoon stevia extract
- 1 oz dark chocolate
- ½ cup almond milk

Directions:

1. Take the mixing bowl and combine the almond flour and baking soda together. Stir the mixture.
2. After this add dark chocolate.
3. Take the separate bowl and put the blackberries. Mash the berries with the help of the spoon.
4. Combine the mashed berries with the almond milk and stir the mixture until you get homogeneous consistency.
5. Then combine the dry mixture and liquid mixture together. Stir it.
6. Add stevia extract and apple cider vinegar. Mix up the mass till you get a smooth dough.
7. Preheat the oven to 375 F.
8. Take the silicon muffin molds and fill the ½ of every silicon form with the dough.
9. Transfer the muffins to the preheated oven and cook them for 20 minutes.
10. When the dessert is cooked – remove it from the oven and chill little.
11. Then discard the muffins from the silicon forms and serve.

Delicious Chocolate fluffy pie

Ingredients:

- 1 cup coconut flour
- 1 large egg
- 4 tablespoon butter
- 1 tablespoon almond milk
- 1 teaspoon baking powder
- 1 tablespoon lemon juice
- 1 cup cream cheese

- 4 teaspoon stevia extract
- 1 teaspoon cocoa
- ½ cup cream
- 1 teaspoon Erythritol

Directions:

1. Take the mixing bowl and beat egg. Whisk it carefully. Add Erythritol and almond milk. Stir the mixture.
2. After this, add butter and coconut flour. Sprinkle the mixture with the baking soda.
3. Add the lemon juice.
4. After this, knead the dough.
5. Take the pie form and cover it with the baking paper.
6. Transfer the pie dough in the form and make the shape of the pie.
7. Prick the dough with the help of the fork.
8. Preheat the oven to 370 F and transfer the pie dough in the oven.
9. Cook the pie dough for 12 minutes.
10. Meanwhile, whisk the cream with the hand whisker until you get fluffy mass.
11. Then add cream cheese and continue to whisk it.
12. When you get smooth and soft mass – add stevia extract and cocoa. Stir the mixture carefully.
13. Transfer the mixture to the fridge.
14. Then remove the cooked pie dough from the oven. Chill it well.
15. Place the cocoa cream mixture in the pie dough and leave the pie in the fridge for 10 minutes.
16. Cut it into pieces and serve it.

Almond Vanilla Chocolate soufflé

Ingredients:
- 1 cup almond flour
- 3 egg whites
- 1 egg yolk
- 2 tablespoon stevia extract
- 1 tablespoon cocoa powder

- 1 teaspoon vanilla extract
- 1 oz dark chocolate
- 2 tablespoon butter
- ½ teaspoon baking powder
- 1 tablespoon lemon juice
- 5 tablespoon coconut milk

Directions:

1. Whisk the egg whites with the help of the whisker until you get strong peaks.
2. After this, add stevia and cocoa powder and continue to whisk it for 30 seconds more.
3. Then add vanilla extract and butter.
4. Mix up the mixture with the help of the mixer.
5. Melt the dark chocolate and combine it with the baking powder and lemon juice.
6. Add egg yolks and mix up the mass till you get smooth and homogenous mass.
7. Then combine the egg white mixture and egg yolk mixture together. Stir it.
8. Add the coconut milk and almond flour.
9. Knead the smooth liquid dough.
10. Take the ramekins and fill the ½ of every ramekin with the dough.
11. Preheat the oven to 375 F and transfer the soufflés in the oven.
12. Cook the dish for 15 minutes - till you get baked surface.
13. Then remove the dish from the oven and serve it.

Delight Donuts with the dark chocolate

Ingredients:
- 3 eggs
- 1 teaspoon baking soda
- 2 tablespoon lemon juice
- ½ cup almond flour
- ½ cup coconut flour
- ½ cup coconut milk
- 1 tablespoon stevia

- 1 oz dark chocolate
- ½ teaspoon salt
- 3 tablespoon butter

Directions:

1.	Take the mixing bowl and combine baking soda, almond flour, and coconut flour together. Stir the mixture.
2.	Crush the chocolate and add in the dry mixture.
3.	After this, beat the eggs in the separate bowl and whisk them.
4.	Add coconut milk and salt. Stir the mixture.
5.	Combine the liquid and dry mixture together.
6.	Add lemon juice, butter, and stevia together. Knead the smooth dough.
7.	Preheat the donut maker and place the dough into the dough maker.
8.	Cook the donuts for 5 minutes.
9.	Then flip them to another side and cook for 4 minutes more.
10.	When the donuts are cooked – remove them from the donut maker gently.
11.	Serve the dish immediately.

Easy grated pie

Ingredients:

- 1 cup almond flour
- ½ cup coconut flour
- 5 tablespoon butter
- 1 egg
- 1 tablespoon stevia extract
- 1 teaspoon Erythritol
- ½ cup raspberries

Directions:

1.	Beat the egg in the mixing bowl and add butter.
2.	Whisk the mixture till you get smooth and homogenous mass.
3.	Add Erythritol coconut flour. Stir it.
4.	Add almond flour and knead the non-sticky dough with the help of the hands.
5.	Then mash the raspberries and combine them with the stevia extract. Stir the mixture.

6.   Separate the dough into 2 parts.
7.   Take the tray and cover it with the baking paper.
8.   Grate the 1 part of the dough in the tray.
9.   Place the raspberry mixture in the grated dough.
10.   Then grate the second part of the dough.
11.   Preheat the oven to 365 F.
12.   Transfer the tray with the grated pie in the oven and cook it for 25-30 minutes.
13.   Then remove the pie from the oven and chill it little.
14.   Serve it.

Almond vanilla pudding

Ingredients:

- 7 oz avocado, pitted
- 2 tablespoon stevia
- 1 teaspoon Erythritol
- 1 cup almond milk
- 1 teaspoon vanilla extract
- 1 teaspoon lemon juice

Directions:

1.   Peel the avocado and chop it roughly.
2.   Transfer the avocado to the food processor and blend it till you get smooth mass.
3.   Then add almond milk and blend the mixture for 2 minutes more.
4.   After this, add lemon juice, vanilla extract, and Erythritol.
5.   Blend the mixture for 30 seconds.
6.   Transfer the pudding to the freezer for 5 minutes.
7.   Then remove the pudding from the freezer and ladle it in the serving glasses.
8.   Serve the dish immediately.

Raspberry Lemon Popsicles

Ingredients:

- Immersion Blender (Helps to blend the mixture smoothly)
- 100 grams of Raspberries
- ½ Lemon Juice
- ¼ Cup of Coconut Oil
- 1 Cup of Coconut Milk (Carton)
- ¼ Cup of Sour Cream
- ¼ Cup of Heavy Cream
- ½ teaspoon of Guar Gum
- 20 drops of Liquid Stevia

Directions:

1. Add all the ingredients into a container and make sure you use an immersion blender to blend the mixture together
2. Continue blending and add the raspberries into the mixture and mix until smooth
3. Strain the mixture and throw away any leftover raspberry seeds.
4. Pour the mixture into the mold you want and set the popsicles in the freezer overnight or for a minimum time of 2 hours
5. Once frozen, run the mold under hot water ad dislodge the popsicles
6. Serve when you want or store in the fridge for a great snack!

Yummy Chocolate Orange Truffles

Ingredients:

For the Filling:
2 tablespoons of heavy cream
3 ounces of dark baking chocolate

1 tablespoon of farm butter
1/2 teaspoon of orange extract
2 drops of liquid stevia
2 tablespoons of fine erythritol
Coating:
1 teaspoon of fine erythritol
1 teaspoon of orange zest – prepare just before making up the recipe
2 teaspoons of natural cocoa powder

Directions:

Set your stove to medium-low and set up a double boiler. Melt the chocolate in this while stirring constantly.
Add in the rest of the ingredients for the filling and stir until well-combined. Take off the heat and continue to stir for another few seconds.
Chill in the refrigerator until solid enough to make balls out of. Divide into nine equal portions, and roll into balls.
Coat with the coating and chill for a few hours. Serve cold.

Yummy Vanilla Coconut "Ice Cream"

Ingredients:
1/4 cup of good quality cocoa butter
1/4 cup of good quality coconut oil
1 teaspoon of vanilla essence
1 tablespoon of natural coconut (shredded)
12 drops of stevia

Directions:

Set your stove to medium. Mix together everything except for the coconut, and place in a pot on the stove.
Heat until it is all liquid, stirring continuously. Switch off the stove and add the coconut.

Decant the mixture into a silicone tray with twelve compartments, and freeze until completely set. Best served straight out of the freezer.

Double Cream Lemon Cheesecake

Ingredients:

2 ounces of double cream
8 ounces of plain cream cheese (softened)
1 teaspoon of erythritol
1 tablespoon of freshly squeezed lemon juice
1 cup of sour cream
1 tablespoon of vanilla essence

Directions:

Mix everything until well combined, and allow to sit in the refrigerator for at least two hours. Serve and enjoy

---

Creamy Rasperries Decadent Cheesecake

Ingredients:

2 ounces of double cream
8 ounces of plain cream cheese (softened)
Half a cup of raspberries (mashed up)

2 pieces of very dark chocolate (finely grated)

Directions:
Mix together all the ingredients (except the dark chocolate) until properly combined and leave in the refrigerator for at least two hours to set.
Top with the grated chocolate and serve.

Weekend Cocoa Coconut Brownies

Ingredients:

1 cup cocoa powder
2 teaspoons stevia powder extract
2 large eggs
1 cup almond flour
½ cup shredded coconut
1 teaspoon vanilla
½ teaspoon baking soda
½ cup chopped almonds
½ cup coconut milk
1 cup coconut oil, melted

Directions:

Prepare a square baking pan by brushing it lightly with olive oil. Preheat the oven to 350°F.
Place the baking soda, coconut and almond flour in a mixing bowl and blend thoroughly. In another bowl, whisk together eggs, vanilla, stevia, cocoa powder, coconut milk and coconut oil. Combine both mixtures together then gradually fold in the almonds.
Pour the brownie mixture into the pan and bake in the oven for 30 minutes. Let the brownies cool before slicing it into 9 squares.

Coconut Chocolate Almond Squares

Ingredients:

120 grams dark chocolate chips
1 cup shredded coconut
1 cup almond flour
3 tablespoons coconut oil
1 ½ cups almond butter
¾ cup coconut sugar

Directions:

Heat the almond butter and 2 tablespoons of the coconut oil in a saucepan over medium-low flame. Once the ingredients have melted, turn off the heat. Fold in the almond flour, coconut sugar and shredded coconut into the saucepan and mix well.
Pour the almond mixture into a square-sized baking pan and set aside.
Heat the chocolate chips and remaining coconut oil in a saucepan over medium flame until the chocolate melts. Mix well.
Pour the melted chocolate mixture on top of the almond mixture, making sure that the top of the dessert is evenly-coated. Refrigerate for 2 hours then slice the dessert into 20 almond squares.

Honey Chocolate Zucchini Brownies

Ingredients:

1 cup gluten free semi-sweet chocolate chips
1 ½ cups shredded zucchini, drained
1 cup almond butter
1 large egg

1 teaspoon cinnamon
1 teaspoon baking soda
½ cup organic honey

Directions:

Preheat the oven to 350°F and lightly grease a 9x9 baking pan.
Combine the zucchini, chocolate chips, egg, almond butter, honey, baking soda and cinnamon in a mixing bowl.
Pour the mixture into the baking pan.
Bake the brownies for 45 minutes. Slice into squares and serve.

Fresh Berries Flaxseed Coconut Pudding

Ingredients:

2 cups full-fat coconut milk
1 cup fresh strawberries, stems removed
½ cup blueberries
½ tablespoon stevia
½ teaspoon vanilla
3 tablespoons flaxseeds

Directions:

Place the coconut milk, strawberries, mangoes, stevia, vanilla and flaxseeds in a blender and pulse until the ingredients are mixed well.
Pour the mixture into 2 bowls and place it in the freezer for 1 hour. Serve chilled.

Butter Vanilla Crispy Pecan Bars

Ingredients:
- 1 cup coconut flour
- 1 cup butter
- 25 drops Stevia
- 1 teaspoon vanilla extract
- 3 oz pecans
- 2 egg yolks
- 2 tablespoon almond flour
- 1 oz dark chocolate

Directions:

1. Take the mixing bowl and combine coconut flour, almond flour, and butter together.
2. Add egg yolks and vanilla extract.
3. After this, add stevia.
4. Crush the pecans and add the nuts in the mixture.
5. Take the hand mixer and mix the mixture carefully.
6. Then knead the non-sticky dough with the help of the hands. Add more flour if desired.
7. Preheat the oven to 365 F.
8. Roll the dough and make the small circles from the dough.
9. Transfer the circles to the tray and put the tray in the oven.
10. Cook the cooked for 15 minutes.
11. Meanwhile, melt the dark chocolate.
12. When the cookies are cooked – remove them from the oven and chill little.
13. Then sprinkle the cookies with the melted dark chocolate.
14. Dry it little and serve immediately.
15. Enjoy!

Easy Keto Mocha Chocolate Cake

Ingredients:

2 tablespoons wheat protein isolate, 1/2 ounce
2 tablespoons almond flour, 1/2 ounce
2 tablespoons cocoa
1/4 teaspoon baking powder
2 tablespoons butter, melted
3 tablespoons plus 2 teaspoons granulated Splenda or equivalent
liquid Splenda
1/4 teaspoon vanilla
1 tablespoon water
1 egg
Mocha Cream Frosting

Directions:

Melt the butter in a 2-cup glass measuring cup. Stir in the Splenda, vanilla and water. Sift the wheat protein isolate, almond flour, cocoa and baking powder together; stir into the butter mixture.

Break the egg into the measuring cup and mix well with a fork. Scrape down the batter with a small rubber spatula.

Cover with plastic wrap and vent by cutting a small slit in center. Microwave on HIGH 1 minute until nearly set, but still a little moist on the top.
Cook about 10 seconds or so more if too moist.
It will dry a bit as it cools. Invert onto a small plate; cool completely.
Frost with Mocha Cream Frosting or just slice cake and serve topped with a dollop of the frosting.

Cinnamon Carrot Cake

Ingredients:

1 cup unblanched almond flour (3 1/8 ounces or 92 grams)
1 cup finely ground unsweetened coconut (3 1/8 ouces or 92 grams)
1 teaspoon baking powder

1 teaspoon baking soda
1/4 teaspoon salt
1 1/2 teaspoons cinnamon
1/4 teaspoon ground ginger
1/8 teaspoon ground nutmeg
1/8 teaspoon xanthan gum
1 cup granular Splenda or equivalent liquid Splenda
1 1/2 teaspoons vanilla
1/2 teaspoon pineapple extract, optional
2 tablespoons oil
1 teaspoon blackstrap molasses
2 eggs
1/4 cup heavy cream
4 ounces carrot, finely grated (about 1 large carrot or 1 cup loosely packed after grating)
Frosting:
8 ounces cream cheese, softened
1/2 cup unsalted butter, softened
1/2 cup granular Splenda or equivalent liquid Splenda
1 teaspoon vanilla

Directions:

Put everything except the frosting ingredients in a medium mixing bowl and beat well with an electric mixer until you have a very thick batter.
Spread in a greased baking pan. Bake at 350° for 25-30 minutes.
The cake is done when it no longer feels spongy when you lightly press it in the center.
Cool completely before frosting. Store the frosted cake in the refrigerator.

Beat the frosting ingredients in a small mixing bowl with an electric mixer until fluffy. Spread over the cooled cake.

Vanilla Apple Cake

Ingredients
1 6-ounce McIntosh apple
1/2 cup butter, softened

4 ounces cream cheese, softened
1 cup granular Splenda or equivalent liquid Splenda
5 eggs, room temperature
1 teaspoon vanilla
6 1/2 ounces almond flour, 1 1/2 cups plus 2 tablespoons
1 teaspoon baking powder
1 1/2 teaspoons cinnamon
Pinch salt

Directions

Peel and core the apple then chop finely. In a medium bowl, cream the butter, cream cheese and Splenda.

Add the eggs, one at a time; blend in the extract.

Mix the almond flour, baking powder, cinnamon and salt; add to the egg mixture a little at a time.

Gently fold in the apples.
Pour into a greased 8x8-inch cake pan. Bake at 350° 35-40 minutes.
The cake will be golden brown and firm to the touch when done.

Easy Splenda Almond Vanilla Cake

Ingredients
2 tablespoons butter
1 egg
2 tablespoons water
1/4 cup granular Splenda or equivalent liquid Splenda
1/4 cup golden flax meal
1/4 cup almond flour
1/3 cup vanilla whey protein powder (1 scoop)
1/4 teaspoon baking powder
Pinch salt

Directions

Melt the butter in a 2-cup glass measure in the microwave.

Add the egg, water and liquid Splenda, if using; mix until well with a fork until blended. If you're using granular Splenda, combine it with the dry ingredients instead of the wet.

In a small bowl, mix the remaining ingredients.

Pour the dry ingredients into the wet ingredients and stir until combined.

Scrape down the batter.

Cover the measuring cup with vented plastic wrap and microwave on HIGH for 1 to 1 1/2 minutes until set.

Lemon Grind Vanilla Pound Cake

Ingredients
2 cups Carbalose flour
2 cups granular Splenda or equivalent liquid Splenda
1/2 teaspoon baking soda
1 teaspoon vanilla
1 teaspoon lemon rind, from 1 small lemon
2 tablespoons lemon juice, from 1 small lemon
1 cup butter, softened
1 cup sour cream
4 eggs

Directions

Blend all of the ingredients on low speed to combine. Beat 3 minutes on medium speed.

Pour into a large heavily greased bundt pan.

Bake 300° for 65-70 minutes or until well-browned and firm to the touch.

Cool 15 minutes in the pan; turn out and cool.

Tasty Keto Almond White Buns

Ingredients
2/3 cups almond flour
3 eggs - set one egg white aside
1/2 tsp salt
1/2 tsp baking powder
2 tbsp xylitol
4 tbsp olive oil

Directions

Preheat oven to 350F.
Beat 1 egg white in bowl until stiff, set aside.
Mix other ingredients in bowl, then fold the egg white in gently, to avoid breaking the egg white do not over fold. The egg white will provide some height in the buns.
Drop dough from a tbsp on cookie sheet and spread outward into circles but not too thin, you should get 6 balls out of the batter. Use additional spoon full's if needed for balls until batter is gone
In a preheated oven bake at 350F until buns are golden brown.

Delicious Flaxseed Bread

Ingredients
2 tbsp ground flaxseed meal
1 large egg, whole
1 tbsp butter, salted
1/2 tsp Baking Powder

Directions

Mix all ingredients in a large bowl, and microwave for 2 minutes.

Serve and enjoy

Cinnamon Apple Flax Muffins

Ingredients:

3 eggs
1/4 cup oil
2 tablespoons butter, melted
6 tablespoons water
2 teaspoons vanilla, or 1 teaspoon each vanilla and caramel extract
1 teaspoon blackstrap molasses, optional
1/2 cup granular or liquid Splenda
1 cup golden flax meal
1/2 teaspoon baking soda
1/2 teaspoon baking powder
1 teaspoon cinnamon
2 packets apple cider mix (sugar free)
Pinch salt

Directions :
In a medium bowl, whisk the eggs well. Whisk in the oil, butter, water, vanilla, molasses and liquid Splenda, if using.
In a small bowl, combine the dry ingredients, then whisk them into the egg mixture well. Let stand 5 minutes. Whisk well, then spoon into 12 muffin cups with paper liners. Bake at 350° 15-17 minutes, or until they are browned and seem set to the touch.
Cool about 10 minutes on a rack then remove from the tin. Store in the refrigerator.

Butter Almond Flour Sugar Cookies

Ingredients :

3 ounces almond flour
1/8 teaspoon salt
2-3 tablespoons granular Splenda
2 tablespoons butter, softened
1/4 teaspoon vanilla
1 egg white

Directions:

Mix all of the ingredients well in a small bowl. Everything should be moist and the dough should hold together. Freeze about 15-20 minutes to firm up the dough.
Drop the dough by teaspoons onto a parchment or silicone lined 12x17" baking sheet. Roll each piece of dough into a ball.
Cover the balls with plastic wrap and take a baking powder can, that has about an 1/8" rim around the bottom, and press down firmly over each ball of dough.
Be sure to press all the way down to the baking sheet. Peel off the plastic wrap and discard. Prick the cookies with a fork.
Bake at 325F° for 15-20 minutes, or until golden brown.

Lemon Vanilla Cookies

Ingredients
1/2 cup butter, softened
1/3 cup granular Splenda
1 teaspoon lemon extract
1 teaspoon vanilla
1 teaspoon lemon zest, from 1 small lemon
1 egg

1 cup almond flour
1/3 cup vanilla whey protein powder
1 teaspoon baking powder

Directions

Put everything in a medium bowl and beat with an electric mixer until creamy. This will only take about a minute.
Using a 2 teaspoon cookie scoop, scoop 24 balls of the dough onto a silicone or parchment-lined baking sheet. Place them 6 balls across and 4 balls down on the sheet.
Cover the dough balls with a sheet of wax paper. Very gently press them down with the bottom of a glass or small bowl to about 1/4-inch thick.
Carefully remove the wax paper and bake them at 350° about 8-12 minutes or until golden brown.
Cool on a wire rack. Serve and enjoy

Walnut Banana Muffins

Ingredients :
4 ounces almond flour
1/2 cup golden flax meal
1 teaspoon baking powder
1/8 teaspoon salt
1 ounce walnuts, chopped
1 cup granular Splenda
2 tablespoons butter
1 teaspoon banana extract
1/2 teaspoon caramel extract
1 teaspoon vanilla
2 tablespoons heavy cream
2 tablespoons water
2 eggs

Directions :

In a small bowl, stir together the almond flour, flax meal, baking powder, salt, nuts and granular Splenda, if using.

In a medium microwave-safe bowl, melt the butter in the microwave. Stir in the liquid Splenda, if using, the extracts, cream and water.

Add the dry ingredients and the eggs to the butter mixture; stir with a wooden spoon until well blended. Fill 6 paper-lined muffin cups with the batter, dividing it evenly among them.

You can spray the liners with cooking spray, but they don't seem to stick too much. Bake at 350° 15-20 minutes, until the tops are golden brown.

Serve warm or at room temperature. Store in the refrigerator.

Heavy Cream Keylime Pie

Ingredients:

1 small package sugar free lime jello
1/2 cup boiling water
8 oz cream cheese, softened
1 tbsp lime juice, one small lime
Lime peel, finely grated, one small lime
1/2 cup heavy cream

Directions

Dissolve the jello in the boiling water, stirring for 3 minutes. Beat the cream cheese in a medium bowl with an electric mixer until smooth.

Gradually beat the jello into the cream. Add the lime juice and rind.

Add cream and whip until fluffy. Pour into a pie plate that has been sprayed with nonstick spray. Chill until set.

Almond Peanut Butter Muffin

Ingredients
2 teaspoons butter
1 tablespoon natural peanut butter

2 tablespoons flax meal
2 tablespoons almond flour
1 tablespoon sugar free syrup, caramel or vanilla flavor
1 egg

Directions

Melt the butter and peanut butter in a cup in the microwave, about 20 seconds. Add the remaining ingredients and mix well.
Scrape down the batter from the sides of the cup. Microwave on high 1 to 1 1/2 minutes or until just set.
Serve and enjoy

Splenda Coconut Flour Bread

Ingredients :
3/4 cup coconut flour
1 teaspoon baking powder
1/2 teaspoon salt
6 eggs
1/2 cup unsalted butter, melted
2 tablespoons granular Splenda

Directions

Sift the first 3 ingredients into a small bowl; set aside. In a medium bowl, whisk together the remaining ingredients well.
Add the dry ingredients and whisk until the batter is smooth with no lumps. It will look a bit like cornbread batter.
Spread in a greased pan and bake at 350° for 40 minutes.
Remove from the pan and cool on a rack. Serve and enjoy.

Yummy Banana Chocolate Mini Tarts

Ingredients:

Crust
- 2 large egg whites
- 2 tablespoons coconut flour
- 1 tablespoons erythritol
- ¼ cup chia seeds

Filling
- 4 tablespoons almond butter
- 2 tablespoons coconut oil

Top
- 4 tablespoons carob powder
- 1/4cup erythritol
- 1 ripe bananas
- 2 tablespoons half-and-half
- 1 vanilla pod
- 1/2 teaspoon cinnamon
- Pinch of nutmeg

Directions:

1. Preheat the oven to 350 ° F.
2. Grind the chia seeds in a food processor until they resemble flour.
3. Add the coconut flour, erythritol, and egg whites into the chia seed powder and process until combined.
4. Divide the mixture into 4 and cover the bottom of some small tart tins. Bake for about 8 minutes.
5. Melt together the almond butter and coconut oil.
6. After the crust is ready, let cool a little bit and cover with the coconut oil-butter mixture. Put in the fridge for 30 minutes.
7. Meanwhile, mash the banana and combine with carob powder, erythritol, the seeds from the vanilla pod, cinnamon, nutmeg and half-and-half. Blend until smooth and creamy.
8. Remove the tarts from the fridge, top with the blended banana mixture and return to the fridge for at least an hour before serving.

Hazelnut Cornbread

Ingredients :

3/4 cup almond flour
1/2 cup hazelnut flour
1/2 cup Carbquik
1/4 cup soy grits
1 teaspoon baking powder
1/2 teaspoon salt
4 tablespoons salted butter, melted
3 eggs
1/4 cup heavy cream
1/4 cup water
1/2 cup granular Splenda

Directions

Combine the first 6 ingredients in a small bowl. In a medium bowl, mix the butter, eggs, cream, water and Splenda.
Stir the dry ingredients into the wet ingredients until well blended, but don't over mix. Pour into a greased 8x8" baking pan.
Bake at 400° 15-20 minutes or until nicely browned and and firm to the touch. Cool in the pan on a rack before serving.

Vanilla Creamy Keto Jello Cake

Ingredients
Cake:
3/4 cup butter, softened

6 ounces cream cheese, softened
1 cup granular Splenda or equivalent liquid Splenda
7 eggs
1 1/2 teaspoons vanilla
1 1/2 cups almond flour (160 grams or 5 5/8 ounces)
2 1/2 ounces unsweetened coconut, ground fine (3/4 cup ground)
1 1/2 teaspoons baking powder
Gelatin:
1 package sugar free strawberry gelatin (or any flavor)
1 cup boiling water
1 cup ice water

Directions

In a large bowl, cream the butter, cream cheese and Splenda with an electric mixer. Add the eggs, one or two at a time; blend in the vanilla. The batter will look curdled.
Mix the almond flour, coconut flour and baking powder; add to the egg mixture a little at a time.
Beat about 1 minute until fluffy. Spread the batter in a greased 9x13" glass cake pan.
Bake at 350° for 30 minutes.
The cake will be golden brown and firm to the touch when done. Cool the cake on a wire rack.
While the cake is cooling, prepare the gelatin according to the package directions.
Chill until the outside edges are just starting to set up but the center is still liquid.
Slowly and evenly pour the liquid gelatin over the cake.
Chill 2-3 hours. Frost with the Whipped Topping.

Tasty Coffee Cheesecake

Ingredients :

1 packet unflavored gelatin
1/2 cup coffee, cold or room temperature
2 teaspoons instant coffee granules
2 cups heavy cream
16 ounces cream cheese, softened
1 cup granular Splenda
1 teaspoon vanilla

Directions

In a medium bowl, whip the cream with 1/2 cup of the Splenda until stiff. Place the whipped cream in the refrigerator until needed.

In a small pot, sprinkle the gelatin over the cold coffee and let soften 5 minutes.

Heat and stir over low heat to dissolve the gelatin completely. Do not boil. You can also dissolve the gelatin in the microwave by heating it about 30 seconds or so on HIGH.

Stir until completely dissolved. Stir in the instant coffee granules until dissolved. Cool to room temperature.

Add the remaining 1/2 cup Splenda and the vanilla to the cooled gelatin mixture.

Beat the cream cheese until creamy and smooth. Gradually beat the gelatin mixture into the cream cheese until well blended and slightly fluffy. Chill the batter until slightly thickened, about 20-30 minutes, stirring every 10 minutes to prevent lumps.

Very gently fold in the whipped cream a little at a time. Spread in a greased 9-inch pie plate and chill until set, about 5-6 hours.

Stevia Gingerbread cookies

Ingredients:
- 3 eggs
- 1 teaspoon ground ginger
- 1 teaspoon cinnamon
- 5 tablespoon butter
- 1 tablespoon lemon juice
- ½ teaspoon baking soda
- 1 cup almond flour
- 50 drops stevia
- 1 teaspoon vanilla extract
- 1 teaspoon cardamom

Directions:

1.	Take the mixing bowl and combine cardamom, almond flour, baking soda, cinnamon, and ground ginger together. Stir the mixture gently.
2.	After this, add eggs and mix up the mixture with the help of the hand mixer.
3.	Add butter and continue to whisk the dough.
4.	Then add stevia and lemon juice.
5.	Knead the dough with the help of the hands and transfer it in the fridge for at least 10 minutes.
6.	Meanwhile, preheat the oven to 365 F.
7.	Remove the dough from the fridge and roll it.
8.	Make the gingerbread men.
9.	Transfer the gingerbread men in the tray and put in the preheated oven.
10.	Cook the cooked for 15 minutes.
11.	Then remove the cookies from the oven and chill them well.
12.	Serve it immediately.

Cinnamon Maple Mug Cake

Ingredients:
2 tbsp. almond flour
1/2 tsp. maple extract
2 tbsp. butter
2 tbsp. crushed pecans
7 drops stevia
1/2 tsp. baking powder
1/4 tsp. cinnamon
1 tbsp. erythritol
1 large egg

Directions:

1. Add all ingredients to a mug and mix completely.
2. Microwave on high for 55 to 60 seconds.
3. Tap the mug against and plate and the cake will fall out.

Vanilla gelatin cake

Ingredients:

- 1 teaspoon vanilla extract
- 3 tablespoon gelatin powder
- 2 tablespoon stevia extract
- 1 cup cream
- 1 cup almond milk
- 1 teaspoon cinnamon
- 5 tablespoon water

Directions:

1. Combine the cream and almond milk together, stir the mixture and preheat it until warm.
2. Then boil the water and transfer it to the bowl.
3. Add gelatin powder and stir it carefully until gelatin powder is dissolved.
4. After this, add stevia extract and vanilla extract. Stir the mixture thoroughly till you get homogenous mass.
5. After this, pour the gelatin mixture in the warm cream liquid whisk it thoroughly.
6. When you get smooth mass – add cinnamon.
7. Preheat the cream liquid until boiled and remove the liquid from the heat.
8. Chill it little and pour the cream mixture into the silicone mold.
9. Put the silicon form with the cake in the freezer and freeze it for 2 hours.
10. Serve it.

Vodka Ice Cream

Ingredients:

3 tbsp. butter (browned)
25 drops liquid stevia
1/4 cup heavy cream
1/2 tsp. xanthan gum
2 tbsp. vodka
2 tsp. butterscotch flavoring
2 tbsp. erythritol
1/4 cup sour cream
1 cup coconut milk
1 tsp. sea salt

Directions:
1. If not already done, brown your butter on low heat.
2. Blend all of the ingredients with a food processor, blender, or immersion blender.
3. Pour the mixture into your ice cream maker and follow instructions.
Enjoy!

Coconut Mocha Ice Cream

Ingredients:

2 tbsp. erythritol
15 drops liquid stevia
1 tbsp. instant coffee
1 cup coconut milk
1/4 cup heavy cream
2 tbsp. cocoa powder
1/4 tsp. xanthan gum

Directions:

1. Thoroughly blend all ingredients, except for the gum, in a blender or food processor.
2. Blend on lowest setting and slowly add the xanthan gum.
3. Pour the mixture into your ice cream machine and follow manufacturer's instructions.
Serve and enjoy.

Chocolate Macaroon

Ingredients:

1/3 cup coconut (shredded and unsweetened)
3 tbsp. coconut flour
1/4 cup coconut oil
1 tsp. vanilla extract
1/2 tsp. baking powder
1 cup almond flour
2 large eggs
1/3 cup erythritol
1/4 tsp. salt
1/4 cup cocoa powder

Directions:

1. Preheat your oven to 350☐F.
2. Thoroughly mix all dry ingredients.
3. Now slowly add all the wet ingredients, while stirring continuously.
4. Use your hand to roll out the balls and place on a greased baking sheet.
5. Bake for 15 to 20 minutes
Serve and enjoy.

Nutmeg Butter Cookies

Ingredients:

2 tbsp. butter
1/8 tsp. nutmeg
1 tsp. vanilla
2 tbsp. heavy cream

1/8 tsp. cloves
1/4 tsp. ginger
1/4 tsp cinnamon
2 tbsp. swerve sweetener
1 cup macadamias
3/4 cup cashews
1 pinch salt

Directions:

1. Add all the nuts to a food processor and pulse until smooth.
2. Heat a pan on medium and brown your butter. Mix in the swerve.
3. Now add the heavy cream and stir. Remove from heat and add to nut mixture in food processor.
4. Toss in the vanilla and all spices. Continue to process and make sure no lumps remain.
5. Process until you get your desired consistency.
Enjoy!

Caramel Peanut Butter Milkshake

Ingredients:

2 tbsp. Sugar free caramel syrup (such as SF Torani)
7 ice cubes
1 tbsp. MCT oil
1/4 tsp. xanthan gum
1 cup coconut milk
2 tbsp. peanut butter

Directions:

1. Toss all of your ingredients into a blender, and blend until you get your desired consistency.
2. You can tailor the amount of ingredients until you get the taste and consistency you want.
Serve and enjoy

Tasty Strawberry Milkshakes

Ingredients:
2 tbsp. Sugar free strawberry syrup (such as SF Torani)
7 ice cubes
1 tbsp. MCT oil
1/4 tsp. xanthan gum
3/4 cup coconut milk
1/4 cup heavy cream

Directions:
1. Toss all of your ingredients into a blender, and blend until you get your desired consistency.
2. You can tailor the amount of ingredients until you get the taste and consistency you want. Enjoy!

Yummy Almond Coconut Fat Bombs

Ingredients:

2 tablespoons almond butter
1 cup softened cold-pressed coconut oil
3 tablespoons unsweetened cocoa powder
2 tablespoons organic honey
1 teaspoon vanilla
½ teaspoon sea salt
1 cup shredded coconut

Directions:

Place the almond butter, coconut oil, cocoa powder, honey, vanilla and sea salt in a food processor and mix until smooth and creamy.
Form the mixture into 16 candy balls. Roll each ball into the shredded coconut and place on a parchment-lined sheet. Refrigerate the candies for 1 hour then transfer them in an airtight container.

Delicious Vanilla Watermelon Creamsicles

Ingredients:

2 cups watermelon chunks, deseeded
1 ¾ cups full-fat coconut milk
1 teaspoon vanilla
1 tablespoon organic honey

Directions:

Puree the watermelon in a food processor and pour it into a bowl, making sure to discard seeds. Place the fruit puree back into the food processor then pour in the honey, vanilla and coconut milk. Process until the mixture becomes smooth and creamy.
Pour the watermelon mixture into 4 molds and place popsicle sticks through the dessert.
Place the popsicles in the freezer for 4-5 hours.

Prosciutto Cup Muffin

Ingredients
- 1 slice (1/2 oz.) of prosciutto
- 1 medium-sized egg yolk
- ½ oz. grated Parmesan cheese
- ½ oz. Brie cheese, diced
- 1/3 oz. mozzarella cheese, diced

Directions:

1. Set and pre-heat oven at 4000 F.
2. Get a muffin tin that has around 1 ½″ deep and 2 ½″ wide hole.

3.   Fold the prosciutto in half to make it squarish.
4.   Put it in the muffin tin hole to completely line it.
5.   Put the egg yolk in the prosciutto cup.
6.   Gently top the egg yolk with the cheeses to avoid breaking the yolk.
7.   Bake for approximately 12 minutes or until the yolk is warmed and cooked, but still runny.
8.   Allow the muffin to cool for around 10 minutes before taking out of the muffin pan.
9.   Serve and enjoy!

Tasty Chocolate Chia Pudding

Ingredients :
- ¼ cup of chia seeds
- 1 cup of heavy cream
- 2 Tbsp. of granular Swerve or erythritol
- 2 Tbsp. of cocoa powder
- 1 Tbsp. of chocolate chips, sugar-free

Directions:

1.   Set aside the chocolate chips, then mix the rest of the ingredients in a medium-sized bowl. Allow the mixture to sit for no less than 15 minutes, while stirring occasionally.
2.   Divide equally among 4 cups.
3.   Garnish each cup with the chocolate chips previously set aside.
4.   Dessert is best enjoyed cold. It may be refrigerated for a maximum of 3 days.

Low-Carb Coconut Pumpkin

Ingredients:

1 teaspoon cinnamon

1 cup canned pumpkin puree
½ cup organic honey
1 cup almond butter
1 teaspoon baking soda
1 tablespoon melted coconut oil
1 egg
1 teaspoon vanilla extract

Directions:

Place the pumpkin puree in a mixing bowl. Add in the cinnamon, honey, almond butter, baking soda, coconut oil, egg and vanilla extract. Mix well.

Pour the batter into a square 8x8 baking pan. Bake the dish in a preheated 350°F oven for 30 minutes.
Slice into squares and serve.

Keto Blackberry Muffins

Ingredients:

- 1 cup almond flour
- 1 teaspoon baking soda
- 1 tablespoon apple cider vinegar
- ½ cup blackberries
- 1 tablespoon stevia extract
- 1 oz dark chocolate
- ½ cup almond milk

Directions:

1. Take the mixing bowl and combine the almond flour and baking soda together. Stir the mixture.
2. After this add dark chocolate.
3. Take the separate bowl and put the blackberries. Mash the berries with the help of the spoon.

4.   Combine the mashed berries with the almond milk and stir the mixture until you get homogeneous consistency.

5.   Then combine the dry mixture and liquid mixture together. Stir it.

6.   Add stevia extract and apple cider vinegar. Mix up the mass till you get a smooth dough.

7.   Preheat the oven to 375 F.

8.   Take the silicon muffin molds and fill the ½ of every silicon form with the dough.

9.   Transfer the muffins to the preheated oven and cook them for 20 minutes.

10.   When the dessert is cooked – remove it from the oven and chill little.

11.   Then discard the muffins from the silicon forms and serve.

Delight Chocolate Butter fluffy pie

Ingredients:
- 1 cup coconut flour
- 1 large egg
- 4 tablespoon butter
- 1 tablespoon almond milk
- 1 teaspoon baking powder
- 1 tablespoon lemon juice
- 1 cup cream cheese
- 4 teaspoon stevia extract
- 1 teaspoon cocoa
- ½ cup cream
- 1 teaspoon Erythritol

Directions:

1.   Take the mixing bowl and beat egg. Whisk it carefully. Add Erythritol and almond milk. Stir the mixture.

2.   After this, add butter and coconut flour. Sprinkle the mixture with the baking soda.

3.   Add the lemon juice.

4.   After this, knead the dough.

5.   Take the pie form and cover it with the baking paper.
6.   Transfer the pie dough in the form and make the shape of the pie.
7.   Prick the dough with the help of the fork.
8.   Preheat the oven to 370 F and transfer the pie dough in the oven.
9.   Cook the pie dough for 12 minutes.
10.   Meanwhile, whisk the cream with the hand whisker until you get fluffy mass.
11.   Then add cream cheese and continue to whisk it.
12.   When you get smooth and soft mass – add stevia extract and cocoa. Stir the mixture carefully.
13.   Transfer the mixture to the fridge.
14.   Then remove the cooked pie dough from the oven. Chill it well.
15.   Place the cocoa cream mixture in the pie dough and leave the pie in the fridge for 10 minutes.
16.   Cut it into pieces and serve it.

Icy Watermelon & Cucumber Sorbet

Ingredients:

1 ½ cup diced cucumber meat
4 cups watermelon chunks, deseeded
2 tablespoons lime juice
2 tablespoons Erythritol
1 cup crushed ice
Directions:

Combine the cucumber, watermelon, lime juice, Erythritol and ice in a blender and mix for 15-20 seconds. Pour the mixture into a stainless bowl and freeze for 2 hours.
Take out the sorbet from the freezer and let it stand for 5 minutes. Scoop the sorbet into individual cups and serve.

Yummy Lemon chocolate Donuts

Ingredients:

- 3 eggs
- 1 teaspoon baking soda
- 2 tablespoon lemon juice
- ½ cup almond flour
- ½ cup coconut flour
- ½ cup coconut milk
- 1 tablespoon stevia
- 1 oz dark chocolate
- ½ teaspoon salt
- 3 tablespoon butter

Directions:

1. Take the mixing bowl and combine baking soda, almond flour, and coconut flour together. Stir the mixture.
2. Crush the chocolate and add in the dry mixture.
3. After this, beat the eggs in the separate bowl and whisk them.
4. Add coconut milk and salt. Stir the mixture.
5. Combine the liquid and dry mixture together.
6. Add lemon juice, butter, and stevia together. Knead the smooth dough.
7. Preheat the donut maker and place the dough into the dough maker.
8. Cook the donuts for 5 minutes.
9. Then flip them to another side and cook for 4 minutes more.
10. When the donuts are cooked – remove them from the donut maker gently.
11. Serve the dish immediately.

Yummy Vanilla Almond Butter Fudge

Ingredients

- 1 cup of unsweetened almond butter
- 1 cup of coconut oil
- ¼ cup of coconut milk
- 1 tsp. of vanilla extract
- Stevia (to sweeten/to taste)

Directions:

1. Combine the almond butter with coconut oil and melt until soft.
2. Put all the ingredients in a blender.
3. Process until everything is well-blended.
4. Pour the blended mixture into a baking pan.
5. Refrigerate for around 2 to 3 hours or until it sets.
6. Remove from the refrigerator and cut into around 12 pcs.
7. Serve and enjoy immediately.

Favorite Coconut Grated Pie

Ingredients:

- 1 cup almond flour
- ½ cup coconut flour
- 5 tablespoon butter
- 1 egg
- 1 tablespoon stevia extract
- 1 teaspoon Erythritol
- ½ cup raspberries

Directions:

1. Beat the egg in the mixing bowl and add butter.
2. Whisk the mixture till you get smooth and homogenous mass.
3. Add Erythritol coconut flour. Stir it.

4. Add almond flour and knead the non-sticky dough with the help of the hands.
5. Then mash the raspberries and combine them with the stevia extract. Stir the mixture.
6. Separate the dough into 2 parts.
7. Take the tray and cover it with the baking paper.
8. Grate the 1 part of the dough in the tray.
9. Place the raspberry mixture in the grated dough.
10. Then grate the second part of the dough.
11. Preheat the oven to 365 F.
12. Transfer the tray with the grated pie in the oven and cook it for 25-30 minutes.
13. Then remove the pie from the oven and chill it little.
14. Serve it.

Cheesy Creamy Lemon Bars

Ingredients

- 4 oz. of melted butter
- 1 cup of pecans
- 3 oz. of unflavoured powdered gelatine
- 8 oz. of softened cream cheese
- ¼ cup of coconut flour
- 1 Tbsp. of lemon zest
- 2 Tbsp. of fresh lemon juice
- 1 cup of boiling water
- ¼ cup of granular Swerve

Directions:

1. Mix the pecans, melted butter, and coconut flour in a small-sized bowl.
2. Spread the mixture into an 8x8" baking dish or silicone glass. Set aside.
3. Put the gelatine in a medium-sized bowl with boiling water. Stir for around two minutes.

4. Add the rest of the ingredients into the bowl.
5. Thoroughly mix until all the lumps are gone.
6. Pour the mixture over the pecan crust.
7. Refrigerate to set.
8. Divide into 8 individual bars.
9. Best served chilled.

Dark Chocolate Orange Truffles

Ingredients

For the Ganache
- 3 oz. of baking chocolate, unsweetened
- 2 Tbsp. of heavy cream
- 2 Tbsp. of confectioners Swerve
- ½ tsp. of liquid orange flavor
- 2 drops of stevia glycerite
- 1 Tbsp. of butter

For the Coating
- 2 tsp. of unsweetened cocoa powder
- 1 tsp. of confectioners Swerve
- 1 tsp. of orange zest, fresh

Directions:

1. Melt the chocolate over medium heat setting in a small-sized double boiler, while stirring slowly.
2. Add the butter, Swerve, cream, orange flavor, and stevia to the chocolate. Stir until everything is well-blended.
3. Take out of the heat. Continue to stir for around 10 seconds more.
4. Refrigerate the saucepan for around 1 hour or until the ganache congeals.
5. Use a spoon to scoop the ganache and make 9 balls from the mixture. Do this while wearing plastic gloves to keep the chocolate from sticking to your hands.
6. Create a coating powder by mixing the confectioners Swerve, orange zest and cocoa powder on a plate.

7. Thinly coat the ganache balls by rolling each ball through the coating powder.
8. To achieve the best consistency, refrigerate if the room temperature is over 70° F.

Peanut Butter Chocolate Fat Bombs

Ingredients:

4 tablespoons butter
4 tablespoons coconut oil
4 tablespoons heavy (whipping) cream
2 tablespoons powdered peanut butter, like PB2
2 tablespoons unsweetened cocoa powder
1 teaspoon pure vanilla extract
1 teaspoon stevia, or other sugar substitute

Directions:

To a medium microwaveable bowl, add the butter and coconut oil. Microwave on high in short 10-second intervals until the mixture begins to melt. Once melted, add the heavy cream. Whisk thoroughly to combine.
2.
Mix in the powdered peanut butter, cocoa powder, vanilla, and stevia.
3.
Pour the mixture evenly into an ice cube tray. Freeze for at least 1 hour to solidify, preferably overnight.
4.
Enjoy within 2 hours.

Delux Strawberry Basil Ice Cups

Ingredients:
- 6 tablespoons cream cheese
- 4 tablespoons creamed coconut milk
- 2 tablespoons butter, unsalted, at room temperature
- 2 tablespoons powdered erythritol or Swerve
- Liquid Stevia drops to taste (optional)
- A handful fresh basil leaves
- ½ cup fresh strawberries + extra to garnish
- ½ teaspoon vanilla extract

Directions:

1.   Add cream cheese, creamed coconut milk, butter, erythritol, Stevia, and vanilla the blender and blend until smooth.
2.   Remove half the blended mixture and set aside.
3.   To the other half that is in the blender add strawberries and blend until smooth.
4.   Divide the mixture into 5 silicone muffin cups.
5.   Clean the blender and add the blended mixture that was kept aside. Add basil leaves and blend until smooth.
6.   Divide the mixture and spoon into the muffin cups above the strawberry layer.
7.   Place thinly sliced strawberry slices on top.
8.   Freeze for a few hours until set.

Vanilla Strawberry Shortcakes

Ingredients:

For shortcakes:
- 6 ounces cream cheese
- 4 tablespoons erythritol
- 6 large eggs, separated
- 1 teaspoon vanilla extract

- 1/2 teaspoon baking powder

For filling:
- 2 cups whipped cream
- 20 medium strawberries, sliced

Directions:

1.   Beat egg whites until light and fluffy.
2.   Add cream cheese to the yolks along with vanilla extract, erythritol, and baking powder. Beat until smooth and creamy.
3.   Add whites and fold lightly into the cream cheese mixture.
4.   Grease 2-3 large baking sheets. Line with parchment paper or silpat.
5.   Drop large spoonfuls on the baking sheet. Leave space between 2 shortcakes.
6.   Bake in a preheated oven 300°F for about 25 minutes. You can bake in batches.
7.   Spread whipped cream on all the shortcakes. Lay strawberry slices on half the shortcakes. Cover with the remaining shortcakes.

Cinnamon Baked Ricotta Custard

Ingredients:

- 2 large egg whites
- 2 large eggs
- 1/2 cup half and half
- 1 1/2 cups ricotta cheese
- 1/4 cup erythritol or to taste
- 1/2 teaspoon vanilla extract
- 2 tablespoons ground cinnamon

Directions:

1.   Add ricotta and cream cheese to the mixing bowl and beat with an electric mixer until smooth and creamy.

2. Add erythritol and beat until well blended.
3. Add remaining ingredients and beat until well blended.
4. Transfer into 8 ramekins. Take a large baking dish. Pour enough hot water to cover 1 inch from the bottom of the dish.
5. Place the ramekins inside the baking dish.
6. Bake in a preheated oven at 250 degrees F for about 45 minutes or until set.
7. Remove from the oven and cool.
8. Sprinkle cinnamon.
9. Serve either chilled or at room temperature. Enjoy

Chocolate Cake in a Mug

Ingredients:
- 2 eggs, beaten
- 4 tablespoons cocoa powder
- 4 tablespoons sugar substitute of choice or to taste
- A pinch salt
- 2 tablespoons heavy cream
- 1 teaspoon vanilla extract
- ½ teaspoon baking powder
- Cooking spray
- Whipped cream to serve
- Berries of your choice to serve

Directions:
1. Mix together cocoa, sweetener, salt and baking powder in a bowl.
2. Add cream, vanilla, and egg and mix well.
3. Pour into mugs greased with cooking spray. (½ fill it)
4. Microwave on high for about 60-80 seconds until the top of the cake is slightly hard.
5. Cool and invert on to a plate. Serve with whipped cream and berries.

Conclusion

Thank you again for downloading this book!
I hope this Keto 500 recipes book was able to help you to stay healthy

If you enjoyed this book, then I'd like to ask you for a favor, would you be kind enough to leave a review for this book on Amazon? It'd be greatly appreciated!

Thank you and good luck!

65560383R00206

Made in the USA
Lexington, KY
16 July 2017